THOMSON

COURSE TECHNOLOGY

Professional ■ Technical ■ Reference

going
DIGITAL

THE PRACTICE AND VISION OF DIGITAL ARTISTS

By Joseph Nalven and JD Jarvis

Digital Process and Print Series

Harald Johnson Editor | C. David Tobie Technical Editor

ISBN: 1-59200-918-2

Library of Congress Catalog Card Number: 2005922187

Printed in the United States

05 06 07 08 09 BU 10 9 8 7 6 5 4 3 2 1

Publisher and General Manager, Thomson Course Technology PTR:
Stacy L. Hiquet

Associate Director of Marketing:
Sarah O'Donnell

Manager of Editorial Services:
Heather Talbot

Marketing Manager:
Heather Hurley

Executive Editor:
Kevin Harreld

Senior Editor:
Mark Garvey

Digital Process and Print Series Editor:
Harald Johnson

Marketing Coordinator:
Jordan Casey

Project Editor and Copy Editor:
Dan Foster, Scribe Tribe

Technical Reviewer:
C. David Tobie

Thomson Course Technology PTR Editorial Services Coordinator:
Elizabeth Furbish

Interior Layout Tech:
Jill Flores

Cover Designer:
Mike Tanamachi

Indexer:
Kelly Talbot

Proofreader:
Sandy Doell

THOMSON
COURSE TECHNOLOGY
Professional ■ Technical ■ Reference

Thomson Course Technology PTR, a division of Thomson Course Technology
■ 25 Thomson Place ■ Boston, MA 02210 ■ www.courseptr.com

Dedication

Always in my heart and mind: my wife Sally, and our three children, Zack, Cammy, and Marlo.

—Joe Nalven

To my mother and father, and his father who has a little something to do with every sentence I write. To Brice Howard and all the artists at the National Center for Experiments in Television who inspired me in those days. And, to Myriam.

—JD Jarvis

Foreword

The Electric Dynamic in the 21st Century

The 21st century offers promises, possibilities, and challenges that are unique from any other time in recorded history. As humankind attempts to address these issues, it is equipped with a number of tools that were, for the most part, not even imagined at the dawn of the previous century. Central to these tools is the development, adoption, and proliferation of the various devices conventionally known as computers. The often quoted comparison to the invention of the printing press works on many levels, for not since the proliferation of readily affordable and available books and periodicals have education, commerce, science, and the arts been so affected. It is, of course, in the area of art that we are here most concerned, but to separate art today from its collaborative partners in engineering, communications, and industry is to miss the true significance of the computer art revolution—the simultaneous expansion of both convergence and divergence.

Digital art history, of increasing interest to a number of scholars, can be categorized in a number of different ways. The era of mainframe computing, followed by the era of personal computers, and on to networked interactivity and wireless mobility are all paradigmatic shifts that embraced increasingly greater populations. For this growing number of voices in the digital arts community, the significance of the desktop computer revolution put into the hands of a variety of artists the tools that allowed them to express their work without the advantages or disadvantages of the institutional system. The proliferation of these low-cost tools has both created a professional class of digital artists as well as, equally interestingly, a new category of folk artists, where everyone from children to their grandmothers have begun to manipulate their photographs, create their own music, design their announcements, and edit their films. Certain software graphics programs have become household names to artists and non-artists alike. This is so unlike the early days when computer art was created with mainframe computers. The good news is that now anyone can make a movie; the bad news is that now anyone can make a movie. Obviously, the intrinsic aspects of talent, taste, and accomplishment still are as important today as in the time of da Vinci.

How Will Digital Art Differ from the Arts of the Past?

There has been some reluctance by the conventional art community to immediately accept computer art. Issues such as archiveability and collectibility are at the core of the controversy. Like photography and video art before it, digital art has had to re-conform the traditional interpretation of contemporary art history to include itself in an artist/activist process that I call *hacking the timeline*. No doubt, in time, an honest telling of the arts of the mid to late 20th century will include the pioneering efforts of artists in the mainframe, desktop, networked, and wireless art movements as well as the activists who worked on their behalf. Perhaps art history will be taught as separate strands of timelines, as in the histories of classical music and jazz.

We must come to expect, and even embrace, the notion of change as the only constant. For the future, art resulting from the continuance of collaboration between the engineers, programmers, and the artists themselves (and in certain cases the melding of all these skills into a single individual) will pave the way into territories that today we cannot imagine, much as how the early 20th-century thinkers failed to perceive the innovations that they were to experience in the decades ahead. Like Isaac Newton, who acknowledged that he was able to innovate because he had "stood on the shoulders of giants," we stand as an artistic community, and as a species, on the continuous verge of cultural developments that can both create as well as destroy. It has often been the artist who has been best equipped to inform the community as to the perils that lie ahead, as well as the joys and realizations that will result in the avoidance of impending peril. With art as its beacon, humankind will use its electronic light to shine into the future, illuminating new discoveries in all areas of the creative process.

With its clarity of insight and open approach to the challenges and opportunities afforded artists by *Going Digital*, this book contributes much to that necessary illumination. Artists, gallery owners, curators, and jurors of art competitions alike will find this text essential and helpful as this new ground is broken and explored.

Michael Masucci

EZTV Media

Acknowledgments

The authors would like to thank Harald Johnson for taking on this project and showing us what authors do these days. Our thanks to editor Dan Foster and all the folks at Thomson Course Technology PTR, including Kevin Harreld, Heather Hurley, and Kristin Eisenzopf, who lent their expertise and care to seeing this project through. Our thanks also to layout technician Jill Flores and technical reviewer C. David Tobie. And, many thanks to all the artists who created work, got organized, and did what is sometimes the hardest thing to do concerning one's work: They talked about it.

Whom This Book Is For

This book was written to include a variety of audiences. Artists, photographers, and imagemakers of all types will find this book useful and informative. *Going Digital* will also help gallery owners, artists' guilds, art collectors, and art jurors who are challenged today to include and categorize an ever expanding array of new art forms for exhibitions and competitions. This book will also help anyone who wants a better understanding of the intricate similarities and differences that make digital art unique to the world of fine arts. Students should find the discussion of digital history, production techniques, and the aesthetic decisions made by artists as they develop work specifically for this book interesting and helpful. Regardless of your level or the approach you take toward art, the discussion and use of these new tools and the fresh vision of these artists provide clear insight into the rapidly developing field of digital art.

About the Authors

Joe Nalven learned skill sets including mechanical and architectural drafting early on in his education in a technical high school. Those skills helped frame his cut-and-paste collages for several decades. During his career as a cultural anthropologist he developed a better eye for composition while using photography in ethnographic research in Colombia, Mexico, and the United States. He moved into digital imaging in the late 1990s and has cultivated an "I can do that" attitude as he engages in a silent dialogue with the world of perception and imagination. He is one of the founders of the Digital Art Guild and the editor of its Webzine, www.digitalartguild.com. He also serves as one of the co-moderators for the Digital Fine-Art Yahoo Group. Joe's art and thoughts are available at www.digitalartist1.com.

Number Three

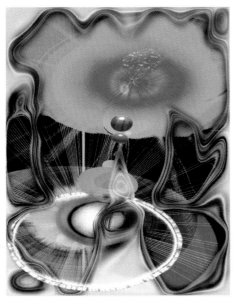

Birth of the Egg

JD Jarvis has accumulated a long career in TV production and graphic design. He earned a B.A. in mass communications and an MFA in video and mixed media, and he has written many articles on topics related to digital art, which have been widely published electronically and in the print media. His artwork has been featured in the Ylem Newsletter, *IEEE Computer and Applications* magazine, Northern New Mexico Gallery Guide and EFX, Art and Design. With some international exhibitions and other honors, he is encouraged to continue to create art and digital prints from his electronic studio in Las Cruces, New Mexico. JD's artwork and writing can be seen at www.dunkingbirdproductions.com.

Contents

Harmonious Horse 2 by Troy Eittreim (www.eittreim.com)

1

Following the Path to Digital Art

It has become popular when discussing digital art to search back for the earliest precedents in both science and art for the development and use of computers. In doing this, a "computer" is often defined by its loosest and most pliable definition—a device that offers a human operator controls for making predictable and repeatable results. Often that task has been to mimic human actions, and, in this light, it appears that computers go back as far as the late Renaissance. But the idea and the desire to build a bridge to the divine order of nature, a physical link whose shining achievement would be an artificial human being, is as old as the myths of ancient Chinese, Egyptian, Greek, and Arab cultures.

Leonardo da Vinci applied a mechanical metaphor to human movement and the articulations of machines. He spoke of *forza*—what he took to be the secret principles of life. He also laid the groundwork for automatons and robotics. Of course, early examples are crude attempts compared to the machinations of even our most common everyday appliances. The elaborate mechanical boxes upon which doll-like figures mimicked the actions of humans playing musical instruments and moved about in order to simulate dance fascinated those who were privileged to see them (see Figure 1.1.). More importantly, these mechanical boxes began the race for finer motions and increased functionality.

Figure 1.1 This automaton created by Henri Maillardet in the early 16th century carried within its cams and cogs the mechanical information to produce four drawings and three poems. Such mechanized works were exhibited throughout the Royal Houses of Europe.

Courtesy of The Franklin Institute of Science Museum, Philadelphia, PA.

More function requires more control and precise timing of nearly simultaneous events. And so, two channels of research and development evolved: one channel for articulation and motion and another for control and choreography of that movement; one channel for input and output, and another for processing and planning. The computer we have come to recognize is this later module, which times, coordinates, stores, and directs the *forza*. This *forza* is now electrical, and the artificial computer brain is the essential center of man–machine integration.

But, analog computing, operating with numbers and represented by measurable quantities of gear rotations, voltage, or resistance, could only go so far. Aside from the gates, envelope shapers, and filters found in electronic synthesizers of the '60s and '70s, the clockworks of analog computing have changed little since Leonardo's time. Until, that is, right in the middle of the last century, when in 1946, ENIAC (Electronic Numerical Integrator and Computer), the world's first digital computer, was introduced (see Figure 1.2). The numbers upon which this computer operates are expressed directly as digits of a decimal or binary system. And a new race for speed, miniaturization, and increased numbers of simultaneous calculations was on.

Figure 1.2 These four technicians are actually working inside the ENIAC computer that is installed in the three walls and equipment racks that surround them. The ENIAC was the world's first decimal-based digital computer. It was programmable and was employed mainly by the U.S. Army to calculate bomb and ordnance trajectories.

Courtesy of the U.S. Army and the Smithsonian Institute.

Also in the '40s, Norbert Wiener coined the term "cybernetics" (from the Greek "kybernetes," meaning governor or steersman) for the science of comparing communication and control systems, such as the computer and the human brain. This science brought attention back to the articulation, input, and output branch of computer research. Wiener's studies emphasized man–machine symbiosis, and in doing so added a different kind of fuel to the accumulated mythology of the quest for artificial life. His work focused on the interface and integration of humans with their machines—not as a Hollywood "cyborg," with bits and chunks of humans sewn into robotic armature, but as functional units or terminals upon which humans could navigate the hidden and nearly immaterial workings of the computer's electrical *forza*.

By 1951, with the patenting of UNIVAC, the world's first commercially available digital computer, the size of a digital computer had gone from two rooms full of electrical wires, tubes, and amplifiers to only one room. Ten years after UNIVAC, Theodor Nelson created the terms "hypertext" and "hypermedia" to describe a new space for writing and reading in which text, images, and sounds could be electronically linked by anyone on a network. In 1964, the RAND Corporation, a Cold War think tank, proposed the Internet as a communication network without central authority in order to be safe from nuclear attack. And, by 1968, with a concept that would hold great significance for visual artists, Douglas Engelbart introduced bitmapping, windows, and the direct manipulation of on-screen information to digital computing—all by way of a "mouse." This was a seminal moment in the development of establishing a symbiotic connection between the electrons flowing through a computer processor, an image on the computer screen, and the hand of the artist.

Bitmapping assigns small "bits" of a computer's memory to each screen pixel. Using the computer's binary code to turn some pixels on and others off, the computer screen becomes a controllable grid—a glowing, two-dimensional space. The mouse, which controls the screen cursor, becomes the proxy for the artist's hand as it moves around manipulating the computer's data space. And, as we know, two-dimensions—a way to make lights and darks and a means to leave one's mark— is all an artist needs to get busy. Indeed, this is all the artists of Chauvet Cave, Lascaux, Aboriginal Australia, or Daraki-Chattan required to set human beings to the task of making art.

The Cyborgs Among Us

As with berry juice and charcoal, type and ink, pigment and canvas, or pixel and code, artists have always sought to use the latest technology to make art. The computer, which of course has also been used for military, communication, counting, and calculating purposes, is no different. Art is often the open field from which, free of the need to produce practical results, human imagination is allowed full rein to play, to leap forward and to conceive, if not produce, the impossible. In spite of the amazing advances of the last 50 years, science and technology in its over five-hundred-year quest to create intelligent, artificial, human-like life has, thus far, failed. By contrast, literature and visual imagery (especially in the genres of science fiction and fantasy) dissolve the interface between biological evolution and technology (see Figure 1.3). Anything is possible in art, and often the job for science and technology is to catch up. In a very real way, when digital artists sit down before a pixel screen to do what artists have always done, they become the cyborgs of those distant technological dreams.

When science and technology do catch up with art, things do not often appear as imagined. There are no tubes running from foreheads, no glowing eyepieces or artificial limbs, no gleaming metallic torsos or bionic feats of strength. Rather, a normal human being sits down before a glowing screen—the computer monitor—that links us intellectually and physically to a highly maneuverable system of both deep self-reference and expanded global awareness. Virtual spaces glimmer into the real world. The non-tangible is made material. Creating, communicating, marketing, and distributing, all from the point of a digital computer interface, the cyborgs are already among us—and some, as always, are artists.

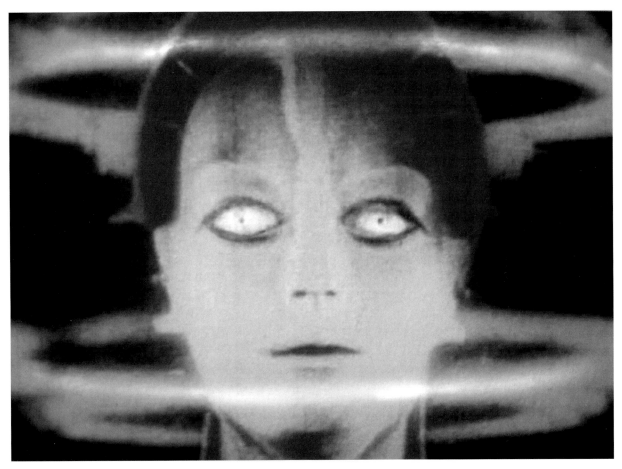

Figure 1.3 A scene from the Fritz Lang classic visionary sci-fi movie *Metropolis*. Film's first cyborg gets her first look at the brave new technological world that has created her.

The Transparent Revolution

Since digital computing did not begin until 1946, limiting our discussion to "digital art" considerably reduces the historical field of computer-integrated art. Graphic output has always played an important role in what these computer hardware and software tools are meant to do, and artists were often called in to aid designers in the early stages of R&D. Many early digital artists wrote their own software programs in order to solve their aesthetic problems, as do many Web and installation artists today. Analog and digital computing shared the developing art scene for quite a while. With the first public exhibitions of computer art held in 1965 (first in Stuttgart, Germany, and later that same year at the Howard Wise Gallery in New York), computer, if not digital, art had its toe in the door. And, by the end of the '60s the stage for the proliferation of the sort of digital art we see today was set with the first Ph.D. in computer graphics awarded to Ivan E.

Sutherland for "Sketchpad," a program he developed for interactive computer graphics (see Figure 1.4). His interface would prove to be the model for today's advanced drawing pads and pressure-sensitive tablets that allow for freehand cursive line input.

Figure 1.4 In a photograph appearing in his 1963 M.I.T. Doctoral thesis, Ivan Sutherland is seated at the "Sketchpad" operating module. "Sketchpad" was developed as an operator interface, which performed many of the same duties as a "mouse." This development led the way toward the pressure-sensitive tablets that many digital artists employ today.

Figure 1.4 © Sutherland, Ivan Edward, Sketchpad, a man-machine graphical communication system; published 1963. Courtesy of M.I.T. Format: BK. Location: Institute Archives – Collection 3 and Barker Library-Microforms. Thesis E.E. 1963 Ph.D.

As more such developments were made during the '70s and early '80s digital computing became more ubiquitous. Engelbart's bitmapping and Sutherland's interactive interface research saw fruition in the form of the "desktop" metaphor for a graphic user interface (GUI) developed in the early '70s by a team of researchers at Xerox PARC in Palo Alto, California, which was later popularized and marketed by Apple Computing in 1983. Artists finally had a much more user-friendly device for manipulating images directly without the need to design special code. Along with this desktop interface came an often overlooked phase in the development of current digital art: the adoption and integration of digital computer graphics into the world of commercial art, advertising, and publishing.

Commercial art directors set in motion much of what we see today—first, in terms of typography and typesetting, and later in page design, layout, and photographic manipulation. Along the way came the Macintosh. This new type of computer was important for integrating computers into existing workflows. When the Macintosh first came on the scene, many typesetters decried the fact that this new device did not possess the capabilities to finely control the spacing and setting of type. In addition, resolution was crude and color control was almost non-existent. Quality suffered and turf was lost. A single art director could change and control all aspects of a project from inception through design and right up to production. Millions of people who had no idea about the "rules" of design felt no loss when those rules were broken, and they now had control over the creative process. There was no going back. Expanding the creative bandwidth and getting more control of the overall process into fewer, and generally more creative, hands was found to be more efficient and would prove to win out over preserving worn out standards and traditional ways. And, when one part of a system goes digital, the rest of the system must follow in order to support it. The effects of new digitally derived media tools were already being felt—the individual was gaining more control over the entire production process.

Today, and for the foreseeable future, this creative bandwidth will continue to increase. The majority of images flooding our senses each day are made digitally. These new art-making tools have revolutionized commercial and fine art, photography, television, music, and film, and as such the term "digital art" is spread so thinly across so many artistic endeavors that, as an art movement, it is virtually transparent. It is often hard to notice something in front of your face and even harder to see something that is neatly embedded everywhere. But, if it is so widespread, is it fine art? If it is so transparent, what does it look like? Good questions. The answer begins by exploring the links between art made in traditional ways and art made using digital tools.

The Links Between Traditional and Digital Media

What does digital art look like? This is a slippery topic. Making the answer difficult is the chameleon-like ability of digital art to simulate the appearance of many traditional media and genres. So, it is often difficult to tell when work has been executed digitally or to what degree digital tools have played a role in the production of an image. In addition, certain commonly held beliefs, two of which are in direct opposition to one another, add to the camouflage about what digital art is and obscures its scope. For example, one idea based on digital imagery of nearly a generation ago, holds that computer art is boxy or pixelated with sharp vertical and horizontal lines and jagged diagonals (see Figure 1.5), that colors are uncontrolled and super saturated, and that the predominate forms hinge on infinite swirling repetitions. The image is likened to the children's favorite "Spirograph" (which, by the way, is a good example of an analog computer). Oddly enough, this idea survives today in spite of the converse belief that digital art serves mainly to create seamless realistic environments and characters that are indistinguishable from photographic reality. These limited views blind us to the expressive potential of digital imagery; these views also reflect the confusion and various degrees of acceptance for digital art tools within our culture.

There is also the belief that making digital art is an automated pastime requiring no more knowledge or artistic input than punching the "art" button. This beachcomber model for sitting back while the computer does all the work, and then simply choosing the best shell on the beach, is a misconception born out of computer phobia. If taken to its logical extreme, this misinformed belief would stifle exploration of the unique and fresh imagery that emerges directly from the digital

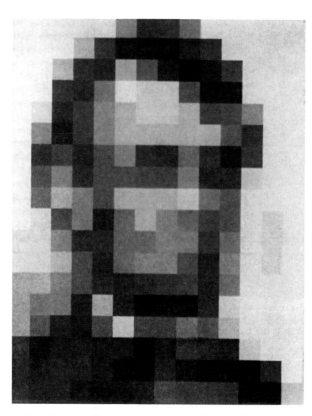

Figure 1.5 This image created by scientists at Bell Labs in 1973 nearly became the icon for digital imaging of the time. It was designed to determine the absolute minimum information required for a person to recognize a well-known face. Interestingly, once a person recognizes Lincoln in this image it becomes nearly impossible to not see the face. Human beings, as it turns out, are very well adapted for filling in missing information.

Figure 1.5 © Leon D. Harmon by permission of the Estate of Leon D. Harmon.

system. To ignore this potential and not utilize imagery that is derived from inside the digital matrix would be a serious artistic and conceptual loss. Plus, this attitude exemplifies another dilemma faced by digital artists. On one hand our culture holds that art ought to be something that is difficult and time-consuming to produce. A good deal of the value we attach to art is based on the amount of time and material sacrificed in its production. On the other hand, our culture wants to believe that its current technology is perfect in decreasing human drudgery and meeting the assumed need for efficiency and speed in the things we do. Digital computers, now the undisputed darlings of our culture of technology, have been designed and heavily marketed exactly as the answer to our need for this ease, efficiency, and speed. Digital artists, then, find themselves trapped in the cultural conundrum of using computers, which ostensibly make all things simple and easy, to make art, which is valued for being something that is difficult and time consuming to create. There is a cultural love/hate aspect to both our art and technology, and digital art finds itself at the front of both battles (see Figure 1.6).

Figure 1.6 *Rom-24* by Gerhard Katterbauer (www.katter.at). 3D modeling and photography were brought together in 3D environmental software to create this image. It is part photo, part sculpture, part theater in construction and application of lighting. It is a good example of art that finds itself "in-between" several genres of tools and art.

Sharing the front lines is a new form of media culture rising up to meet the new century. Possessing the capacity to convert all sorts of visual, aural, and textual information into binary code, and then store or transmit that code over a network barely limited by time or distance, the term "hypermedia" seems appropriate to describe this new state of media culture and all the associated digital tools. The sense of "hypermedia" used here signifies the expansive nature of new media tools and techniques beyond Theodor Nelson's original intent of that term to describe media-rich links within hypertext documents. Whereas mass media sought to reach into individual lives with generalized messages, the proliferation of hyper-media tools has changed the emphasis and flow of media so that individuals can shape messages that reach out to a general, even global, audience. And this audi-ence, in turn, is the source of yet more media; on and on it goes into a hyper state of communication and connectivity. Digital art is but one aspect of this growing hypermedia culture. The importance of recognizing this as a new culture allows us the latitude to consider that, while it is born out of the culture and makes aes-thetic comments upon that culture, the work may not necessarily have been exe-cuted digitally. If, indeed, there is an overriding culture and aesthetic of hypermedia, it must extend beyond a single set of tools. Just as Surrealism, Dada or Pop Art found expression in painting, literature, film, and theater, hyperme-dia will continue to spread its influence into all these forms and more. Appropriately, as noted earlier, commercial art was one of the first bastions of mass media to feel the pressure of hypermedia and to adapt to the potential of its dig-ital tools and adjust to the increase in creative bandwidth those tools bring about.

Commercial art was the stepping-off point for digital imaging and the place where it first reached a level of maturity. In the 1950s, the long held cultural fascination for realism in western European art joined with the popularity of psychoanalysis to form a heady combination of surrealistic imagery, dreams, sex, and marketing. This sort of imagery brought a spotlight onto photography and, in particular, photo-manipulation. In this context, photography, photographic manipulation, and collage have become primary aspects of current digital art. Eyes cannot easily draw away from the tabloid photos that seem to present the most unlikely things, nor can the illusion of airbrushed perfection be ignored. When digital tools arrived in the 1980s, these illusions increased in number and magnitude, to the point where such a time worn notion as "seeing is believing" is no longer a given.

Photography is also important to digital art by virtue of its long and bumpy path into the realm of fine arts and therefore serves as a model for most digital work that aims at that lofty goal. Photography was the source of fine art's first "point and click" dilemma. There is little doubt that photography relieved some western artists of the need to continue in their paintings the singular pursuit of realism, thus opening a path for explorations into Impressionism, Cubism, and Expressionism. But, when photography began to seek its own place in high art, the seeming ease with which the images could be made and the widespread pop-ularity among common and untrained individuals for making photographic images stood squarely in the way. The taint of technology that appears to remove the artist's hand from the direct manipulation of the work was another roadblock.

Digital art has seen this same sort of struggle, but as with photography, such resistance dissipates as more people learn about the intricacies and skills required to produce a really strong and effective digital image (see Figure 1.7).

Figure 1.7 *Via Nuevoa* by Peter L. Hammond (www.peterhammond.com). The photo-collage process by which this image was made can be recognized easily, but the resulting art remains wonderfully colorful and even mysterious.

This path is somewhat more complicated for digital painting. With its lack of many of the sensual pleasures, such as the smell of paint, the feel of wet pigment spread upon canvas, the play of texture and light, many may wonder how digital painting is painting at all. Similarities between traditional and digital painting include: the remarkable ability for digital software to mimic the appearance and behavior of many traditional and natural media; the linkage between the earliest human desire to make a mark and to employ the latest technology in doing so; and the lasting dependence on traditional overarching principles of composition, line, texture, form, and rhythm to construct an effective composition (see Figure 1.8).

Figure 1.8 *Agaves on the Edge, Summer* by Cher Threinen-Pendarvis (www.pendarvis-studios.com). This image is an excellent example of how digital tools can be used to mimic the appearance of traditional painting and drawing media.

However, while there are these links to most traditional and natural media, a digital paint brush represented by a cursor on the screen can be programmed to produce a resulting "brushstroke" of amazing and unique complexity. Patterns and complete images can be placed onto the screen with a single stroke. Filters driven by mathematical algorithms perform hundreds of complex rearrangements of pixels with controllable, predictable, and yet surprising results. By saving versions of an art piece as it develops or by employing "undo" functions that remove recent manipulations to restore an image to an earlier state, the artist's spontaneity is preserved throughout the creative process (see Figure 1.9).

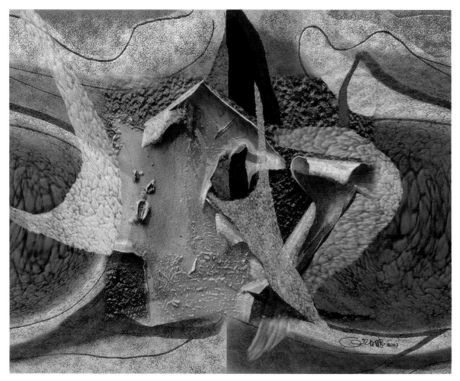

Figure 1.9 *Composition* by Vijay Bhai Kochar (www.vijaybhai-digitalvisions.com). With the addition of texture generators, layering effects, cut and paste, and "brush-looks" simulators, the digital painter's palette has been expanded to include some expressive new tools.

Compare the digital to the traditional painter. The traditional painter finds the piece becoming very precious as it nears completion. The irredeemable nature of paint plus the expense of costly materials and time spent bringing the piece to the point of completion can make a traditional artist reluctant to take chances that might destroy the work.. With digital working methods there is nothing holding a digital artist back from experimenting with a last-minute, spontaneous idea, because all work saved before that risky maneuver can be redeemed almost instantly. As a result, digital artists have more time and freedom to deal with composition, to explore completely an image's possibilities, and to follow and preserve divergent streams of thought while working on a piece.

The Velocity of Imagination

Digital painting does have its drawbacks. Most random effects that occur with natural media cannot be duplicated in digital media without hard work, attention to detail, and patience. For example, when one splatters paint across a canvas, the results are ultimately a random consequence of gravity, viscosity, and absorption, but the pattern is recognizable and somewhat predictable. Sprinkling salt on wet watercolor has identifiably different results than stippling paint with a toothbrush. These actions are random and happen automatically without much artistic effort or exertion of control, since control is, in the first place, what the artist is trying to relinquish or avoid by using these techniques. Painters have used these random procedures for hundreds of years to add spontaneity and looseness, as well as surprise, to their work (see Figure 1.10).

Figure 1.10 *Mossy Glen* by JD Jarvis. The randomness of ink splattered or dripped onto paper was scanned, then carefully composed in digital layers and mixed with applied gradients to combine the spontaneity of some traditional painting techniques with the control and colorations of digital processes.

In the mid '70s, another seminal moment in the development of digital image making occurred when mathematician Benoit Mandelbrot brought to attention what he called "Fractal Geometry." Mandelbrot, who had been working on modeling the fluctuations in cotton futures, was able to show how infinitely repeatable mathematical forms occur in what was often considered random or free-flowing structures within nature (see Figure 1.11). While working at IBM's Watson Research Center, he had developed some of the first computer programs to print graphics. He used these facilities to demonstrate how his fractal geometry could describe complex natural forms, such as cloud formations, the distribution of leaves and twigs on a tree, the shape of a coastline, or the infinitely self-iterating form of a seashell. In combination, fractal mathematics and digital computing brought a new kind of image to art making. Patently beautiful and seductive, fractal images seem to display the math of the infinite (see Figure 1.12). But beyond this distinctive imagery, fractal algorithms have come to direct the behavior of many of the filters and other image-manipulating subprograms that digital artists regularly employ to generate special visual effects that are then integrated into their artwork. Fractal geometry has made it possible for artists to model their own photorealistic landscapes, architecture, and environments in a virtual three-dimensional space.

Figure 1.11 This early image was created from a fractal equation named for the mathematician himself. In the 1970s, Benoit Mandelbrot coined the term "fractals" to describe his simple mathematical formulas that yield complex visual results.

Figure 1.11 © 1982 Dr. Benoit B. Mandelbrot, IBM Thomas J. Watson Research Center.

Figure 1.12 *Marine Scene* by Michael Sussna (www.sussna.com). This contemporary fractal image demonstrates the depth and patent beauty of fractal geometry put to the purpose of creating art. Fractal images appear fresh and new, and yet remain somehow familiar. We recognize the mathematics of nature in these designs.

In the case of digital painting, filters and fractal generators perform algorithmic image distortions or apply pixels in patterns that provide the sort of random, yet predictable, results analogous to traditional randomized painting techniques. By exploring and piling action upon action, the digital artist can guide the imaging system to present unexpected and beautiful results. As with splattered paint, the resulting forms can suggest meaning to the artist's imagination as well as suggest new directions to the developing composition. As the artist works back and forth between steering the process and relinquishing control to the caprices of the tools, a symbiotic dance is performed and nurtured between maker and what is being made. This visual "jam session" gives rise to imagery that the artist could not have imagined without the spontaneous interface between the artist's psyche, his or her hand, and the work as it evolves in the moment.

Digital technology facilitates and expands the bond between human artist and emerging work. This is due mainly to the speed with which the technology can respond and display the results of what a moment ago was only contained in one's mind. Making digital art in this fashion is very much like having a conversation with something perceived to be infinitely deep and yet intimately personal. The computer supplies the depth of infinite visual variety and possibility while the human mind supplies the imagination, warmth, and the connection to meaning. Many digital artists express the exhilaration of having a tool that works as fast as their imagination.

Digital art has much in common and shares many links with traditional art making. As with any artistic tool, such as a brush or a camera, digital imaging systems can be utilized for expressing any variety of artistic styles or personal statements. Between the 50s and 80s, Pop Art emerged and flourished as a stylistic art movement during a time when many of the major developments in digital computing were being made. Only a few Pop artists made limited use of digital computing, but, as an art movement, Pop Art laid some important groundwork for digital art to follow into the galleries and museums. Pop introduced and made acceptable what had been considered commercial processes, tools, and materials for the creation of fine art. Pop Art reflected on mass media and the immediate culture that formed around it, using that media conceptually and materially in the production of work. Computers, by the same token, are now used pervasively in all sorts of commercial creative endeavors and are themselves a current cultural phenomenon as well as a means of commenting on that phenomenon. Making art digitally is a perfect conceptual fit for most aspects of the Pop aesthetic. And yet, digital art is not Pop Art. Digital art has a much broader scope.

Aesthetics form around both tools and vision. There are aesthetics for the broad field of painting, and there are aesthetics for particular art movements, such as Surrealism or Pop Art. "Digital" is both an all-encompassing set of tools and an emerging cultural aesthetic. It can be many things to many people. So, what is it, really? (See Figure 1.13.)

Figure 1.13 *I Had No Earthly Idea* by Werner Hornung, (horning@wanadoo.fr). This image utilizes nearly all the manipulation, painting, and digital techniques available. The synthesis of tools, processes, and styles shows the way to an expressive and versatile new way to make art.

The Real Thing

As noted, a large percent of 2D visual digital art is presented and displayed in the form of prints. Printing is a time-honored form of image making. It involves the preparation of a matrix by either etching a negative or engraving a positive version of the intended final image onto a stone or some form of plate. This matrix or ground is inked and brought, under pressure, into contact with a substrate, usually made of paper. The image is transferred from matrix to substrate, and a print is born. When photography arrived on the scene, much of the physicality of printmaking was traded in for photochemical action. The stone or metal matrix could be easily pointed to or examined as the source of the image, but the photographic negative is much more ephemeral and does not easily under direct examination reveal the nuances of the finished work. The role of a matrix, of sorts, was retained, but little else remained except for the concept of making multiples of a particular image. It hardly seems like "printing" at all. However, the terminology stuck. It was a comfortable way to categorize and deal with a new technology.

This matrix is dematerialized even further with the arrival of digital printing. In the context of digital technology, the print matrix or the original object of art is not an object at all. Digital art is created and exists primarily in a state of encoded binary information that cannot be seen or accessed without the implementation of a viewing or imaging device—a computer monitor screen or printing system. Making this encoded digital original into an object—making it material—depends as much on the performance of the imaging system as it does on the artwork itself. One without the other is nothing. So, in precise terms, any direct viewing or printing of the binary code is a "production" of the artwork, not a "reproduction." Of course, like many traditional printing methods, digital technology is used to make reproductions of art that originates outside the computer. Art executed in some other medium can be photographed or scanned into the computer and reproduction prints can be made. These are commonly called *giclée* prints. But, when the art is composed and created directly inside the CPU there is no such original work of art to "reproduce." Rather, there is a formless original artwork that must be produced, replicated, or otherwise made tangible in order to be present to our experience in the first place.

This somewhat confusing distinction does have some precedent in other art forms. Poetry, for example, is art that shares a similar formless, encoded state until it is read. As with digital, the book or binary file is present, but the act of reading or decoding is required to evoke the art from its form of storage or transmission. Music is a coded art that requires performance to be appreciated. A film is just a long transparent ribbon on a metal reel until it is projected; only then does it become the film we experience and enjoy. With digital technology, as with video and film, the variety of divergent technical means by which the art can be viewed requires a different definition of the term, "original work of art." Using the terminology of these other technologically driven art forms, the digital original is more like a "master file" rather than a static or fixed object. Viewing the digital original on a computer screen requires different nuances in color and the balance of lights and darks compared to the same digital file as it is printed on paper. Differences in papers, inks, and printing systems require adjustments in the digital original in order to produce the best replication of the file as a physical print. And, viewing the art on the Web requires still more manipulations of the original master file to optimize its presentation. As a nearly intangible, ever active, always amendable entity requiring evocation in order to be brought to our awareness, this master file resembles an idea or thought much more than an object. And, while most will agree that art ought to be made of something, no one will deny that art begins in the form of a thought or an idea (see Figure 1.14). Certain ideas and images have survived many permutations of human culture and thrive today like ancient transmissions of knowledge or long-held dreams. Art may come and go, but these ideas are "archived" in our genes.

Figure 1.14 *Ancient Transmission* is a "mixed artist and media" piece with input from Leonardo da Vinci, Man Ray, Kai Krause, Benoit Mandelbrot, and hundreds of graphic software programmers. Concept and design by JD Jarvis.

The sum of our discussion to this point has been to depict the manner by which digital computing grew from a long-held human obsession to create a lively, if not living, interface between man and machine. We have recognized how digital imaging tools are connected with, and have expanded upon, the techniques and capabilities of the traditional forms of photography, collage, mark-making (in drawing or paint), and printing. We have glimpsed how the techniques of digital art suggest a new synthesis of many existing art forms, genres, and styles. We have examined how this new synthesis challenges old paradigms, causing us to consider, for example, the dematerialized nature of the digital original. This dematerialized state, in turn, leads to various mechanized means to visualize and materialize the digital original. We are thereby confronted by art that conveys complexity and the artist's passion, but it is presented with an aloof and mediated technological patina. We have acknowledged how the principals of mimicry, facsimile, simulation, and illusion inform the emerging digital aesthetic. We have noted that, as a device integral to modern culture, the computer represents both the tool and the medium to both shape and express this culture. We have touched on the liveliness of an as yet unaffected body of diverse art which, by virtue of its democratization, has gained much, and has much, much, more to offer.

What does digital art look like? If looking at the work raises questions as to whether it might be a painting, print, or photograph, and the answer is "yes" to all three, then it is most likely a piece created from within the emerging digital aesthetic.

LB Surfer by Jack Davis (www.software-cinema.com/htw/)

2

Looking at Digital Art

Looking and seeing are two different things. This chapter takes our first step in scanning the world of digital art. We discuss how one looks at objects and how one is influenced by the words that describe them, how digital art is composed with imaging software, and how such art is often discussed. The discussion is deepened considerably as each of the featured artists in the following chapters takes the reader on journeys into creating digital art in their particular style. After reviewing what these artists have done, a discussion about *seeing* digital art and categorizing digital art becomes more meaningful. At that point it will be easier to attend to what we have been *looking* at, but may not have been able to *see*.

Understanding What It Is

Understanding art is at once simple and complex—simple, when viewers look at an image and say, "I like it" or "I don't like it"; complex, when someone asks "What makes this a good (or bad) image?" or "What makes this a strong (or weak) image?"

Some viewers may anticipate difficulty in understanding digital art because of the toolsets digital artists use to create their work. Caution may overcome the viewer who is uncertain of making any judgment without being able to tell exactly what the artist is doing. When we look at a painting we understand what is going on in the production of that picture. Or do we? We understand that the artist is rubbing a pigment onto a prepared ground. We know the color comes in tubes and the artist usually uses brushes. But, most of us do not understand the chemical composition of the pigments or understand the interaction of many of the additives put into pigments. Do we ask who wove the canvas cloth or who created the pigments? But still, recognizing that these days the artists themselves did not grind the pigments or prepare the ground does not devalue the painting. We *understand* painting, but perhaps we do not *know* it as deeply as we think we do. We *look*, but what do we *see*?

Digital artists enlist a new set of tools for the making of their art. Tools understood to be complex, cold, unforgiving, and restrictive. You have to use digital things in just the right way or the whole mechanism freezes up—and then what? Can images made by such mechanized and restrictive means be art? Clearly, this understanding of computers is incomplete, which sometimes causes us to overlook the art and instead focus on how, and by what tools, the images are made. However, lacking the comfort of *knowing* the deepest aspects of the tools should not be allowed to distract us from *understanding* the art. Regardless of our knowledge of the processes and tools used to make art, the age-old rules of composition, color theory, quality of the line, and the rhythm of patterns remain in force. One does not need to know how an image was made in order to value it, aesthetically.

Some viewers of digital art may be fearful of being tricked. As with the proverbial picture painted by the hand of a monkey or the trunk of an elephant, how do we know a piece of digital art is indeed something over which a human being diligently and honestly toiled. There can be no doubt that soon monkeys will be using computers to make digital art and perhaps receiving the same critical acclaim and patronage that their oil painting friends enjoy. Art trickery is nothing new and certainly not particular to digital art. But here again, the question really isn't about the art but rather the trustworthiness of the artist or the exhibitor. In either case, whether the doubts one harbors about digital art concern the use of certain tools or the authenticity of the artist's intent toward the work offered, education and familiarity hold the best remedies.

You can expect further pressure on the visual arts to retool for digital image making. Even if one pursues traditional oil painting, for example, there is still an advantage in being able to use and understand digital imaging techniques. The versatility of digital is critical in commercial production techniques for speeding up the process and offering more choice. While there is a learning curve to acquiring digital skills, the advantages of these tools lie in the ability to further explore more variations in composition, nurture more avenues of thought, synthesize styles, and output the images quickly for further development and study.

The production and expression of art, as with much of contemporary culture, has been affected in many ways by digital technology. To be wise about evaluating how the process gets done and how to value the output, the viewer is required to make an intelligent assessment. The first step is framing a discussion that embraces all art—digital or otherwise—and this step needs a laser-like focus on what a viewer really *sees*.

Talking About Art

Discussion can distract from the enjoyment of art. However, discussion can also add insight into the artist's intent, life story, and the tools the artist uses to create a specific artwork. Discussion and comparison between artists and art styles should not be viewed as competition but rather as a prime method for enhancing enjoyment and understanding of the very human urge to create.

One way of comparing artists is to look at how they treat similar subject matter, whether a common landscape, portrait, or a bowl of fruit. But the comparison is made more difficult if the artists are not looking at the same landscape at the same time of day, during the same season, standing in the exact same location, with the same perspective of what is viewed. An effective comparison needs some common or uniform elements—some anchor points. But do we know exactly what we are comparing when we look at art? Perhaps not. A fanciful example will sharpen this premise.

A Show at the Museum of Art: *Black on White*

Suppose you walk into the Museum of Art—a museum with a new exhibit called *Black on White*. The room housing the exhibit is small and set off from the regular exhibits of 18th-century landscapes. The room traditionally houses exhibits dedicated to the boundaries of the human imagination.

You approach the first image. It appears to be a line, more or less straight and more or less textured with shades of black. The line is inscribed on a fabric that looks like white canvas. The title plate says, "Unknown Artist. Carbon dated to 8000 BP. Southwest USA. Found inside a recessed area of cave. Thought to represent hunting weapon with magical qualities" (see Figure 2.1). You might wonder about magic as a much needed adjunct to the harsh surrounds of life thousands of years earlier. Life without the constant light and noise of contemporary life—a life without modern shelter and weapons. As much as can be inferred from life in a primitive technological period, art likely expressed magical desires to control the environment.

You walk over to the next image and it looks remarkably the same: a black line on a white canvas. The title plate says, "Artist: Emilio Velez. A Lone Tree on an Alaskan Snowscape as Seen through Snow Goggles" (see Figure 2.2.). As you think about the artist's description, you might nod in agreement: "Yes, there is the brilliant white snow. The snow goggles prevent me from being overwhelmed and blinded by the whiteness of the snow. The tree looms up—a solitary pole of blackness." The artist's intent is clear, revealing, and persuasive.

Figure 2.1 *Hunting Weapon with Magical Qualities.*
Unknown artist. Carbon dated to 8000 Before Present. Southwest U.S.

Having fully absorbed the impressions crafted by the artist of a black tree on white snow, you now walk to the next painting. This image appears to be the same as the previous image—a line, more or less straight and more or less textured with shades of black. You look at the artist's description and it says, "Frank Morton: A Picture of the Universe." Aha. You recall the story of the well-known photo-astronomer.

Figure 2.2 *A Lone Tree on an Alaskan Snowscape Seen through Snow Goggles* by Emilio Velez.

He took a photorealistic image of the object (the universe) and placed it on white canvas. A naturalistic approach to image making. Again, the artist's intent is clear, revealing, and persuasive (see Figure 2.3).

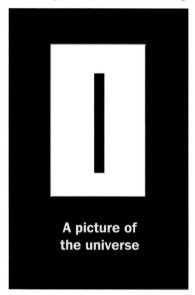

Figure 2.3 A Picture of the Universe by Frank Morton.

You continue on through the exhibit. The next image looks strikingly like the last three, except this one is labeled, "Noemi Parvet: The Number One." It's an abstraction codified as blackness on whiteness, and, again, the artist's intent is clear, revealing, and persuasive (see Figure 2.4).

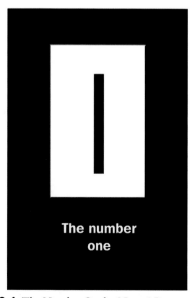

Figure 2.4 *The Number One* by Noemi Parvet.

You now come to the fifth image. Again, the resemblance is remarkable, but here the description states, "Xingua-Jun: Black Color on White Canvas." It is what it is, not a fiction or symbol of something else, but only itself, as if to say, "There is no art, but just color on canvas" (see Figure 2.5). Wanting to appear modern and "with it," you grudgingly accommodate this piece; after all, the artist's intent is clear, revealing, and persuasive.

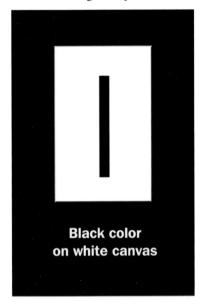

**Black color
on white canvas**

Figure 2.5 *Black Color on White Canvas* by Xingua-Jun.

In thinking back on the exhibition thus far, you realize that you just experienced the breadth of the visual artistic endeavor—from magical object, to impressionistic, to naturalistic, to abstract expressionist perspectives and, of course, the nihilist who claims there is no art, but simply ego put to canvas in the nature of colored inks.

Yes, there are different traditions and individual styles within these visual perspectives, and it is very much worth the effort to appreciate these variations. One might also argue that by stepping back we can understand the limits of human thought and, by way of those limits, understand the unity of the visual artistic endeavor—at least in terms of the human experience up to this point in history. But even with these limits, the variety of human expression is immense.

With this one black line on a white canvas, we have already seen five distinct pictures: a magical line, a tree on a snowscape, a picture of the universe, the number one, and black paint on white canvas. The physical markings are the same, but the context—defined by words—sets them apart as different "objects" or different perceptions of visually identical objects.

The human experience is not a closed enterprise. Our imagination is inflected by the world of words. These are the words we are taught and learn to use in a particular cultural space; they are words that we bend and shape to our particular needs.

The curator of this show, *Black on White*, helped pave the way to show that with the same starting point there are many ways to concoct artistic imagery. To be sure, the curator's work invites further discussion to amplify what we see and discuss within the artistry of each object.

And now, you notice that there is a sixth image. This image is also a black line on a white canvas. The title plate reads, "Chefren 2: That Thou Art" (see Figure 2.6). The artist notes that he had seen the earlier show and was doing a reinterpretation of the earlier images. This artist explains that he was conveying the relationship between his idea and the pixels within a digital imaging program. He further notes that this image is, in fact, a collage of all the other images presented in this exhibit and that his work is a synthesis of all the styles and contextual statements presented, and, as such, his digital art work constitutes something new and unique in art.

Figure 2.6 *That Thou Art* by Chefren 2.

The curator of the show was skeptical. The curator had been tempted to exclude this sixth image because it looked like derivative art. Nothing unique in this black line on white canvas. He was even more disturbed by the notion that it may have been made by a machine.

The curator finally decided that he did not know enough to categorize this art-work. Maybe it was a new style of art or a new technology that reframed how reality might be perceived. The curator saw the crowds around this last image and accepted the digital artist's intent as a matter of faith.

This fanciful example takes the point of view of a curator who presumably knows a field of art and who looks back over a period of time. By contrast, this book looks forward in time and is an adventure in art making. Our curator attempts a conclusion about existing art rather than setting the stage for an experiment. The question becomes, "How can one craft an experimental approach to explore making art with digital-imaging software while, at the same time, keeping the same laser-like focus used in discussing the *Black on White* exhibit above?"

How Did You Do That?

Before explaining how this experimental approach would work, some basic understanding of digital imaging is required. A useful starting point revolves around the frequently heard question concerning how computer art is made.

When the artist is confronted with the question, "How did you do that?" there is an assumption that the answer will somehow explain what the viewer likes or dislikes about the image. Often, the viewer loses the sense of mystery as a result of the explanation and at the same time gleans nothing more from the explanation than, "Oh, the computer did it." This discussion is not helpful to the viewer or the artist.

Still, the question "How did you do that?" is worth asking even though the details are incomplete. This question opens the door to taking a first look at the inner workings of art going digital—a good place to start before discussing particular artist visions and styles, which will be the subject of the artists featured in this book. This is the process that digital and computer graphic artists use (varying, of course, with the specific digital toolsets of the imaging software), and which is helpful in identifying some of the elemental considerations in digital composition.

Transforming a Rock Formation—
A Digital Imaging Example

The first comparison in discussing image transformation is to look at the *before* and *after* images—ostensibly the *original* and the *final* image. However, there is a minor, but important, difference between the before image and how original it is. In the image discussed here, the original image of the rock came out of a digital camera as a JPEG file. For the purpose of this discussion, the image has been slightly adjusted—cropped, selectively blurred where the rock was worn and pock marked, and the brightness and contrast bumped up. The interest here is different from the typical photographic objective. The goal in this discussion is to focus on transforming an image (and an adjusted "original," or "before," image works just fine), which is quite different from that of a photographer who wants an untouched photograph to serve as a reflection of reality.

Next to the "before" (or adjusted original) image is the final one. "Finality," of course, is arbitrary in the sense that it is a momentary stopping point; the artist may continue to change the image, perhaps to create a series of "final" images, perhaps to adapt it for commercial use, or perhaps to save it as a backdrop for yet another image (see Figure 2.7).

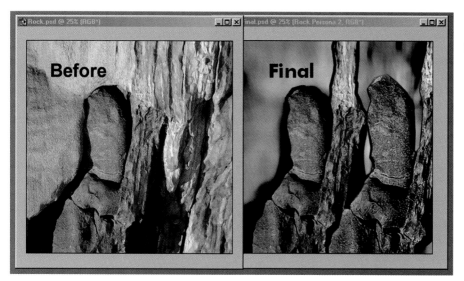

Figure 2.7 Comparison of the "before" (adjusted original) and "final" image.

What happened between the "before" and the "final" image? What are the important things to learn, and what things are not significant for the discussion here? The last question, "What is not significant here?" leads the discussion into the subject matter of books about technique that go into great detail on how to use specific imaging software, such as Painter, Photoshop, KPT, Lightwave, Maya, Dogwaffle, Photo Studio, and many more.

In a far more elaborate fashion, the featured artists of this book (beginning in Chapter 4) will take three uniform source images, or "seed images," as we'll call them (see Chapter 3) and will use their personal art style to create a new composite—a new vision. In the pages that follow, the discussion of technique is balanced with discussion of each artist's decisions about composition.

But first, the more general question in making—or for that matter, in viewing—any digital images is how to locate the artistry in the image.

Did the Computer Do It?

The question about whether the computer created the artwork can be asked again, whether about the simple transformation of the rock image or about the far more complex transformations that appear in the following chapters. Should any credit be given to the digital-imaging program relative to the artistry of the image?

Of course, the answer is yes and no.

Just as the oil painter who uses a brush must credit the brush, so too the digital artist must credit the digital imaging program. And, in this comparison, the greater credit goes to the mind and sensibilities of the artist rather than to the tools of his or her craft.

At another level, the question can be re-asked, "What about the duplicating of the rock image?" (See Figure 2.7.) A traditional painter would have painted the second figure himself, but the digital artist would simply clone (copy) it.

Well, what about this concern? In one respect, this question merely restates that oil painting uses a different toolset and manner of application than digital imaging, and that difference in toolsets is already known. So what if one draws with a brush on a canvas, or uses a digital brush or mouse to draw or paint in a digital-imaging program, or simply uses the computer's iterative powers to duplicate and place the objects. In all cases, it is the mind of the artist that is making choices and applications.

Perhaps there is another question to ask that involves a specific technology, such as a camera, which captures images differently than a painter does. From a neutral point of view, shouldn't each technology be given its due? Or are some technologies—like oil and brush—somehow superior to other technologies like a camera or computer imaging? Of course, each person will have his own take on the value of the various media; the purpose here is to show how art works within the digital medium and not to position it as *better* or *stronger* than any other medium. In this sense, it is simply another tool that an artist might employ.

Down by Robert "Beto" Ambler.

Specialized digital tools, adjustments, mathematical formulas, and filters are part of the digital-imaging craft. The applications of these are what the computer-imaging software does. But these applications do not occur automatically; the artist must know how, when, where, and to what extent to use these applications to demonstrate artistry. The more important and expansive part of the answer to whether the computer did it becomes: "And let me count the ways!" However, this *counting the ways* in which a digital artist undertakes art making is easily swamped by the sheer variety of techniques and imaging software; so, it is helpful to eliminate some of the variation in order to allow the focal points in the creative process to emerge.

For this reason, artists featured in the following chapters have been limited to the same starting point—to the same three uniform source images. From that point, the adventure begins, and we can better understand how each artist makes use of the immense number of ways the computer provides for crafting imagery.

Seed Image 1

Seed Image 3

Seed Image 2

3

In the Beginning, There Were Three Images

Comparing art made by different artists is always problematic—the more so when the art made by these various artists began at different starting points, which is, of course, the usual case. But what if the artists started in the same place? With identical images as their source of inspiration?

One premise of this book is that by restricting our featured artists to the same starting point—three pre-selected "seed images"—variations in individual styles and techniques become more transparent and finely drawn. In addition, by circumscribing their imaginations at the very beginning of the process, the artists were forced to craft their way toward an understanding of what these pictures meant to them. That struggle between craft and making art lead to some interesting revelations about what it is that a digital artist does differently, as well as what is absolutely shared and similar between digital and traditional media. That premise and the adventure of this book begins with three seed images—a woman, an urban grid, and a canyon—that have been given to the artists featured in this book as their identical starting point.

The previous chapter underscored the importance of context and how language and culture shape our perception. In that chapter, the hypothetical example showed how several images that all appeared identical—namely, with a black line on a white canvas—could be viewed as different things when the language used to describe each work led the viewer into a different context for each image. And now the context is broadened considerably with images rich in color, shape, form, and content, reaching into different aspects of the human condition. This is particularly so with the use of photographs for capturing different aspects of the human condition—a person, a built environment, and a natural landscape. In terms of visual currency, the photograph has become the dominant medium and makes a good reference for the artists to begin their creative adventure in this book.

With the billions of photographic images available today, the problem of selecting just a few is challenging. Which images would be best? Perhaps it may not matter what initial images are chosen, and a random choice would suffice. After all, this selection is not meant to be a scientific experiment. However, as an adventure in art, some forethought about the selection of the initial photographic images will make the transformative process of each featured artist a bit more intriguing. Beyond the previously mentioned fact of the widespread use of photographs, there are other reasons to select photographs as the common reference point. Why should we choose photographs rather than paintings or prints as our seed images? This has to do with the notion of agreement—of people seeing, as much as possible, the same thing. The use of photographs as seed images removes one more layer of interpretation. And, even though the time-honored notion that a photograph somehow fixes reality into a permanent state of truth—that "photos do not lie"—is rapidly undergoing re-examination and change, for the most part, a photograph represents a form of visual agreement. We see in a photograph essentially what we are meant to see. The fact that in the context of digital manipulation a photo is merely a starting point—without the baggage of truths or lies—will become sharply evident as we go along.

So what types of photographs should be considered? How about the photographic quality? What size, color, shape, perspective, and distance from the viewer should be represented in these photographic images? We discussed all these questions, and more.

Why These Three Images?

Art reflects humanity in important ways—in different historical moments, in different cultures, in times of crisis as well as in meditative and jubilant moods. Art also reflects how individuals see themselves and how they see others. In sum, art reflects the myriad ways in which the human condition is experienced and fantasized about. This includes "seeing" landscapes, flowers, animals, the stars, and bacteria. In this way, the images considered for this book began with the question, "What is central to the human condition?"

The comparison of the artists included in this book could not have too many starting points; that would make the comparison ineffective. So, three images were selected—definitely a tight constraint, but also a tight focus. This type of comparison can be repeated—and well it should—with different types and number of starting points to continue this experiment in teasing out differences in art styles and production techniques.

The selected images were chosen to represent several different environments in which individuals find themselves: the social and personal environment represented by the image of another person (Figure 3.1), the built environment represented by an architectural image (Figure 3.2), and the natural environment represented by one of our best known canyons (Figure 3.3). Other environments merit attention, but these three provide a good beginning within our framework. We provided these three images to each of the participating artists with the request that they use no other photographic images in their artwork.

Figure 3.1 *Female Figure Seated* (Seed Image 1) by Joe Nalven.

Figure 3.2 *Architectural Detail* (Seed Image 2) by Joe Nalven.

Figure 3.3 *Grand Canyon View* (Seed Image 3) by JD Jarvis.

This selection of images represents the type of photographs taken by many camera enthusiasts. In the following chapters, the featured artists will deform and manipulate these images, and then resurrect them as new images. Given the guidelines provided to the artists to use these photographs as starting points, the use of "better" photographs would have misconstrued the role that our "seed" images play. This is not a book about photography, but a book that uses photographs as source images—images that will be transformed with digital toolsets. In this sense, the wiser decision is to use photographs that are "good enough," rather than picture perfect.

A Method for Making Comparisons

The method of having artists work with the same uniform source images has several advantages: the comparison of images can provide a window into each artist's creative process by seeing how the image evolves; also, the comparison can provide a basis for talking about art styles, especially in relation to the new digital imaging technology that more and more artists are using. As mentioned earlier, our method would be an adventure in ideas and, if properly constructed, would be a springboard for talking about and appreciating art making in the twenty-first century.

The method itself merits a closer look. As previously noted, the starting point is providing a core number of digital artists with the same photographic images. The artists are given an equal amount of time to construct their own image from these initial photographic images or to use them as inspiration, especially where their own style does not use photography (for example, a painter who paints from objects or a fractalist who uses mathematical formulas). At the same time, the artists were asked to keep a journal to document their decisions—whether to crop the original photographs, whether to superimpose them, whether to add texture and color, and the large array of other compositional decisions. This is the core process that the artists use to construct their images. A second-tier discussion compares the artists' work processes and results in terms of the paths they set for themselves and also includes general observations about the commonalities of making art digitally.

But there is a lot more that these digital artists will consider—these are the specific turning points that reflect their individual aesthetic choices. At the outset, decisions will focus on how to use the uniform source images. Those who prefer to paint may use the photographic images only as points of reference as they craft their own painting that is evoked from these photographs. This painting, of course, occurs inside a software program on the artist's computer. The next set of decisions may involve mixing painting with photography, perhaps using elements of the photographic images and melding them together with "brush" tools or applying an algorithmic filter or changing the blending mode across several layers; perhaps even painting out areas of the emerging image. Then, there are digital artists who use fractal plug-ins to generate elaborate patterns. They will make yet other decisions on direct or inspirational use of these initial photographic images.

While this book is not intended to be a tips and tricks book, nor will we attempt to explain all the various digital imaging software, the artists will illuminate their image creation process to show where and to what extent their techniques optimize their styles.

Discovering the Paths to Creativity

Art styles can be effectively compared when the starting point for each artist is the same. Many of the similarities and differences are immediately visible to everyone. This immediacy allows viewers to discover their likes and dislikes as they see what the artists have done to transform the common starting point and to aid them in making judgments about what makes an image *strong* or *weak*. The art critic, museum curator, and individual collector have more specific notions of the *goodness* or *strength* of an art work, but the specialist's judgment in no way undermines popular notions about what is appealing in the millions of images found in magazines, movies, or television, as well as art galleries and museums. The popular eye is as important to this experience as the specialist's.

Beyond the immediacy of seeing different artwork emerge from the same starting photographic images, it will be possible to identify important differences in how each artist works and how each artist conceptualizes a style of art. This method of working with uniform seed images minimizes the variation at the point of departure—every reader can see the identical starting point. It is transparent; there are no hidden tricks. Unlike painters or photographers who look out upon a common landscape or model, this method fixes the point of view, the color, lighting, and other content. By constraining the variation in the starting point for each artist, the understanding of the creative process becomes clearer, partly by what is seen in each artist's steps along the pathway and partly by what the artist describes in documenting his or her deep creative processes.

Some unasked questions remain. Will this comparison and hard work yield a digital aesthetic? Will there be some conclusion made about digital creativity? Will this approach only show how digital toolsets are used? Or, will digital art emerge as a distinct and separate art form? More likely, these questions will make sense after reading and viewing what each artist does and says.

The show begins.

The Wind Catcher

4

Ileana Frómeta Grillo

Prior to discovering digital drawing in 1988, Ileana studied traditional media in her native Caracas and California, including drawing, painting, sculpture, and photography. The pictures she creates are compositions of figures and characters created in Corel Painter combined with textures and images captured with her digital camera. Unless suggested by someone, the main image comes to her as a loosely drawn sketch. "I carry my digital camera wherever I go, and store the images taken on CDs for later use. I later select a sketch that grabs my attention and use it as the foundation for a finished picture of the main figure. The process of selecting the images to enhance the figure is more intuitive. I look through the pictures from my photo library and put those that fit in a folder. Then it is a matter of blending and placing the layers together in Photoshop until I achieve the desired composition." In reflecting on her personal approach to creating art, Ileana emphasizes that she does her best work subconsciously by allowing images, associations, feelings, and thoughts to seep into her mind over time until she feels the *aha* moment that finally pulls her to the computer to engage the piece physically.

Ileana's first digital project was a children's book, *La Bicicleta de Nubes*. Her work has been featured in magazine and book publications such as *Design Graphics*, *Agosto*, *Digital Output*, *IDEA*, *EFX*, *Mastering Digital Printing*, and *Secrets of Award-Winning Digital Artists*.

First Impressions

I began by opening the three seed images in Photoshop and placing them side-by-side on my computer screen in a single file and made a print on my desktop printer. In the days following, I would open the page with the three images and glance at them—observing them—until their elements came into focus in a three-dimensional way. I began to identify prominent elements in each image and to discover associations between them that would help me integrate them into a unified piece. One technique I used here was to print the seed images and place them around the house where I could see them casually as I went about my day. This was the starting point for creating *The Wind Catcher*.

My first impressions of the three seed images were as follows.

The Figure (Seed Image 1)—The image of the woman was the first thing that I noted. I felt relieved to see a woman included as one of the three images since my figurative pieces often include women, and womanhood is a running theme throughout much of my art. This was a good starting point. The other two images seemed foreign by contrast.

The Grid (Seed Image 2)—I found it difficult to relate to the grid-like structure. It felt metallic, heavy, stark, and unappealing, and I immediately felt that this image would be the hardest to integrate. It seemed to be the opposite of what I like to convey in my pieces—a sense of openness and space. This is not an image that I would have selected on my own to incorporate.

The Landscape (Seed Image 3)—The rocky landscape did not offer much contrast from the metallic structure, and combined they appear more architectural and less dynamic. I felt, however, that it had a wider color range, and I sensed intuitively that the landscape would become the bridging element between the figure and what I would call "the grid."

The Process Unfolds

I opened Photoshop and grouped the seed images into one folder. I then saved each image in *psd* format and placed them in separate folders ("Figure," "Rock," and "Grid"). I also created an additional folder ("Patterns and Textures") in which

I would place elements or sections of the seed images that caught my attention. Using this arrangement, I was able to keep derivative versions of each seed image in their respective folders.

My initial thoughts began with translating the seed images into my visual language. My overall working theme would be "womanhood"—a transition between two worlds; however, I would use these themes only as loose guiding lights. I noticed that there are striking elements in this beautiful woman's face. I love the pose, but her countenance seems a bit stern (defiant? confident? rebellious? arrogant?). I played a bit with the order of the images. The composition with the woman in the middle seemed to elicit more free associations. I liked it even better when I inverted the rock landscape image.

A Name Comes to Mind

I brought each image as a separate layer in Photoshop into one canvas and created different arrangements by playing with the scale and overall composition. I felt a stronger pull when I placed the image of the woman in the middle and the rocky landscape in the background. This particular arrangement seemed to have a Native American look, and the imagery that I developed carried this theme. The grid image was flipped and stretched horizontally underneath the figure. Normally at this juncture I tend to free-associate names that fit the composition that I am most drawn toward. In this case the title *Winds of Change* came to mind. But as the image progressed, the titled also changed and finally became *The Wind Catcher*. The composition that I created, although rudimentary, seemed like a good guideline, so I saved it in the seed folder for later use.

Creating the Figure

I decided to use the woman's photo as a starting point in order to create a figure with a more universal appeal. This included changing the outfit, softening the facial features, and eliminating the tattoos and piercing.

The work on the figure began by opening the seed image in Corel Painter IX and creating a clone: File > Clone. I used the Tracing tool to create a pencil outline of the figure. Select All > Delete, then click Tracing Paper > Create Outline with Pencil Brush. I saved the outline version in riff format (Corel Painter's native format) and made the changes necessary to fit the image that I was looking for using the Pencil Brush and the Eraser tools.

Using the seed image as reference, I began to paint and model the skin tones using colors from my own custom palette. The colors were applied with the large and Soft Chalk brushes and then blended in with the Just Add Water variant in the Brush Palette. By the time I got an acceptable picture of the skin tones, I had created 18 versions of this outline (see Figure 4.1).

Figure 4.1 Ileana painting the woman's face with her custom palette.

Next, I added movement to the hair with the Airbrush tool as a way of creating a more dynamic element and to give more volume to the figure.

I felt that the color and texture of the dress would be determined by the background composition, so I left it blank.

Each time I added a significant element to the picture, I numbered it sequentially and saved it in the Figure folder. Finally, I drew a selection around the figure of my final version, changed it into a layer (by clicking on the image with the Pointer tool), and saved it as a *psd* file.

The figure of the woman wouldn't be finished until it was placed against the background, so I saved the most complete version in *psd* format, selected the outline, and opened it as a layer into Photoshop (see Figures 4.2 to 4.4.)

Figure 4.2 Outlining the figure.

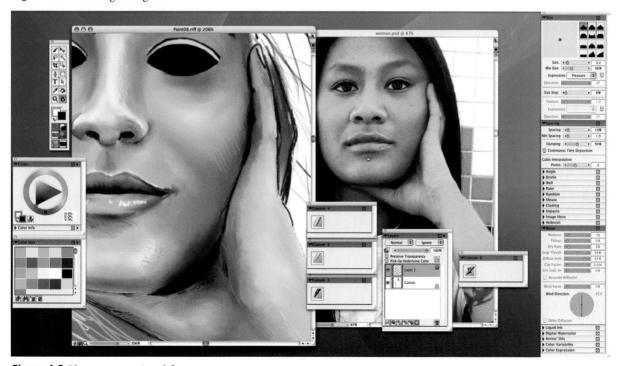

Figure 4.3 Photo versus painted face.

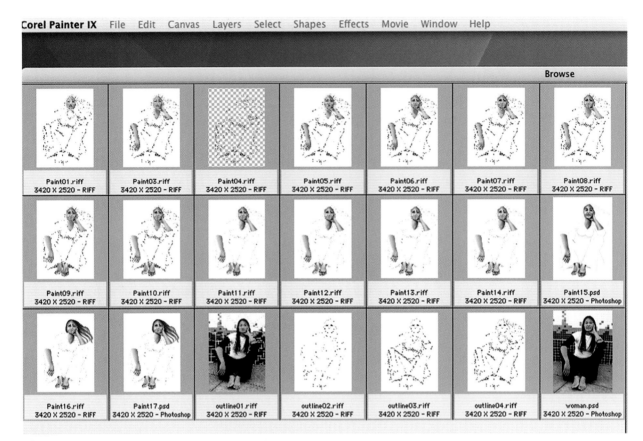

Figure 4.4 Variations of a woman as shown in the browser.

Creating Patterns

In an effort to counteract the rigidity of the background images, I selected elements that I could use to make the whole imagery more dynamic. I was drawn to the colored tiles behind the seed image of the woman and created a multi-layered composition by grouping them as separate layers in Photoshop.

By opening the layered tiles in Corel Painter, I was able to create a Nozzle brush that allowed me to spray the tiles and create interesting patterns and textures (see Figure 4.5). At this point I didn't know how this brush was going to be incorporated into the final image, so I saved it as a Tile Nozzle brush in the Painter library and hoped that I would use it at some point in time.

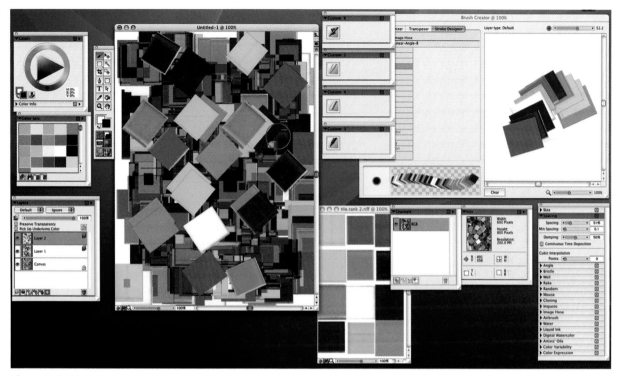

Figure 4.5 Tile hose.

Next, I began to create a tile wall by first selecting (using the Marquee Selection tool) the portion of the image that included the tile wall behind the seed picture of the woman.

Using the Stamp tool, I covered the figure with the tile pattern. This pattern was layered, and a duplicate of it was flipped vertically in order to create a tile wall. The layers were grouped, collapsed into a single layer, and saved in the Patterns and Textures folder.

I then used the Stamp and Clone tools to create a tile wall (see Figure 4.6).

Although I liked the positioning of the grid image at the bottom, it still felt out of place.

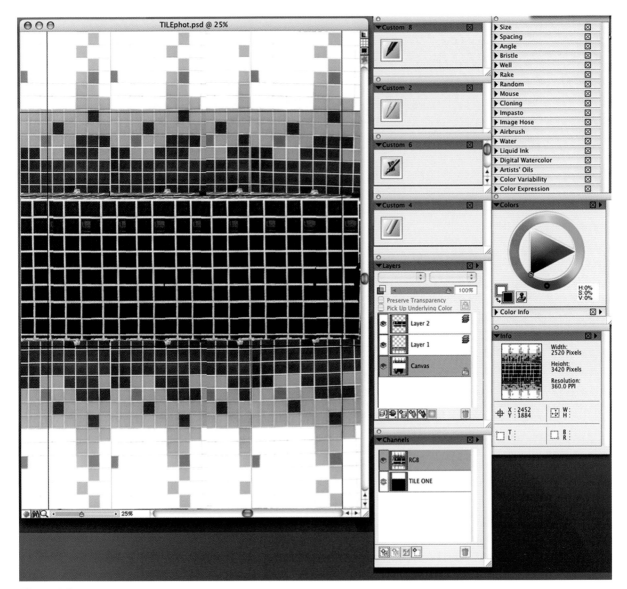

Figure 4.6 Tile wall.

In order to soften and liven up the steel structure, I opened the image in Painter, selected the black (Select > Color Select > Black) and painted it over using the Large Grainy and Soft Chalks with bold-colored strokes. I was much happier with the results (see Figure 4.7).

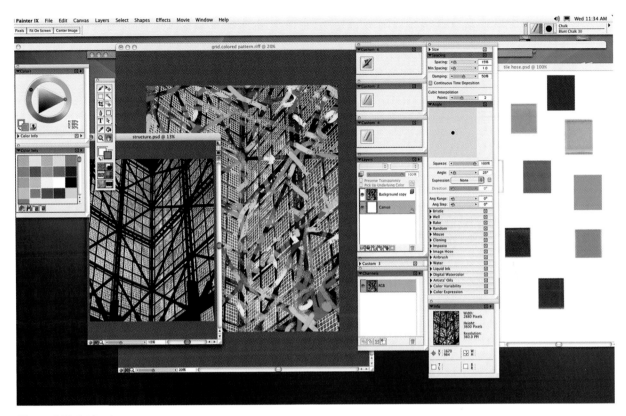

Figure 4.7 Grid color.

The Blossoming of the Image

I began by opening the figure layer in Photoshop and transferring the other seed images as well as the patterns I had created into separate layers (see Figure 4.8).

This is really where the fun begins for me. The gears at this point shift from the exploratory to the intuitive. At this point the mystery begins, and I find myself playing with the different layers until I find a composition that *feels* right. As the image evolves I establish a dialogue with it, and it is that discourse that dictates each step in my process. The picture gives me the feedback; the dialogue with the imagery dictates the final outcome. It is hard to explain this process in clear steps because I don't know what the final outcome is going to be. It requires surrendering to the process in hopes of finding your own voice in the completed image.

I opened the Photoshop file that included the composition I had saved in the seed folder and used it as a starting point for the assembly work.

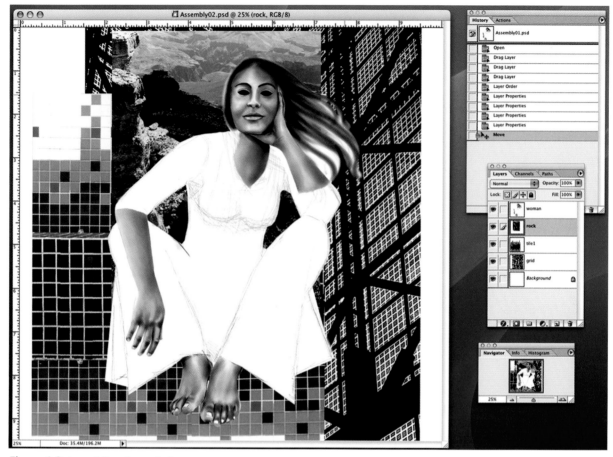

Figure 4.8 Assembling the seed pictures.

The rocky landscape provided a sense of space and openness, so I decided to stretch it further and make it the backdrop to the entire image. I placed the black grid at the bottom. To make it less stark and heavy looking, I placed the colored version as a layer on top and played with the Blending and Hue/Saturation modes until I found a more pleasant design that could be integrated with the background (see Figure 4.9).

I also selected and layered sections of the background landscape and colored it by experimenting with the Channel Mixer, Blending and Hue/Saturation modes. The *tile wall* pattern was brought in as another layer, and I played with the positioning and effects until I found an arrangement that I found satisfying. Finally, I added the layered version of the woman's figure I had worked on earlier and placed it in the foreground. I saved the file in a new folder that I named Assembly. I recorded the progress of the assembly work by saving the various versions that I numbered sequentially into this folder.

Figure 4.9 The assembly process—finding a way to integrate the black grid into the background. Note also the emergence of the layering of the dress folds.

After I came up with a background design that I was happy with, I saved the image and re-opened it in Painter in order to add the final touches on the woman's figure. I also selected and layered sections of the background landscape and colored it by playing with the Channel Mixer, Blending, and Hue/Saturation modes. I followed the same process with the tile wall pattern I had created.

An Unexpected Technical Glitch

I did encounter some technical difficulties as I lost some of the Photoshop effects once I opened the image in Painter and could not recover them. Unfortunately, the latest version of Corel Painter cannot preserve all the Photoshop effects.

Luckily, I always keep a duplicate of the last image I have worked on, so I went back to Photoshop and flattened the layers with the effects in question. The flattened version opened up fine in Painter.

Finishing Touches

The goal here was to integrate the figure into the background. Using the Soft Chalk Brush, I added colored highlights to the skin tones that reflected the surrounding landscape and blended it in with the Add Water Brush. I also worked on the hair using the Airbrush tool.

The next task was to choose the highlights and design for the dress that matched the background. I opened the file in Corel Painter, selected the dress, and filled the selection in an off-white color (Effects>Fill).

With the dress selection still active, I created a duplicate layer and sprayed the selection with the Image Hose using my own Nozzle Pen with the tile pattern that I had created and saved in the Nozzle Library (see Figure 4.10).

I combined the two dress layers by experimenting with the different blending options until I found the combination that fit best. I then used the Eraser tool to more effectively reveal the woman's figure in conjunction with the dress folds. I highlighted certain areas to give a more three-dimensional effect. Using the Image Hose was a totally unexpected technique for me; I had never tried it before. The resulting pattern seems to fit the Native American feel that I was getting from the overall image.

It is interesting to compare both the differences in the dress and the hair in the different stages of completion (see Figure 4.11). For the hair, I used the Spray Paint tool to complete the sketch—adding more hair, darkening it, and adding appropriate highlights. For the dress, as already noted, I used my Nozzle Pen to spray on a tile pattern.

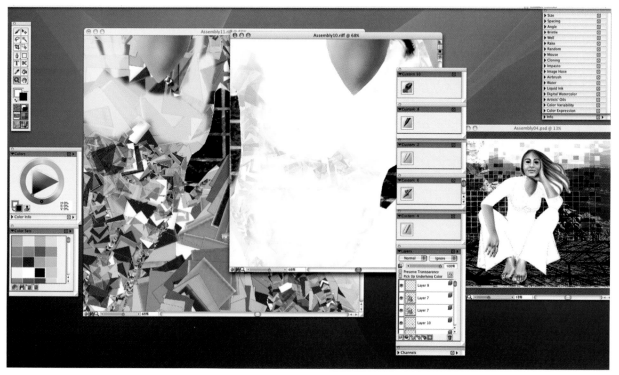

Figure 4.10 The tile patterns are sprayed on the dress with Ileana's Nozzle Pen.

Figure 4.11 Different stages of image completion focusing on the dress and hair.

Another way of comparing the different stages of the assembly process is shown in Figure 4.12. The image in the lower right-hand corner shows the separate layers in the background behind the nearly complete figure of the woman. At the far

Figure 4.12 Comparing stages of assembling the image.

left is the final image itself. Between these two are intermediate stages. For example, in the middle image, the grid structure lays over the bottom portion of the
dress while in the upper right-hand image that grid element is eliminated, giving
way to the sprayed-on tile pattern. Also, you will notice the grid pattern in the
lower right-hand portion of the intermediate stages moving from blue-dominant
colors to a reddish coloring, giving way in the final image to a vibrant weave of
bright reds, yellows, oranges, and the like. This resulted partly in the overlaying
of the colored grid seen in Figure 4.7.

Another way of looking at the development of *The Wind Catcher* is by laying it
side by side with the original seed images (see Figure 4.13). Here, you will see
obvious changes in the woman's clothing and shaping of the hair while retaining
her seated posture. However, the use of the Grand Canyon may be less obvious;
it has become absorbed into the background with varying degrees of visibility. The
seed image of the metal grid has been absorbed into the floor on which the woman
sits. This grid element interacts with that part of the Grand Canyon image that
also occupies this area. The use of blending modes and effects such as
Hue/Saturation disguises the obviousness of these original images.

Figure 4.13 Comparison of the original seed images with the final image.

Yet another way of understanding how the final image was composed is by looking at all the layers that have been assembled, or collaged and montaged, together (see Figure 4.14). This compositional approach allowed me to grab various elements of the seed images and integrate them in a way that I could not have done with traditional methods. *The Wind Catcher* was my reaction to the rigidity of the original images. The pulling in of the various elements, the use of color, and how they are arranged was my way of arriving at my sense of how the image ought to look.

Figure 4.14 The final image showing all the layer elements.

Printing with the Right Color

I printed a copy of the picture on my Epson 2200 on Enhanced Matte paper. The colors mostly reflected what I had on the screen (it helps to keep your monitor calibrated), so there was no need to make any changes to the color profile.

Saving and Storage

I burned a file with all versions of the picture onto a DVD. On my hard drive I keep a folder of this image with a layered version and a flattened version as well as keeping a saved version in stn (Genuine Fractals) format. This will allow me to change the size, ppi, and format without losing information.

Last Words

I stopped working on the final composition and let it sit in my mind for a couple of days. It has been my experience that over time some details begin to emerge and I either change them or enhance them. In this case, I felt that the grid at the bottom of the picture was still too overpowering. Consequently, I changed the layer order and erased sections of the black grid to create a more open, colorful design.

I decided to title the piece *The Wind Catcher* to reflect the Native American feeling and the dynamic aspects of the piece.

Artist Profile: Ileana Frómeta Grillo

Artistic Background or Influences: I am heavily influenced by the sounds and sights of my Caribbean upbringing, particularly in the use of bright colors and type of imagery and symbolism that I find attractive. I grew up admiring the works of Latin American artists from the Dominican Republic, such as Candido Bidó, and Venezuelan painter Hector Poleo, to name a few. Both artists' work relied heavily on the use of vivid colors and the interplay between flat and modeled surfaces. My digital imagery also finds inspiration in the work of Gauguin, the *Fauve* painters, David Hockney, and surrealistic painters such as Magritte.

For me, digital art involves the use of one or more digital processes or technologies for its creation. My "art palette" consists of a digital camera, a pressure-sensitive tablet, a computer with specialized software, and a wide-format printer for its final output.

In the Garden

System Profile: Apple G5 (2.0GHz dual processor), Apple 23" high-definition cinema display, ATI Radeon 9600 Pro AGP 64MB (with dual display support), 3.5GB RAM , 160GB hard drive, Pioneer DVR-106 DVD-RW, Kensington ExpertMouse Trackball, Wacom Intuos II 6" × 8" USB graphics tablet, Pantone ColorVision SpyderPRO monitor calibration, Dazzle 6-in-1 Digital Media Reader

Peripherals: Canon LiDE 30 Scanner (USB), Epson Stylus Photo 2200 Printer, LinkSys Wireless-G Broadband Router with Toshiba PCX1100 Cable Modem, LTS Daylight Glow Portable Lamp, Tripp.Lite, UPS 400 Uninterruptible Power Supply, Nikon D70 Digital SLR camera

Software and Plug-Ins: Mac OS X 10.3.7 Panther, Corel Painter 9, Photoshop CS, LizardTech Genuine Fractals 2.0

Papers, Inks, and Other Output Preferences: UltraChrome inks

Personal Web Site: www.ileanaspage.com

From Timbuktu to Tempe, The Endless Journey

5

Bruce Shortz

The path that Bruce Shortz followed is as varied as the artistic influences he cites, which range from Immogen Cunningham through Chuck Close, Hiroshi Sugimoto, William S. Burrows, Communist poster propaganda art, Devo, and the Kronos Quartet. Having worked as a chemical engineer, professional photographer, music industry executive, and software designer, Bruce eventually opted to live in Portugal for four years where he reconnected with his art career. He returned to New Mexico in 2001, settling in Albuquerque. Since then, investments in printing and digital equipment have allowed him to further refine his art and pursue a 35-year passion for capturing "real life."

According to Bruce, "real life is your best entertainment value. I have been artistically guided by that self-evident truth for the last 35 years. I see 'real life' as an assortment of artistic statements in patterns, colors, parody, and themes, begging to be recorded. My photographs reflect the notion that 'things are not what they seem,' typically within the context of the 'story within a story'. I'm trusting in my years of artistic experience to present art in a compositionally dignified way—a tap on the shoulder inviting the viewer deeper inside, rather than a hammer blow to the head."

Bruce is a founding member and current president of DA3NM, a professional digital artists league currently centered in New Mexico. He maintains a heavy exhibition record with 11 exhibitions since 2002. He produces his own fine arts prints and does portrait work and prints digital, large-format archival images for other photographers and artists. "I call my work, 'Photographs'. The public struggled with the idea of 'Fine Art Photography' in the 1970s. Now, traditional photography holds some lofty position in the public-art-mind, while most people, using digital tools, are not considered as 'serious'. I'm not buying in to that. I'm a photographer using various and numerous digital tools (infinitely more available and malleable than traditional photographic tools) and thus should probably call myself an 'Advanced Photographer'."

 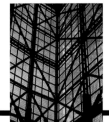 

First Impressions

Since I am visually impelled toward depictions of people, and since my own work shows a predilection for portrait work, of the three source images, Seed Image 1 is a natural choice for me. However, this image offers a number of challenges in terms of the pose, the lighting, and the background. Of secondary interest is the architectural piece, Seed Image 2. Unlike the portrait, where I see promise and potential, I do not have an overall sense of where I might go. The landscape image, Seed Image 3, holds no interest for me. I have been engaged for the last three years in a series of projects that I loosely call "New Portraits." These series of works all focus on portraits in a non-traditional style. I'm trying to stretch the definition of "portraits" as far as I can.

My first thoughts are to extract the face from Seed Image 1 and begin to work with that. I recently viewed a PBS documentary on the evolution of modern man, which describes the human ancestral journey from Africa to India, Mongolia, Antarctica to the Artic Circle, and then down through North America into present day Arizona. By means of DNA testing, scientists can show clear evidence of the African to Asian to Native American link. Seed Image 1 came to my attention the day after I saw that fascinating program! So already I have a general sense of where I am going to go with this process toward a final image. Plus I have a sense of a working title involving the journey "from there to here." Invariably my work involves the "story within a story." All of this intellectualization will be for naught, however, if the final image does not have sufficient artistic merit: composition, color (even if grayscale), color balance, tension, and so on. And if the final image lacks what I call "story" then I should expect the piece to attract very little attention.

I'm not convinced that when viewing art people immediately grasp the artist's intent. And I am not convinced that this even matters. If they will spend just a little time with a piece of art most people will be drawn to its overall aesthetic. If they can get beyond a cursory glance, meaning will emerge—their own private meaning. Often, on learning of the artist's intent, a viewer may feel let down: "I saw something different and more meaningful to me." It's like reading a good book and then seeing the movie; the movie proves to be a disappointment as the reader's imagination can produce more vivid imagery, more developed characters, and perhaps more drama and tension. With that in mind, I will explain my intellectual choices and decisions and lead the reader (and myself) to the conclusion of this project. Think what you may.

My intent is to work solely with the face. I could extract the entire body and modify that. However, initially I see the face as a mask. To me, masks represent a variety of things, including alter egos, hidden feelings, mystery, sensory deprivation, and so on. I shall use the face alone to provide the journey, the search, and discovery—hers and mine.

The Process Unfolds

Figure 5.1 reveals that the photograph is sharp enough, but I'm not pleased with a number of things here. There are not enough lights or shadows to provide good modeling. I need to do a variety of things to improve that to provide a platform from which to work. I find the tattoo and stud interesting, since I plan to trace her ancestral/tribal/primitive roots, and here we see one of the most primitive forms of human decoration on a modern woman! Nonetheless, the ink and jewelry will go, as I want to invoke "primitive" without the physical accouterments. Her nose is perfect for what I want to suggest—that her ancestors, as has been hypothesized, were African. Her lips have a nice, full shape, albeit not highlighted in this photograph. First I pull out the face from the original image with the Lasso tool and Quick Mask and look at its histogram, realizing that I'll have to do a variety of things to give the image more snap and depth (see Figure 5.2).

Figure 5.1 The Lasso selection tool is used to select only the girl's face from Seed Image 1.

I've adjusted levels for a more dynamic color/contrast range, smoothed her face, cleaned up and given the eyes more brilliance, added luster to the lips, and changed the overall skin tone. I've also added sheen with the Diffuse Glow filter (see Figure 5.3). I also created a

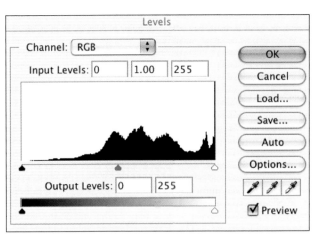

Figure 5.2 The histogram in Photoshop (Image > Adjust > Levels) shows the need to add some visual dynamics to the face image.

duplicate layer switching the Blending mode to Soft Light with Opacity set at 58%. This skin tone may be too red; however, I can change that as I go along. Oh, and I removed her stud (hopefully, it was a painless process). I'm moving toward creating her ancestors (see Figure 5.4).

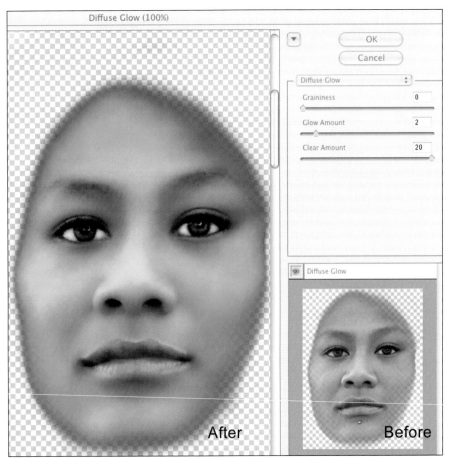

Figure 5.3 Comparing "before" with "after" shows the results of a number of alterations performed on the face, including a Diffuse Glow filter.

One of my favorite plug-ins to Photoshop CS is Flaming Pear's Flexify. This plug-in effectively provides a variety of Points of View that I find very helpful in constructing my art. One must be very judicious with this tool and understand its controls with absolute precision. Using this tool is similar to working with five- or six-point perspective, and allows me to "walk around" the object. To me, this is the essence of composition (all the while realizing that the first rule is that "there are no rules," followed by a thousand rules). I know that I have to construct a map in order to use

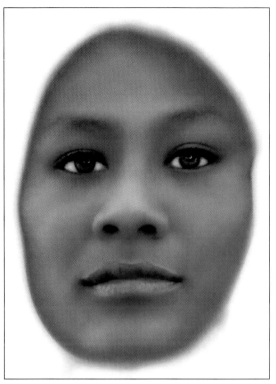

Figure 5.4 With a final adjustment to color (which will probably be adjusted later), the image is now ready for more exploration and manipulation.

Flexify effectively. I also have the idea that I'm looking for several "characters" to be derived from this single image. I'm anticipating creating a mother, father, and a child, plus other characters that may or may not work.

I used the Liquefy tool in Photoshop to create a more childish face, making adjustments to the eyes, nose, and mouth, and bringing in the cheeks and forehead. I also created a more mask-like image to be consistent with the notions I expressed earlier (see Figure 5.5). These will be used in the map I need for the third-party plug-in filter Flexify. I experimented with several other faces (see Figure 5.6). I'm not convinced that I'll use them, but it never hurts to stretch the concepts.

It's with these images that I'm going to build my map(s). There are collisions that occur at the intersection of longitude and latitude within the Flexify plug-in filter. Most of the collisions are controlled. One defines those intersections and then examines the resulting effect (see Figure 5.7).

I know that I can accomplish very quickly what I see (in my mind's eye) as a possible final result without using these kinds of filters. But I know, too, that that old "darkroom magic" exists within experimentation. As I seek the journey of "everywoman" as she moves from the past to the present, I embark on my own journey and find not only her past, but also my own and a truth within that.

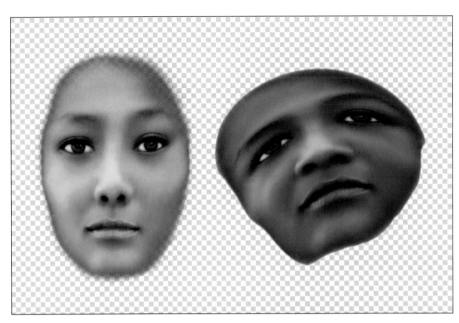

Figure 5.5 The face has been altered to create a child-like appearance (left) and a more mask-like image (right).

As shown in Figure 5.8, the plug-in I intend to use requires some careful preparation of "maps." The maps require that I have up to 75 layers, which I create in order to place the faces along certain intersections. I Hide and Show and Group images into folder sets in order to keep track of what I'm doing. I make use of the History Palette extensively, for I know that once I go into the Flexify plug-in I have to know exactly where I am. I'm also aware that the map figures and the resulting images often look like Poser figures (pre-constructed 3D models). I'm not overly concerned with this, as a lot of people (as seen from advertising and in everyday

Figure 5.6 This is working toward a more African-stlye face. The color is still not right for me; however, I know that I can always change that later. The tattoo is just an idea that I'm not certain I will use.

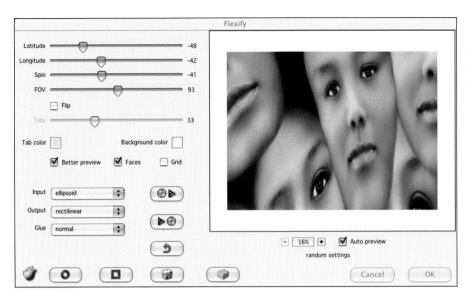

Figure 5.7 The control panel for the Flexify filter gives the artist a lot of control over the outcome and allows for a lot of experimentation and surprise.

life) look like Poser models themselves, with a kind of generic, overly scrubbed, overly made-up face. I also know that the modified characters I am creating come from an original image completely controlled by me.

Figure 5.9 represent various collisions and reconstructions that I have created from my maps. What is difficult to see in these illustrations is a grid system pulled into a spherical overlay on top of the image (which was created in Illustrator. See Figure 5.10).

This grid represents a global trek. I feel convinced at this point that I am going to use the grid. I like its symbolism. Additionally, I've developed a number of characters that I think I want to use: black people, white people, and people-of-color between the two. The African skin tones are what I am seeking. I love these colors and am always fascinated by the range of tones of black skin. I'm discovering

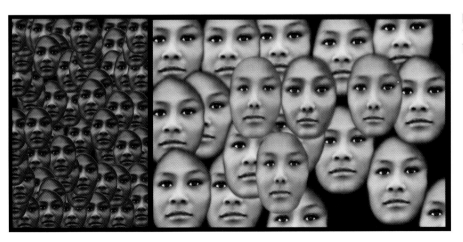

Figure 5.8 An example of the "maps" that are constructed before using the Flexify plug-in.

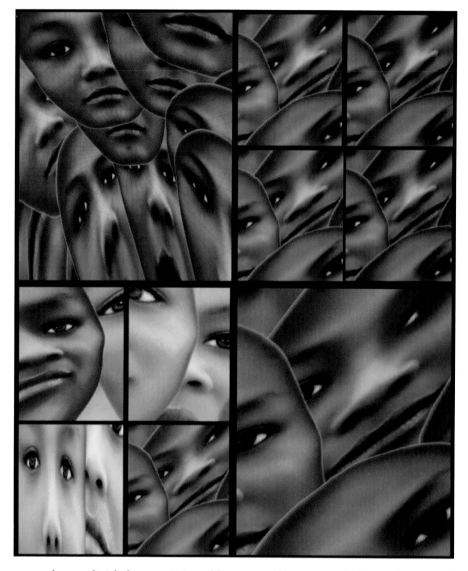

Figure 5.9 Once the "maps" are created, a wide assortment of effects can be created and collected for later use.

young boy and girl characteristics, older men and women, middle-aged men and women—all derived from the single, original seed image. Now that I have my characters, I need to tell the story.

With the images seen in Figure 5.11, I am moving closer to the ideas that I think best exemplify what I am trying to express. I now feel that the ultimate image must be compositionally very simple and striking. My strongest sense is that the final composition contains simply a man and a woman. Despite all of the work that I have done creating young and different types of characters, the final image will not contain those features. I found a "male" character at one of the intersections of a map. This is both a created character and a found character; part purposeful and part chance.

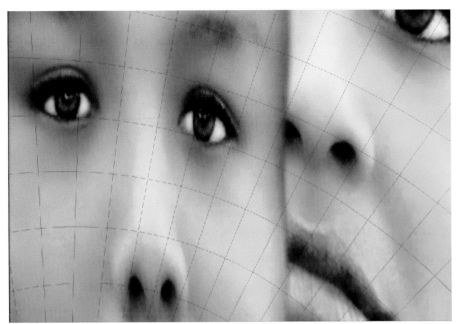

Figure 5.10 A grid representing a globe serves as a reference to the concept of a vast trek and dissemination of human beings. The grid, developed in Adobe Illustrator, has been applied to one of the images developed using the plug-in filter.

The image shown in Figure 5.12 comes closest to my visualization. The "male" image on the right expresses what I call "caution." He peers off to the right, as if scanning the area, making sure that the female is protected. To me, the female face on the left suggests hope. It is this combination of hope and caution that drives the trek forward. There are a few elements that I still need to work with. The man's mouth needs more exposure and the large, flared nostril needs more development. I'm also sensing that the grid that I liked earlier will not work for the final images.

Figure 5.11 As the concept begins to solidify, many experiments are left behind, but the main characters of the "story" have emerged and the piece becomes more focused.

Figure 5.12 A masculine face developed from the seed image is placed behind the altered and improved female face. The expressions on these faces convey the meaning and the concept that has been developed as the piece has progressed.

Despite the call for a 5-inch by 7-inch image size for this project, I see this as a 5-foot by 7-foot print. I keep visualizing this as if I'm walking into a large gallery and see this particular image from about 30 feet away. As I walk closer I see something different than from the further perspective, and because of this I want to apply a "painterly" effect that breaks up the image, making it more abstract the closer a viewer gets. As I am working with primitive characters, I think that the abstract paint strokes will enhance that effect. I really like this idea as expressed most profoundly and famously by Richard Estes's photorealism work. If Dick can do it, so can I. I imagine this piece printed on canvas and varnished to enhance the painterly look.

Figure 5.13 represents variations on a theme. I've used different paint strokes (in Corel Painter) and have fiddled with the position and orientation of both characters. I prefer the painting tools in Painter to that of those in Photoshop. I use a Wacom tablet to paint the strokes using the Clone Brush, which picks up the underlying colors rather than mixing colors on the palette. I have experimented with different brush types and sizes, and different media, oils, acrylics, airbrushes, etc. I've settled on what I am referring to as a "high energy" stroke that, to me, is more abstract than a straight type of brush stroke (see Figure 5.14).

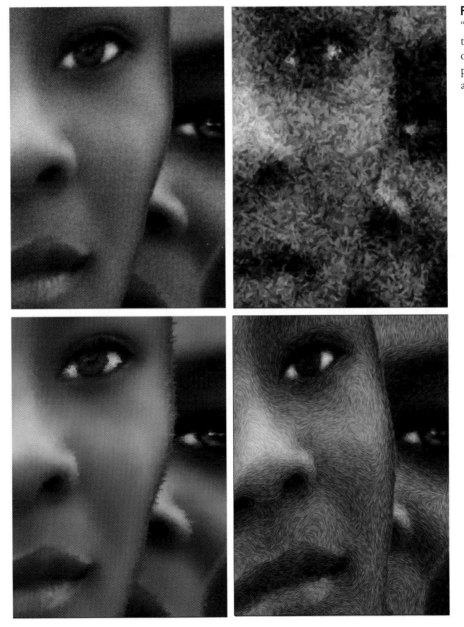

Figure 5.13 Various "brushstrokes" are applied to the image to support the idea of this piece being a very large print, which reveals its texture as the viewer nears it.

Figure 5.14 The brushstrokes applied to the image on the right have a higher energy than the ones applied to the image on the left. This choice is the final decision needed to complete the piece.

The close-up views presented in Figure 5.15 show the details of the brushstrokes applied to the finished image and give an idea of what a hypothetical viewer would see upon approaching the final gallery-sized print. From across the room the image would appear much as a photograph, but as one gets closer and the brushstrokes become more evident, another level of enjoying the image and appreciating the concept is discovered.

Last Words

I've concluded the work confident that it is complete in its quest for the past. The final composition abundantly conveys what I was pursuing. This image expresses strength, purpose, intent, hope, and guarded optimism for the future. This surely is the journey of early man to modern man, although it often doesn't seem as though we've come very far—and this too is part of the final composition. While the image has a "primitive" look, it could very well be modern.

I kept naming the image iterations *Hope and Caution* as a working title. However, I knew that would not be the final title. As simple as the final construct is, I want my final title to be a little more complex, not to confuse or obfuscate, but to add a depth to the image that solidifies the whole concept. So my final title is, *My Parents Went to the Artic Circle and All I Got Was This Lousy T-Shirt*. Just kidding! My real final title is, *From Timbuktu to Tempe, The Endless Journey*. Just as Timbuktu is a familiar city in Africa, Tempe is readily recognized as a Southwestern U.S. city. "The Endless Journey" suggests that the trek between geopolitical points is never over and that history keeps marching on irrespective

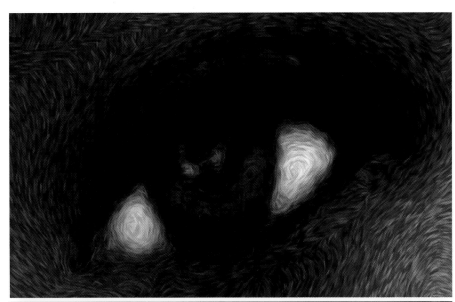

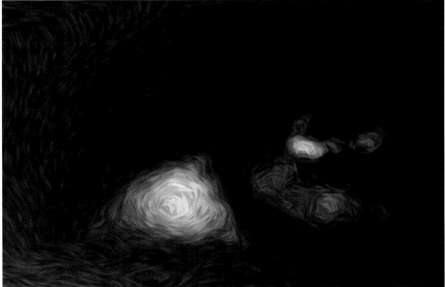

Figure 5.15 These close-ups show the detail of the brushwork applied to the final image.

of political interventions, man-made calamities, or seemingly positive milestones. History treks on with hope and caution.

In the broadest sense, this artwork is consistent with what I normally do, which is to tell a story in a dignified and compositionally sound way. I approach most of my work in an intellectually curious fashion. I believe that there are three key responses to art: an emotional response, an intellectual response, and some combination of the two. My work typically asks the viewer to think, which fires emotional triggers that lead to more intellectual responses. The story can be as deep as one wants. That's my style, and I've kept with that style throughout this exercise.

I don't call myself a digital artist. I refer to myself simply as a photographer. As a photographer with over 35 years of experience, my take is that the tools available in the digital medium represent the greatest unburdening of photography since its inception. By "unburdening" I mean that visualizations no longer have to be restrained by the parameters of the medium. If one can think it, one can capture it on paper (or other medium) more easily thanks to the vast array of tools available today in numerous programs such as Photoshop, Illustrator, Painter, and the like. That's not to say that there is not a steep learning curve with these programs, for there is. I would encourage anyone interested in artistic expression to learn the basics of these types of programs and let their imagination and curiosity run wild. It's easy to transition from traditional tools and methods to the digital toolset. One simply takes the first step and rarely looks back, much like the characters in this composition, *From Timbuktu to Tempe, The Endless Journey*.

Artist Profile: Bruce Shortz

Artistic Background or Influences: Portrait and fine art studio work since the '70s. Many modern photographers and Soviet industrial design of the '60s have influenced my work.

System Profile: MAC G5 2.0GHz Dual Processor, Mac OS X 3.8, 512MB RAM, Princeton 21" monitor, Wacom pressure sensitive tablet

Peripherals: Epson 4870 Photo Scanner, Canon D-60 digital camera, Epson 9600 printer

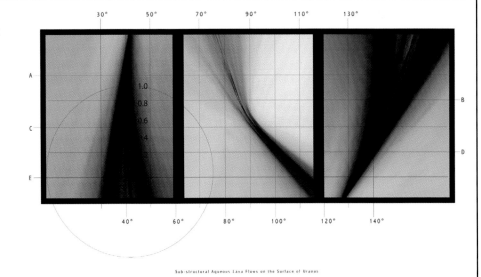

Sub-Structural Aqueous Lava Flows on the Surface of Uranus

Software and Plug-Ins: Photoshop CS, Illustrator CS, InDesign, Bryce 5.0, Painter 9.0, Flaming Pear's Flexify

Papers, Inks, and Other Output Preferences: Brilliant Colors Elegance and Epson Enhanced Matte papers, Epson UltraChrome pigmented inks with Matte Black, big print sizes (smallest and most marketable) around 24" × 30", latest work printed at 44" × 55"

Personal Web Site: www.10000cranes.com

Serenade for the Goozerfish

6

Greg Klamt

Evolving from a background in traditional media, Greg Klamt began working in digital in 1982. He incorporates drawing, photography, painting, etching, serigraphy, natural textures, and other resources with his digital painting techniques to create illustrative visual stories he calls *Possible Moments in Improbable Worlds*. Often Greg begins by creating a space, texture, or design based on intuition and experimentation, then gradually discovers a story in its midst as he works it, following this process in both his visual art and music.

Says Greg, "In my art, I seek to investigate realms beyond my *normal* perception of this world. There are amazing untapped mysteries in the twilight of the subconscious and the infinite depths of imagination. I am inspired by a reverence for nature, a fascination with texture, color, and design, and a great love of the mysterious and absurd."

 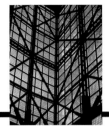 

First Impressions

When I first saw the three seed photos, they seemed fairly ordinary with little story or emotional impact to them. I thought the landscape and architectural features could be sources for creating textures, but were not something that I found interesting by themselves, nor were they images that I would have started working with if it were not for this project. The only element that had any impact on me was the woman's face, which had a mysterious quality that I thought might be worth doing something with, but I did not know what. I was initially disappointed that they were not stronger images until I realized that if the images had an obvious tale to tell, it might have sent all the artists after similar ideas. I dumped any preconceptions about what the project should be and decided to just dive in. In the beginning I thought I would end up with my final piece being more photographic but eventually found more unique ideas.

I have a few exercises that help me initiate ideas when I lack inspiration. This was a good opportunity to make use of them. The following strategies helped launch me in a variety of interesting directions.

- Experiment with creating and layering abstract textures, adjustment layers, layer masks, and color manipulations. This can be a great way to simply inspire a mood, find a good color palette, or even stumble upon imagery that can be worked into more figurative elements. I never know what might appear by simply layering two images—maybe distorting or blurring one of them, changing the color range of one, and experimenting with opacity and blending modes between the two.

- Isolate strong elements in photos or other illustrations and manipulate or repaint them in my own style. This is a great way to begin the creation of original objects or characters.

- Create environments, landscapes, or architectural spaces, and then populate these spaces with characters or objects. I archive a lot of my abstract textures to use later to build architectural elements, clothing, surface textures for landscapes, and the like.

The Process Unfolds

I created all my images in this book using Photoshop 7. In some of my older work, photographs were a central part of my final imagery. I still use photos for textures, reference, or starting points, but rely on them far less than I used to. What you see in this chapter is an evolution of the seed images through various stages and styles, finishing up using my preferred technique in which I rely on memory, imagination, and the role of accidents to help me discover original stories with my unique perspective. The resulting images had very little, if any, of the original content left in them.

I have accumulated a huge library of photographs, textures, and objects that I have created in the past. As I have grown more comfortable with my tools and techniques, the more traditional artistic elements have become less prominent, though I typically still use some of these resources for inspiration and texture. However, for this project, I wanted to use only new textures created from the seed photos and items created from scratch in Photoshop–yet still inspired in some way by the original images.

I actually began this project thinking that my final image might be a photo-composite. I started layering the seed images in different combinations to experiment with textures, moods, and colors, without any idea where I was going. But the creative process moves in its own strange way. I would wrap up many nights feeling like I was going in the right direction, but when I looked at what I had the next day, something would steer me off in a different direction. One night, after about a week, everything started coming together and I found a path that felt right and was really mine rather than based on someone else's images. I finally knew which direction to go. I ended up on a great journey, taking a few divergent routes to new places that I never expected. I now have a lot of leftover images that could be launching points for other works at a later time.

My Creative Process and Working Style

Working in this intuitive painting style, I use as little reference material as possible. If I have photos, I obscure them through distortion or layering with other items. If I am stuck and cannot figure out how something is constructed, I will occasionally take a brief glance at a photo or object—for example, my hand, foot, or something in the room—but will typically not sit with a source and try to replicate proper proportions and shading. There were a few photo elements in this, so I did rely on those for starting points, but once it became my painting style I just went with my gut. This makes me rely on imagination and memory for shape, lighting, detail, and how things fit together rather than relying on reality. It takes a lot longer than using photos, but it is integral to making my individual character come through in my art. This means that often my images are caricatured, strange, and a bit out of proportion, but they have a personality that I enjoy and that is uniquely mine. I prefer this to being able to do photorealistic renderings. I believe that our shortcomings—not just our strengths—define who we are. It is nice when we can make them both work for us. It is not the mistakes we make, as artists and humans, but what we do with them that is more important.

For the images in this book, I sparingly used a few simple filters supplied with Photoshop: Gaussian Blur, Motion Blur, Distort > Polar Coordinates, Add Noise, and Liquify. The rich textures, details, and effects all come from creative painting and layering techniques. My primary painting tools are Smudge, Burn, and Clone, along with standard airbrushes of varying sharpness, and a handful of brushes I made to create textures and clouds. I also use the Transform tool regularly for reshaping and resizing objects. These tools, brushes, and filters are all I use for 95% of my Photoshop work. I tend to be dissatisfied with any effect that looks too obviously digital, or that could have been done by anyone else. I recognize that it is probably obvious that my work is painted on a computer but always hope that the art is seen first, rather than the medium.

Isolating the Woman

Since I did not care for the woman's clothes or her seated position, my first idea was to isolate her face and limbs to eventually create a more interesting pose and design a new wardrobe (see Figure 6.1). I played around with these elements for a while, but it did not inspire any great ideas, so I set it aside to work on some textures to combine with the face.

Abstracts and Experimentation

I thought the grid shape of the building had some potential to make a decent texture, though it would require some manipulation. To create a less grid-like texture, I distorted the photo using Filter > Distort > Polar Coordinates to create an arched pattern that looked more like a vaulted ceiling (see Figure 6.2).

Figure 6.1 Selecting the woman.

I began layering the dismembered body and distorted architecture with the landscape. The results ranged from simplistic cut-and-paste to more interesting layering (see Figure 6.3). These photo composites were a start, but were not interesting me much, so I thought I would try another path. I took the distorted grid, duplicated the layer, blurred it, and played with opacity and blending modes to create a more colorful texture (see Figure 6.4 A).

Figure 6.2 Experimenting with the grid.

Figure 6.3 ■ Simple composites.

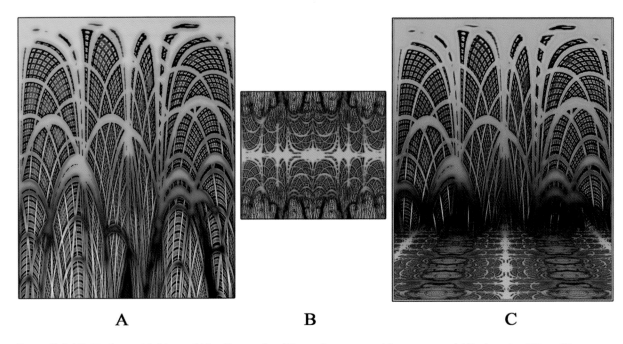

A   B   C

Figure 6.4 (A) Working with blur and blending modes, (B) creating a repeatable pattern, and (C) changing 2D to 3D.

Creating 3D Space from 2D Imagery

To create a repeating texture, I scaled the pattern down, duplicated the layer, flipped it vertically, and merged it with the original. Then I duplicated and flipped that horizontally and merged again. Now I had a symmetrical, repeatable pattern (see Figure 6.4 B). I took the basic pattern and repeated it to fill the whole canvas. Using the Transform tool, I put perspective on it to create a floor and modified the original pattern to make a back wall, transforming the space from 2D to 3D (see Figure 6.4 C).

I enlarged the face from my original dissection of the woman, copied it into this environment, and played with layering to integrate it with the background. I masked out some areas on the different layers, brought in some of the rocks, copied in a couple of variants of the grid and layered them with the face, eventually creating a heavily saturated, comic-like texture on the face (see Figure 6.5).

Figure 6.5 Layering variations.

Divergence

I felt a more graphic approach was required at this point. I found myself trying a variety of alternatives.

Alternative 1: Angled Face

The face seemed more like it had been painted or drawn, especially as I detailed around the eyes and mouth, and the photographic elements did not match. I cropped the image to a less symmetrical aspect and then painted with some of my custom brushes to bring in some new textural elements that hid the photos (see Figure 6.6 A). I liked what came of it—like a close-up of a comic-book page— but it still needed work, so I made it more of an abstract (see Figure 6.6 B).

Alternative 2: Drops Style

I returned to an earlier state to try another idea (see Figure 6.5). It had interesting elements but was flat, symmetrical, and did not have much of a story. I thought I might add some dimension to it—a more tech-looking approach—making use of Photoshop styles.

I usually shy away from digital-looking effects, but they can inspire ideas and, with enough work, look less artificial. I prefer sticking to a more organic, painterly appearance, but it is fun to experiment and a good way to accidentally trip upon new color schemes, textures, or other ideas. I often end up creating textures that I archive for later use.

Figure 6.6 (A) Painting in texture, and (B) making the face more abstract.

I expanded the canvas size and then painted big black dots on one layer and applied an embossed/watery style to it to create a blob texture. I created another layer with more solid black, copied the style from the previous one, and applied it to that layer too. I added a border with an embossed edge. Then I grouped earlier versions of the illustrations with the two blob layers with varying opacity so that different textures and the original face showed through in various areas. I then decided the artificial look was not what I wanted and went back to a previous variation to begin again, but I was able to use some of the textural element that I created in this file (see Figure 6.7).

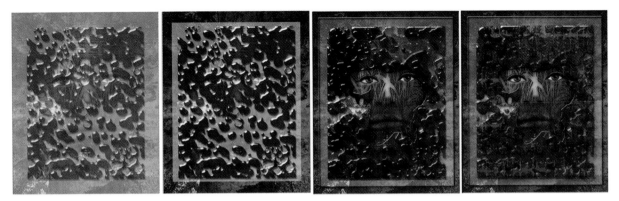

Figure 6.7 Grouping earlier versions with two blob layers.

Locking In on the Main Image: Back to the Organic

I decided to expand and improve the three-dimensional space and reduce the artificial textures. I finally had a mood and color scheme that felt good but wanted it
to be more organic. I copied one of the blob textures into the original 3D space
to layer with the original background. It added some dimension to the texture.

I then copied in the original architectural photo, cut it apart, and transformed the
two halves to add walls to the room (see Figure 6.8 A). I realized that bringing
back in the Grand Canyon rock textures would help. Using the landscape photo
and the Clone tool, I began to paint in a new landscape starting at the bottom
and working into the foreground as well as up the walls of the room. This changed
the entire nature of the image as I built depth, more realistic texture, and a new
environment around the central face (see Figure 6.8 B). (See the demo for the
Clone tool later in this chapter.)

Everything up to this point was foundation, and none of it was highly inspiring
for me, but now I had something drawing me in and it started feeling like my
work at last. At the point where I started building the rocks, I was about 20 hours
into the project. Just guessing, I probably spent 30 to 40 hours working on the
rocks from that point.

The expression on the face was a bit flat, so I decided the mouth should be opened
up. I selected the lower lip area, put it on a separate layer, distorted it (Filter >
Distort > Spherize), and then painted in black on a layer behind the lip for the
opening of the mouth. As I painted in the rock textures, the lower lip got covered
up and the mouth became a cavern (see Figure 6.8 C).

I added a walkway coming out of the mouth/cave. (See the demo for the Walkway
in the following section.) After adding the path I spent an entire day playing with
integrating the embossed layers, the path, and the color of the face and ended up
with generation after generation that was not working.

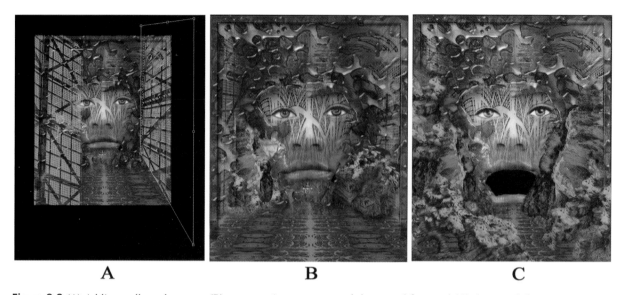

A   B   C

Figure 6.8 (A) Adding walls to the room, (B) a new environment around the central face, and (C) the mouth becomes a cavern.

Demos for Constructing Image Elements

Here, I would like to pause to briefly discuss some of the ways I constructed some of the elements in my images.

Using the Clone Tool to Build a New Landscape

To create the rock landscape, I took a section of the original landscape photo and put it on one layer. I used the Clone tool (checking the box marked "Use All Layers") to sample a texture from a small area of the photo and paint it over a wider area on a new layer. By cloning from a few interesting textures in the seed image, I built an array of new rock surfaces and then used those textures to paint larger and larger groupings of rocks. I then used a smaller brush to add sharper detail to areas that were lacking.

By switching between the Clone tool and the Dodge and Burn tools I can rapidly add shading and highlights, combine textures, and build a variety of new shaped rocks that are much more detailed and interesting than the originals. I can create different sections of rocks with a similar character but with different values of light and dark. (Note the difference between the whiter foreground rocks and the upper golden-shaded sandstone texture.)

Often, if I have some good textures but am unsure what I want to do and do not want to destroy the original, I will create a new layer and clone-paint on that one, checking "Use All Layers" so that I can clone from all the previous textures. This also allows me to play around with masking out sections I do not want on either layer until I get a combination that works. When I am happy, I can merge the layers together (see Figure 6.9).

Figure 6.9 Cloning to build an array of new rock surfaces.

Building a Tiled Walkway

I made a tiled walkway coming out of the mouth and between the cliffs by making a rectangle from a section of the rock, adding noise, and then duplicating and repeating it to make basically a brick wall. I used the Transform tool to put perspective on it and put it in a new document to detail it. I used Filter > Liquify to make the shape more irregular. I then added depth to the edges of the tiles with the Clone tool and added overall lighting with the Dodge and Burn tools. I applied a mask to the walkway to work it in and around the rocks. I added another layer in Overlay mode to apply additional shading (see Figure 6.10).

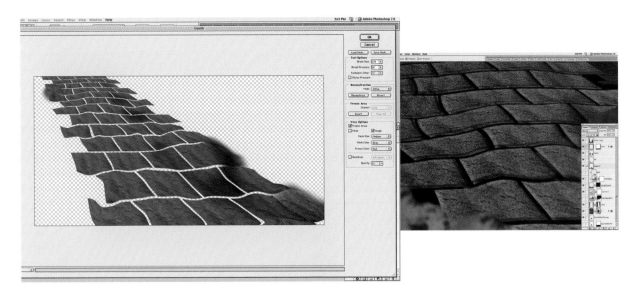

Figure 6.10 The tiled walkway.

Cooking Up a Fish

I was not satisfied with the detail in the eyes—they had been enlarged and were pixilated—so I copied one to a new layer to fix it up. But as I painted around the eye it started to grow a body and eventually became a fish. I have ended up creating a few great characters this way in the past. With a few variant copies of the original, simple fish were transformed in scale and warped and left under the water. (See the demo for Water later in this chapter.)

In order to make a better fish, I copied the original to another file, dissected it into the head, body, and tail sections, and worked on these elements distorting the relative sizes, adding fins and textures, and reassembling the pieces. The texture on the body began with a couple of my custom brushes and then using the Clone tool to paint repetitions and variations of that texture. Then I added the fins and tail and more blending patterns and textures to integrate all the parts (see Figure 6.11).

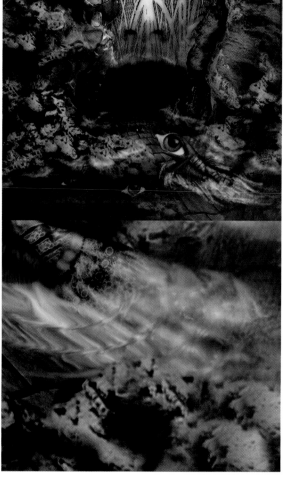

Figure 6.11 A better fish.

Toward the end of the process after everything else was in place, I came back and curved the body shape and improved the detail so it looked more like it was jumping out of the water.

Water for the Fish

The fish had to have water, so I created a new layer, selected the bottom half of the picture, filled it with an aqua-blue, and set the opacity at 30%. I added highlights with an airbrush, duplicated it, and changed the color to fade from bluish to greenish. Once I had a couple of layers that seemed to have the right opacity, I joined them together in a Layer Set and made a mask for the set. This allowed me to mask out the shapes of the rocks with a brush so that the water flowed naturally around their edges.

I continued fine-tuning the layers of water using adjustment layers to fade the color from top to bottom, and gradient masks to vary opacity and color. On another layer, I painted foam in and around the rocks with another of my custom brushes that makes random splashes of white. I also used this tool on another layer to put spray around the fish coming out of the water, and I painted in some drops of water mixed in with the spray (see Figures 6.12 and 6.13).

Figure 6.12 Transparent layers of aqua-blue and hand painted highlights create a believable appearance of water, which is then masked to mimic a "shoreline."

Figure 6.13 The final fish coming out of the water.

The Landscape Takes Over

Now I had a composition that was working. I had characters (the fish and the face in the rocks), depth and texture, a color scheme that felt pretty good, and the shading was starting to come together. I enlarged the canvas at the bottom of the image to make more room for the fish and rocks.

As the rocks became more realistic, it began to feel like the colorful face did not belong in this environment any more. It was comic-like and inorganic. I began painting over it with the existing rock textures using the Clone tool. I spend a lot of time studying rock formations and other details of nature and that has worked its way into my psyche, which made painting the rocks fairly simple and extraordinarily fun.

As I painted rocks over the face I tried to keep some of the shape of the face. I continued detailing the landscape—improving lighting and shading, and cleaning up the rock textures. I transformed the dripping eye into a waterfall, and I also added rocks in the foreground and at the top (see Figure 6.14).

Though the vibe was working, it felt a bit dark and gloomy and there still needed to be more of a story. Why was the fish out of the water? What was it looking at? I needed something interacting with the fish. I began reconstructing the dismembered woman from Figure 6.1. I wanted her to fit my painting style rather than have her look like a photo pasted into this foreign world. I thought, "We can rebuild her and give her a makeover."

Figure 6.14 Making the landscape.

The Woman

I opened the original file with the isolated limbs and head and moved those elements around, experimenting with different positions. I extended the neck with the Smudge tool to start building a torso. I took a section of the neck and duplicated it to a new layer and reshaped it into a triangle to form the shoulders. I added a bit of shading to the triangle, then duplicated and flipped it over the horizontal axis to form the hips. I manipulated the two triangles until they made a rough torso shape.

I positioned the arms and painted legs growing up out of the feet. I left it still very rough at this stage. I then worked with some of my custom brushes and the Dodge and Burn tools on a separate layer to make a dress using the torso as a guide for the shape. I began repainting the face, though this was not what I ultimately ended up with. She ended up looking like she was bowling, and I gave up because it did not work in the picture.

I went back to detailing rocks for a few days but finally got back to the woman and had another idea. I thought she could be feeding the fish. But that would require a completely different pose—more of a side view rather than straight on. I cut the woman's face in half using the spacing of the eye, nose, mouth, and chin to build a 3/4 view. On a separate layer, I painted a new eye and adjusted it so that it was more at the right angle. The face was a bit long and strange but intriguing, and I liked where it was going. I would come back and detail it later after figuring out the final position.

I brought in a flattened version of the landscape, fish, and water to give me a reference background for rough positioning and color scheme. I began tearing her apart and reassembling her to look like she was sitting on the rocks.

In the detailing process, I completely changed the shape of her face, repainted the hair, and repositioned her limbs so she was sitting cross-legged. Continuing to adjust her limbs, I found her hands positioned like she was playing a violin. I quickly sketched out a violin shape with a hard brush just to see how it would look and it worked. So, I started a new image and built a detailed violin, then distorted it to fit her hands. (See the demo for Violin later in this chapter.) At this rough stage, her limbs were all mostly untouched other than building the legs. Once everything was in place, I had to repaint her features so the lighting was right and so it looked more congruent with the rest of the piece and so her left hand was fingering the violin more correctly (see Figure 6.15).

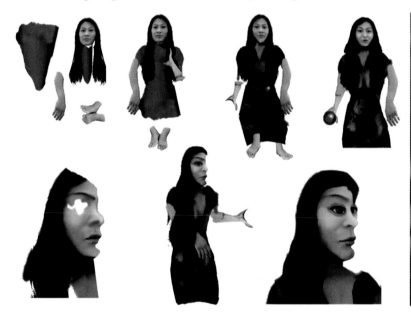

Figure 6.15 Making the woman.

The Violin

I did not want this to be a concert violin, but more of a distant relative from a far-off world. I started by drawing a shape of half the body with the Pen tool and filled it with black. Then I duplicated the layer, flipped it over the vertical axis and merged it with the original half. I isolated a border of a few pixels at the edge of the body and made it a different layer so that it could be a different color. I then filled the center portion with a brown color and duplicated the layer. To make the wood texture, I added noise and applied a motion blur a few times to create streaks. I then used Filter > Liquify to warp the streaks around and make the texture more like wood grain and adjusted the color to a rosewood tone. Then I began detailing the bridge, holes, neck, strings, frets, tuning pegs, and other details. I duplicated the body, reduced it slightly, and offset it to create the side (see Figure 6.16).

Figure 6.16 Making the violin.

I then had to fit together the violin and the woman's body. This required putting some perspective on the violin and fitting it into her hand and neck area. I could not just flatten the whole violin and pull it over. I had to do this in several layers in order to get the side view correct after the distortion. I duplicated the violin file and grouped some of the layers so they would transform together, put some perspective on them, and then made adjustments, drew in the elements that were missing for the side view, and moved these layers to the "woman" file, readjusted them, and repainted a few parts that needed to be fixed. I made a merged version of the woman and violin to put back into the main image.

I also went down a separate path and created a combination of the violin and the fish. This *violin fish* did not connect directly to the original images, nor did it end up being used in the final composition. This derivative path is shown in Figure 6.17.

Figure 6.17 Violin Fish. You just never know where evolution will go.

The Flower

I had cloned the lower lip when I was trying to make the open mouth. I duplicated it again and morphed it to make a tongue, which looked stupid, but it worked as a flower petal. By duplicating and rotating copies, I turned it into a circular layer of petals, and combined progressively smaller layers to make a flower. I stuck a flower on the side of the violinist's head. Later when I was making the foreground plants, I took a section of this to make a side view of the bud and then detailed it (see Figure 6.18).

Figure 6.18 Making the flower.

Erosion of the Landscape

I spent many days detailing the wall of rocks and building them up to the top. As other details evolved, I decided that the rocks were too monolithic. I thought that if there were some sky showing through it would help with the depth. I tried various sky colors and cloud configurations before settling on the final one. After adding the violinist, I realized that the rocks were still distracting from the story and characters, so I simplified them by removing them in stages as I worked on the other elements. Eventually I had removed almost all of them from behind the woman and added the distant water and haze at the horizon to the sky layers. Rather than erasing the rocks, I created a mask for that layer, painted out what I wanted on the mask, and then painted parts of it back in to create the thin tower of rocks in the middle. From there I spent several more nights detailing the landscape (see Figure 6.19).

Figure 6.19 Erasing rock: Erosion of the landscape.

Dancers—A New Image

I like to add little sub-plots and points of interest in the details in my work—little objects that may not be seen at first but become evident only on closer examination. Sometimes they work and sometimes they don't, but they can be inspiration for a totally different image. I thought I would add a few little people standing or climbing on the rocks. I sketched in a simple black silhouette of a figure standing on the rock. I locked the pixels of the layer so any painting I did would apply only to the black, and started painting with some custom texture brushes. I decided to move the figure to another file and enlarge it to work on details. This became the male dancer, and eventually I ended up creating a female figure to go with him and added the balloons (see Figure 6.20 A). I put them back into the original image and tried to make them fit, but it seemed like they needed their own story so I kept them separate. (see Figure 6.20 B). Taking inspiration from the tattoo on the original model's arm, I painted one on the woman.

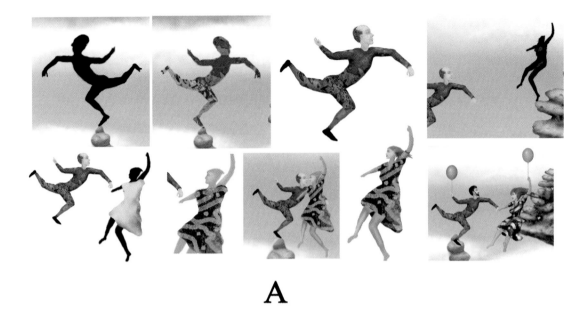

A

B

Figure 6.20 (A) The dancers in the original file and (B) A Dance in the Clouds.

Creating Plants

I wanted more foreground elements—both for alternative textures and for depth. I noticed the flower on the woman's head and figured it had to come from a plant, so I grew one from scratch. I created a leaf shape and added some shading to define the stem and veins. I created a texture on another layer and then experimented with blending modes until it gave me a nice, irregular texture. I made a few copies of the leaf and applied varying levels of opacity to that texture and painted in a bit more texture on some leaves to individualize them. Then I brought them together in clumps of leaves to make the bush (see Figure 6.21). I added flowers and gave them some individuality. I then went in and added individual shading to each of the leaves and flowers.

Figure 6.21 Growing a plant.

Once I had everything in the final illustration, I tweaked the lighting with adjustment layers and detailed the overall shading and lighting by painting in light and dark on a layer in Overlay mode. I also went into some of the elements and added sharper detail where things were a little blurry and repositioned a few elements. The final step was spending a couple of weeks adding details into the rocks (see Figure 6.22).

Figure 6.22 Rock details.

Last Words

I had been through a bit of a creative dry spell before I received the seed images for this project, so it was nice to find some inspiration and I am greatly satisfied with the results, at least at the time of this writing. I often see things that I can improve upon after I think a piece is finished, and, of course, that is one of the great joys of going digital. And maybe it is a bit of a curse as well, as many pieces are never finished—something else can always be added. This was a good reminder that inspiration can come from the most unexpected sources.

More generally, some observations about digital painting are useful. With all art (perhaps more so with digital art), when I notice the medium before I feel or see the art, it can be distracting to the point where I do not even really notice the content of the picture. I like a more organic and professionally crafted look. Examples of distracting elements that I try to minimize include:

- Pixelated edges or artifacts caused by a photo that was blown up too much or manipulated poorly. I blur, paint, or layer low-resolution images with other textures to cover up poor quality resources.

- Edges of overlaid elements that show like a bad cut-and-paste job. I am careful with masking to remove outlines or blur the edges, when necessary.

- Elements pasted into an image but not well integrated, such as having the wrong lighting or detail level to match the rest of the content. This can lend to the artificiality. I try to integrate all elements to feel like they belong in the same space rather than a collage style.

- Obvious filters that dominate, or even show as a prominent feature, in the image. When I do use identifiable filter effects or standard layer-style effects like bevels or embossing, I strive to hide them.

- 3D landscapes without any personality or story. The inherent character of 3D is so artificial that it is difficult to put truly individual style into it without a lot of painting or painstaking work. I also prefer a painterly style to the perfect lighting that comes with 3D. But there are few masters of that medium who make unique and organic work.

None of the digital tools are bad, and pixelated edges are not inherently wrong. But I find that a lack of originality and craftsmanship can distract attention away from what the viewer should be seeing or feeling: the intent of the artist and the content of the image. This applies to any medium, not just digital. When I look at an image, the first thing I want to see and/or feel is the content—not the fact that it is a photograph, fractal, watercolor, or etching. Good art, whatever the medium, elicits an emotional response first.

I challenge myself to work with a very small palette of tools and simple filters because it forces me to master those tools rather than relying on an endless list of effects. It also has helped me improve my skills of observation and perception, and most of all to make sure my own voice comes through in my work. I often end up doing things the hard way, but gain a lot from it.

Artist Profile: Greg Klamt

Artistic Background or Influences: As a child I was fascinated with the fantastic and surreal worlds of artists like Bosch, Breughel, Dali, and Escher, and by a book of photos taken with a scanning electron microscope. The textures that I saw in these little microcosms of nature were just as fantastic as the imaginary worlds of artists. Living in Micronesia for a few years made me aware of the intricate and amazing details to be found in the natural world. I attended college at University of California, San Diego, and took several drawing and painting classes, but the medium I fell in love with was film animation, which lead to my interests in both computer art and music. My work continues to be influenced by all those elements, as well as classical painting, cartooning, graphic design, and a wide variety of other artistic styles.

By the early '90s I was using computers for commercial design and illustration, and for a lot of abstract digital imagery using filter effects, simple 3D modeling programs, and applying effects to photos and paintings. It became important to me to develop my personal style and craft. One of my goals became to bring an organic, natural, and integrated feel to my work—to move beyond the feel of the technology and instill my own style and perspective into my artwork. The digital images that catch my attention do not look like "computer graphics" and rely on story, composition, color, and other traditional aspects common to all good art. I studied more traditional media and practiced working with fewer gimmicks.

When Memory Made Dreams

System Profile: Mac G4 (867MHz, 80GB hard drive, 1.28 GB RAM), Apple 22" Cinema Display, Wacom Intuos tablet

Peripherals: Epson Expression 1600 Scanner, Epson 2000P printer

Software and Plug-Ins: Adobe Photoshop 7.0, Macromedia Freehand, Videodelic, Adobe After Effects for Animation, MOTU Digital Performer

Papers, Inks, and Other Output Preferences: Canvas, watercolor paper, photo prints, occasionally paint on top of canvas prints

Personal Web Site: www.gregklamt.com

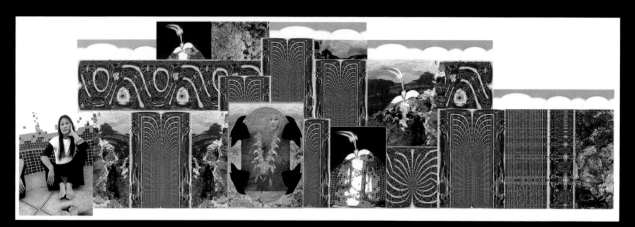

A Girl Can Dream

7

Dolores Glover Kaufman

Having graduated from the Cleveland Institute of Art and Case Western Reserve University, Dolores began her visual arts career with exhibitions around the Cleveland, Ohio area. At that time her works were large colorful abstracts, mainly acrylics on canvas. Soon, she became "caught up in the excitement of photography and never looked back." She combined her exhibit career with teaching and lecturing on art and photography until 1987, when she set up a partnership in a commercial photography studio. Her studio purchased a computer in 1995, and she taught herself digital imaging, "discovering the possibilities for taking photography into the realm of imagination more seamlessly than was possible in the traditional darkroom." Her experience with digital imaging tools inspired her to return to more personal and expressive art making, and she is now exhibiting her digital artwork throughout the Ohio/Midwest region and nationally with recent exhibits in Florida, New York City, Washington D.C., and New Mexico.

First Impressions

Seed Image 1 is a compelling image for me. The first thing that draws my attention is the combination of expression and attitude, which communicate pride and even defiance. The young woman's features, her bare feet, and her tattoo bracelet comprise what appear to be Native American symbols contrast starkly with her modern dress and urban environment. There are definite pictorial and evocative relationships that begin to suggest themselves to memory and imagination. For example, the pattern of the background tiles behind her recall the structure and detailing of the pueblos of New Mexico as well as the repetitive patterns and color of the turquoise and silver bracelets of the Zuni. And the black and white of her outfit against the black and white tiles she so comfortably leans against begin to suggest (to me at least) a kind of truce. The tiled background of Seed Image 1 is recalled in Seed Image 2, but here the urban environment suggests something quite different. In this I see the skeletal forms of an industrial revolution that suggest—with soaring perspective lines intersected by strong diagonals that fill the space crowding out all else—the rapid rise, power, and pervasive force of technology. Seed Image 3 is nature pure and simple. Or is it? After viewing Image 1 and Image 2, it is natural to seek some relationships. Now, from a vantage point on high (as opposed to Image 2 where we look up) we look down upon a landscape that was stolen. With the theft of the land, the culture based upon it was also stolen and then replaced by a new culture of which this young woman is now a part.

To me, art (visual art, that is) is a translation of experience into visual form. This is not an easy task because experience includes all of the sense impressions to which the mind, imagination, and emotions have conferred significance. In order to translate our experiences into visual form we need a visual language, and, as with all languages, different dialects will develop. In the visual arts these different dialects emerge from the different materials (media) employed. So in this era of emerging digital media we also see an emerging language or dialect. Therefore, in addition to the more general visual language that marries line, shape, form, space, and color with the concepts of rhythm, balance, harmony, contrast, and complement, I am also concerned with this new dialect as I attempt to give form to my experiences. The medium, while not the message, is the messenger.

But art can never be a direct translation; it can only evoke. To the viewer, the work of art becomes a new experience absorbed through only one sense. In addition, the viewer's own mind, imagination, and emotions will now be involved and a new, somewhat different experience will emerge. This is the case involving the three seed images with which we, the participants in this book, are engaged. All three images represent a translation of someone else's experiences into visual form. Now these forms will provide new experiences for the artists to translate using the language of art, the dialect of digital, and our own unique voice. So, where shall these three images lead me? I am in as much suspense as you are!

Posing the Question

Before arriving at my current style I did lots of experimenting with digital tools. At first it was simple color correction (though that is hardly simple) in conjunction with my partnership in a photography studio devoted to advertising photography. As my confidence and familiarity with the various tools (mainly Photoshop and Live Picture) grew, however, I began to see possibilities for combining both my personal (and even commercial) photography with my background in painting, which I had earlier abandoned for my new love. It was this hybrid nature that attracted me at first, but it wasn't until I made the decision to restrict myself, temporarily at least, to one tool set within Photoshop (in this case the Hyper Tiling plug-in of Kai's Power Tools) that I was able to begin developing a personal style as well as gain access to the subconscious. To gain access to the subconscious, one must relinquish a bit of conscious control. The sort of collaboration-with-process that this tool provides allowed access to imagery I would not have discovered on my own. And yet, Hyper Tiling provides abundant controls to manipulate forms as they emerge. The collaborative nature of the Hyper Tiling process resonated with me, since I had previously been involved in collaborative work in both my fine art photography and commercial photography. I have always viewed photography as a collaboration between what is, what is seen by the photographer, and what the camera sees.

For me, restriction (ironically) proved to be liberating. While in this "restrictive" period I also limited myself to creating a series of images that all derived from a single parent, or seed. After creating a number of series in this way over a period of a year or so, I ultimately allowed myself the freedom to incorporate unrelated images and use the Hyper Tiling plug-in in less obvious and more subtle ways. My overriding interest in all this is exploration for the purpose of discovery and revelation. Like the scientist, I often start with the question, "What if?" And so, you might ask, what am I searching for? Well, on this expedition I think I'll dig around in digital space in search of the future. Well, maybe not *the* future, but just one possible alternative. So, let's see….

The Process Unfolds

What if, instead of stealing land, isolating people on reservations, and imposing European culture onto native people, our American history had absorbed and blended their culture into our own? If we begin today, what might America's urban landscape look like in 3005? A girl can only dream.

Packing

I'm traveling light. With Photoshop 7 and Kai's Power Tools plug-in installed on my trusty Power Mac G3, I'm all set for my journey into cyberspace. I'm going to start with Seed Image 1, and the first thing I want to do is to duplicate the image onto a separate layer. This is important because I will want to use the seed image over and over again as I experiment with the plug-in (see Figure 7.1). Notice that I have also created a second duplicate that I rotated 180 degrees, but first I will click on the right-side-up layer and choose the Hyper Tiling filter from the KPT Collection.

Figure 7.1 Working in Photoshop, the girl's image has been duplicated twice and one of the copies has been rotated to facilitate later experiments and processes.

Hoisting the Cybersails

Figure 7.2 shows the small set of presets that the Hyper Tiling plug-in provides. If I were to apply one of them, I would get the result shown in Figure 7.3.

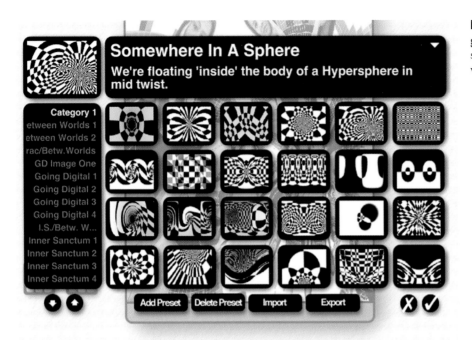

Figure 7.2 These presets can get you started but begin to save your own presets as the work develops.

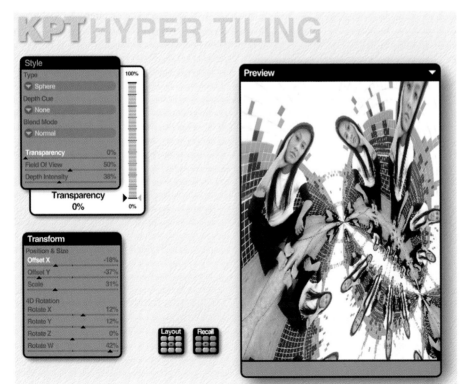

Figure 7.3 Typical results from applying one of the presets from the Hyper Tiling selection can be fine-tuned and altered by experimenting with the control palettes and observing the changes in the preview window.

Well, this composition does nothing for me. The image is typical of a beginner's stab at fractals, with everything generating away from a center point. Also, the heavy repetition of the figure might say something about the population explosion but doesn't relate to my question. The things to note on this figure, however, are the two palettes at the upper left. There you will find an abundance of parameters that can be adjusted in any combination in order to discover an image that resonates with the imaginative task at hand. As you can see, the top palette includes the Style palette, which controls the geometry Type (vortex, pinch, cube, sphere, or cylinder), the Depth Cue (choices are alpha, lighten, darken), and 21 Blend modes (similar to the choices in Photoshop layers). Then, there are sliders to choose percentages from 0% to 100% of such things as Transparency, Field of View, and Depth Intensity. Below the Style palette are the first three sliders of the Transform palette for controlling Position and Size and the last four sliders for control of 4D Rotation. You can start your exploration by clicking on one of the presets shown and then adjusting the sliders until something interesting begins to happen, or you can select one of the styles, null the sliders to midway in order to start from scratch, and go from there. Now, let's see what I can make of Seed Image 1.

Beginning from scratch, one of the images starting to happen for me is seen in Figure 7.4.

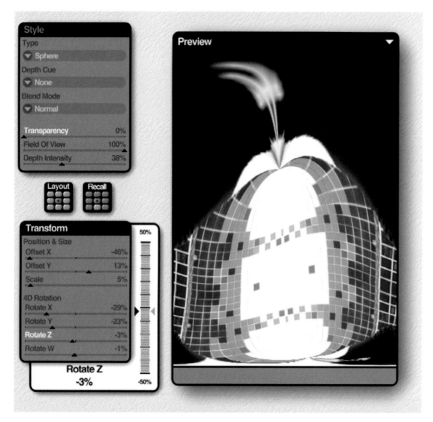

Figure 7.4 Some interesting results begin to appear. Minute changes can present interesting results.

It is still a bit crude and needs some additional work, but I can really see something happening. For one thing, the shape is kind of a cross between a tent and the beehive shaped ovens of the Taos Pueblo in New Mexico that I visited in the summer of 1999. Memories are starting to surface that make me want to go to my archives and pull up the photos from that trip. I can't incorporate them in this project, but they can certainly provide inspiration. And how about that arrow shape! I didn't add that, it just appeared as I slowly adjusted the scale down to 5%. At 6% it wasn't there; at 5% it appeared, and *voila*!—a keeper. But I also see something else happening in this image. I'm detecting a modern building facade superimposed onto the Native American shape. This needs to be strengthened, but I can feel the excitement mount as I save the image to a new layer in Photoshop.

Before proceeding, however, I will also save this Hyper Tiling setup as a preset that I will add to a growing list as I continue to experiment (see Figure 7.5).

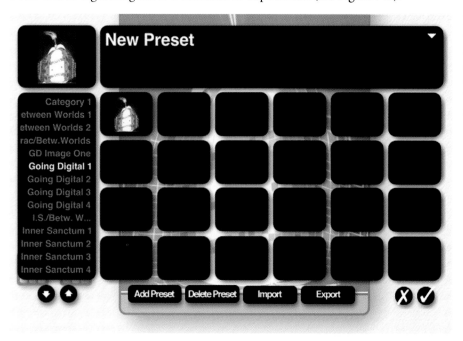

Figure 7.5 Saving presets at this stage of image development keeps the explorations moving quickly and allows the artist to repeat the same results later at higher resolutions.

I've added new categories for this project above the multitude of presets (more exist below the down arrows) that I have developed during the course of creating many series during my "restricted" period. The odd thing is that they aren't really presets in the usual meaning of that word because they apply only to the seed image with which they were created. If applied to another image, I would get wildly different results. So why do I save them? Because I like to do all of my experimenting as low resolution (72 dpi) "sketches" until my ideas have jelled. At that point, I can reproduce the sketch at output resolution by applying the saved presets to the higher-resolution seed images. The presets take up very little hard-drive space, and having them ready greatly facilitates the experimental process.

Cyberwaves in the Cyberwind

I spent the last two days experimenting with all three seed images, and I now have more than three groups of presets from which to begin choosing.

Figure 7.6, which shows the presets saved for just Seed Image 2, will give some idea of the extent to which I go before starting to work in earnest. Beginning with a period of "play" is a very important part of my creative process. It is this "play" that combines an attitude of openness with intense concentration. Because the image changes as I manipulate each parameter, I put myself into a kind of meditative state where I am open to suggestion and yet ready to act when something begins to resonate with the question I am asking. When that happens (and sometimes it doesn't) I know I have tapped into memories and feelings that lie just beneath the conscious mind. As past experiences begin to emerge into consciousness, a feeling of excitement starts to rise and I begin to guide the formation in the suggested direction. Now I am sailing with the wind, not into it. This is what I mean when I say that I view the process as collaborative (or symbiotic). I start my search with a question evoked by the seed image. Interaction with the software becomes sextant and compass as I steer my way into uncharted waters. Although I will use only a small number of the images I have saved as presets, the experience of creating them has provided me with useful imagery and has set me firmly on a course I might not otherwise have found by simply sitting and thinking about where I wanted to go. Thinking and feeling are involved, but these arise from actively following the process.

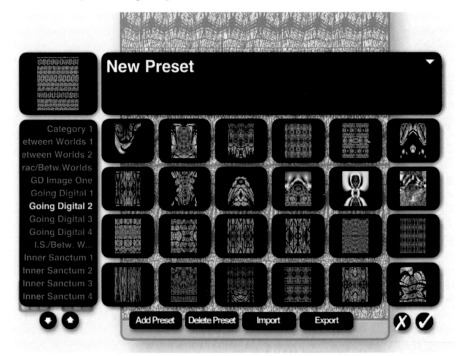

Figure 7.6 One of several collections of presets developed for this project.

So let's see what has evolved from Seed Image 1. One of the saved results that I chose to use is shown in Figure 7.7. As you can see from the Layer palette, this image was created using the seed image rotated 180 degrees. I often do this in order to access different areas (and colors) of the image. Reversing the image accessed the neutral tones of the sidewalk and the girl's clothing, while working with the seed image in its normal position accessed the turquoise and white tiles. You may have noticed also that although the figure of the girl takes up a great deal of the seed image, she does not appear at all in the images brought into Photoshop so far. So how was this done? Did I crop her out or erase her at some point? No, not at all. The image you see now and the layers just below it were solely the result of manipulating the entire seed image and have not yet had any tweaking applied in Photoshop. How then does the figure disappear? Well, remember all those parameters in the Hyper Tiling plug-in? As you move the scale slider in the Transform palette to a low percentage, the figure begins to disappear and the image becomes very abstract. If you move the slider toward higher percentages, the figure will begin to appear in multiples out to infinity. The thing that is so compelling about the Hyper Tiling plug-in is that it does not simply distort an image as the Distort filters in Photoshop do, but instead provides the means to create totally new forms. A complete transformation can take place rather than a manipulation, and that's why I call the resulting images "Transmutations."

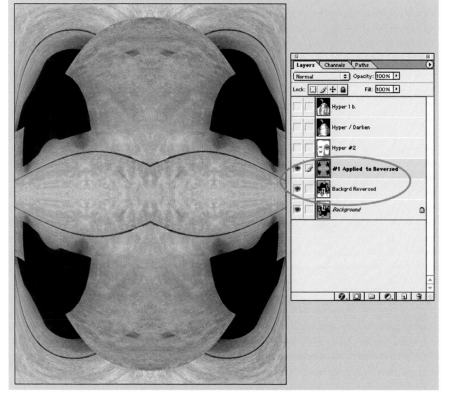

Figure 7.7 This image was chosen from a number of presets developed and applied to the seed image with the Hyper Tiling plug-in.

So why did I choose to save this particular configuration? Well, for one thing I like the oval, almost capsule-like shape that emerges from the background. Can I use that to transport this native girl into the future? I also love the black claw-like shapes that surround and protect the capsule. Bear's claws perhaps? These shapes remind me of the bear claws in two of the Navaho and Zuni necklaces that I inherited from my mother. I think I'll scan those two necklaces for possible use as that is allowed within the guidelines of this project and should help to strengthen the idea taking shape. But first, what can I do with what I have already started?

The first thing I would like to do is combine this image with the seed image on the background layer, so I will turn off the rotated image and experiment with a number of layer modes that combine layers and reveal parts of the underlying image in different ways. I like what happens with the Luminosity mode, but there are a couple of things that bother me (see Figure 7.8).

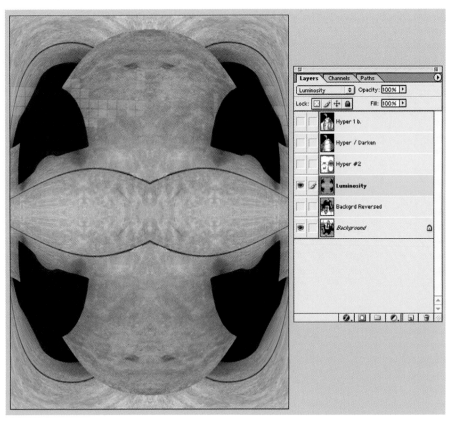

Figure 7.8 Layer modes change the way one layer and another just below it interact. The rotated image has been turned off in order to examine how the layer marked Luminosity interacts with the Background layer.

First, I'm not sure I like that brassiere shape going across the middle, and the face is not well enough defined. For some purposes this might be just fine (more mysterious), but I think I want to go with the idea of transporting the Native American girl to the future. Perhaps this image can serve as a kind of portrait of how she might dream herself into being. So, I need to do two things. I need to remove the unwanted black lines and some other annoying spots with the Clone tool and create a mask (white) for the Luminosity layer so that I can take a brush loaded with black (at various opacities) and paint on the mask to reveal some of the face and the feet. I think I would like to make her emergence from the background a little more subtle and also remove the thin, black, curved lines. I make a copy of the Luminance layer to do that in case I want to return to where I was. Then I will make another copy (see Figure 7.9) of the new layer and set its Color mode at 15% opacity to take the edge off the orange cast of her skin.

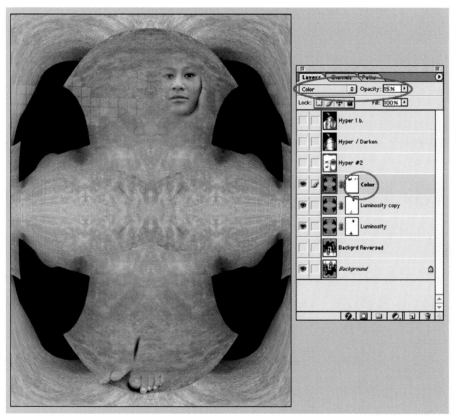

Figure 7.9 The Layers list builds as adjustments are made. The untouched copies of various layers make going back to the beginning of a process easier. Using the Color Blend mode between layers has the interesting effect of allowing the colors of the images below a layer to stain or "seep" into that layer's image.

Now things are starting to get interesting, but there is still a lot of empty space in the middle, so now might be a good time to introduce those two necklaces I scanned (see Figures 7.10 and 7.11).

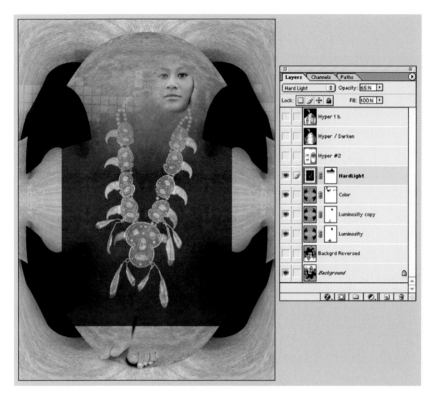

Figure 7.10 A scan of a necklace is added to the composition. The layer is masked to allow the necklace to blend into the image near the girl's face.

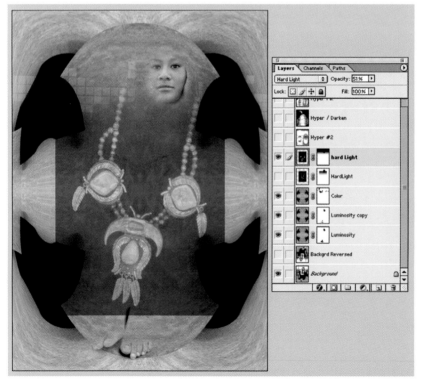

Figure 7.11 Another necklace is "tried on" and blended into the composition.

Here I have set the Blend mode of the layer holding the necklace to Hard Light mode with slightly different opacities. I have also added masks to the layers in order to reveal or conceal. At first I thought of having her wearing the necklace but then decided against that in favor of presenting the necklace as a symbol of ceremony. Can you see the resemblance of the black shapes to the bear claws? To complete the portrait and introduce a reference to the land, which is so important to Native American spirituality and culture, I add one of my saved Hyper Tiling versions of Seed Image 3, set the layer Blend to Soft Light at 64% opacity, and add a layer mask to keep the face from being obscured by the foliage (see Figure 7.12).

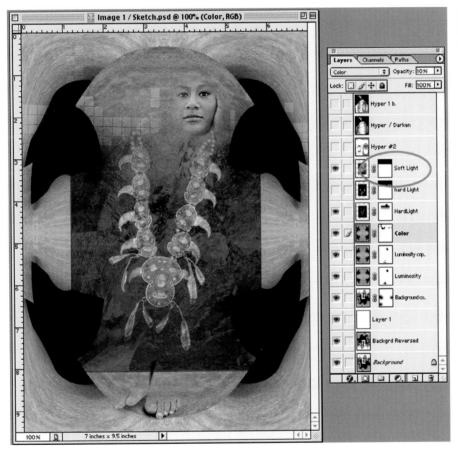

Figure 7.12 A touch of nature from an earlier Hyper Tiling experiment is added.

So are we there yet? Not quite, because the question raised by viewing the seed images in the beginning has not yet been answered, so why stop here? Remember, the question had to do with what America's urban landscape might look like if we could manage to absorb and blend Native American culture into our own. One of the things that inspired this question while viewing the three seed images was remembering a trip I took in 1999 to the Taos Pueblos of New Mexico. At more than 1,000 years old, they are the oldest continuously inhabited communities in the United States. The structures consist of layers, much like modern apartment complexes, but are made of adobe (a mixture of earth, water, and straw) with the roofs supported by large timbers (called "vigas"). Figure 7.13 shows what is referred to as the north house (or "Hlauuma"), and Figure 7.14 shows a detail of the south house (or "Hlaukwina"). While I will not incorporate these photographs into the project at hand, they will serve as inspiration.

Figure 7.13 Taos Pueblo, New Mexico: "North House."

Figure 7.14 Taos Pueblo, New Mexico: "South House."

Beyond structural concerns, some other ideas began to surface as I was working with the Hyper Tiling plug-in on Seed Image 2 and Seed Image 3. In order to blend an ancient culture with the modern, I must take into consideration the technology of the present and of the future. Once that concept took hold I began to steer the Hyper Tiling process in that direction. The first, and most obvious, move was to take Seed Image 2 (the "technology" image) and create patterns that recalled the native patterns on pottery or rugs.

Figure 7.15 shows some of the results of that effort. But then, while I was working with Seed Image 3 (the canyon) I got another idea, more subtle than the first, and I began to steer the Hyper Tiling parameters to create forms from the canyon scene that combined the colors of the earth with precise and hard edged forms that vibrate with the energy of technology (see Figure 7.16).

Figure 7.15 Seed Image 2 was run through the Hyper Tiling plug-in to create a collection of patterns.

The form at the top right of Figure 7.16 is the most organic of the forms and will be used to create the vigas. The one at top left is intermediary between the technological and the organic. So now I have the materials (a technological adobe and some organics) with which to build my structures. Is it worth noting here that the technological adobe could not have been created without the technology of the computer? Any other art tool could not have made the extremely fine and precise grooves that will show up even better at the larger (18" × 24" and up) print sizes.

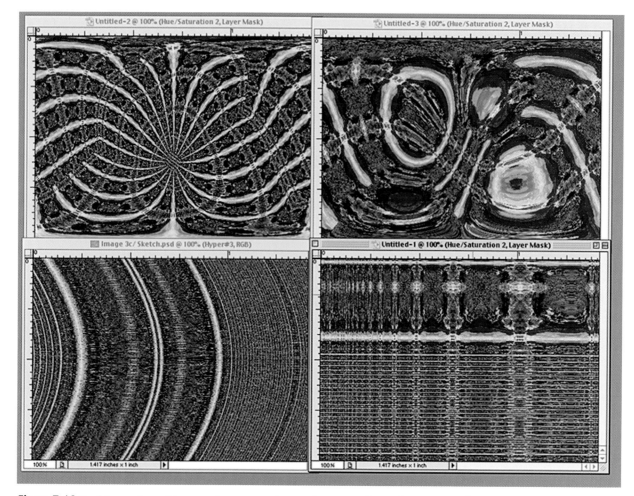

Figure 7.16 Seed Image 3 provides some important colors to the composition references as well as some nice organic shapes.

The other important color that I needed to incorporate was the color turquoise. For the Zuni, turquoise contains the two colors that symbolize the essential elements of life: the blue of the water and the green of plant growth. By using a Hue/Saturation layer I was able to change the blue of the sky in Seed Image 3 to a turquoise, and, as you can see in the final versions, I have used it as both a unifying and an evocative element. The Hyper Tiling plug-in was utilized extensively to create nearly all of the elements, including the clouds, which were made from Seed Image 1. Even Seed Image 1, included in both versions, has been slightly tiled to suggest a tribe. An unmanipulated version of Seed Image 2 was used both to tone down the white areas of Seed Image 1 in *Dreaming Hlaukwina* 3005 and to give greater emphasis to her present environment.

Dreaming Hlaukwina 3005

This second finished image was created by Dolores Kaufman as an off-shoot to her explorations of the seed images. It is common for one image to lead an artist into another. Working with a computer facilitates following several avenues of thought at one time. This working method often opens up digital art to the presentation of a series of images based on a common theme, rather than the creation of a single work of art.

Trimming the Cybersails and Heading to Port

The final versions took shape over a period of several weeks. Arriving at the constructions was accomplished in a state of wakeful dreaming inspired by the experience of photographing the Hlauuma and Hlaukwina of the Taos Pueblos six years earlier. Working with the seed image of the "Native American" girl created a sense of empathy and identity. In Native American thought there is no distinction between what is beautiful or functional and what is sacred or secular. Design goes far beyond concerns of function, and beauty is much more than simple appearance. For many native peoples, beauty arises from living in harmony with the order of the universe. After reading the words of contemporary Native American artist and potter Maria Martinez, I can truly say that, despite the different dialects spoken (digital versus pottery), we both speak the same language.

"Out of the silences of meditation come purity and power which eventually become apparent in our art: the many spirits which enter about us, in us, are transformed within us, moving from an endless past not gone, not dead, but with a threshold that is the present. From this time sense, for this experience deep within, our forms are created."
—Maria Martinez
(www.artsmia.org/surrounded-by-beauty/southwest/martinez_home.html)

Last Words

Since I first began using digital media my work has slowly evolved from an inner to the outer world, while not forgoing the inner, and from the specific to the general, without forgoing the specific. My most recent concerns have been with American culture as manifested in specific geographical areas. My current, "Touring Suburbia" series questions the American Dream by looking at a suburban community in northeast Ohio that is, to me, synonymous with middle Americana. The overriding theme in that series and in this, however, is the human spirit's ability to transcend cultural oppression. I think we all must, in one way or another, overcome the tyranny of culture, and I can only hope, through my art, to show a way.

Artist Profile: Dolores G. Kaufman

Artistic Background or Influences: To be honest, I have never quite "gotten over" Modern Art. The artists and/or movements that have helped to form my aesthetic bias have been the formal structures of the cubists; the sensual rhythms of Modigliani; the pure music of Kandinsky; the combination of whimsy and seriousness of Klee; the sharp-edge, shallow space, and pattern of Matisse; the poetic surrealism of Magritte; and the hyper-real constructions of Rosenquist. As a result I am interested in a marriage of structure, medium, and meaning, and strive for a combination of precision and expressiveness. With the computer I am able to combine my aesthetic bias with working methods that (when I'm lucky) allow me to transcend what I "know." With patience and an attitude of curiosity, the computer can serve as a wonderful tool of discovery.

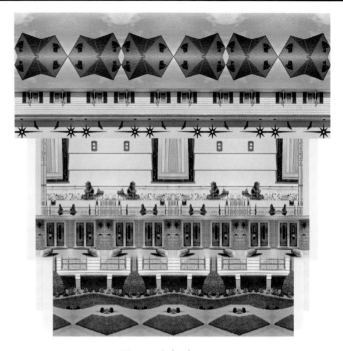

Touring Suburbia No.3

System Profile: Power Mac G3 (400MHz, 640MB RAM), Apple Studio Display 20", Wacom UD1212R pressure sensitive tablet

Peripherals: Microtek ScanMaker 5 (no digital cameras yet), Cannon T90 and Cambo 4 × 5, Epson Stylus Photo2200 printer

Software and Plug-Ins: Photoshop and Kai Power Tools

Papers, Inks, and Other Output Preferences: Illuminata photo rag paper and Epson UltraChrome inks, LightJet prints on Endura Metallic paper for output over 16" × 20", depending on the image.

Personal Web Site: www.dgkaufman.com

Canyon Fog

8

Ursula Freer

As a child growing up in Europe, Ursula Freer's first art lessons came as one-on-one instruction from a master painter. She spent years sketching before she was allowed to touch paints. Then, at age 14, she "decided that I would never be as good as the classical painters I had been given as role models and decided to quit." As an adult, her introduction to Chinese Brush Painting allowed her to develop "a new outlook on art" and then, living in California, she progressed naturally from watercolor to collage and acrylics, "in my search for texture."

Ursula became inspired to get a computer after seeing some of Renata Spiazzi's (Chapter 10) digital work. Renata continued to encourage her, even after Ursula moved from California to New Mexico. With a solid exhibition record dating from 1995 to present, Ursula states, "I have never looked back nor regretted having switched to this amazing medium. The possibilities for artistic expression are virtually endless, and my tendency to get bored has not surfaced once as it had occasionally with traditional media. Having said that, I do appreciate the classical art education that had given me a solid foundation to build upon."

First Impressions

I was struck by how different each of the seed images are. I loved the photo of the girl, but it was a bit intimidating in its perfection. Her expression is rather intriguing; is it self-assurance or defensiveness I see in her face? Her image would most certainly become the strongest component of the composition. The canyon image seemed pretty and colorful, but a bit boring in a "been there, done that" way. Although, I do like the way the distant mountains fade into the background.

When I first received the seed images I had an immediate negative reaction to the grid-like structure (Seed Image 2). I would have, most likely, bypassed it for my work. But, as I thought about the possibilities, I realized the grid could make an interesting contribution. It would force me to work in new ways, and the challenge could result in learning something new. So, this picture made the process interesting. It introduces a tension when combined with the organic shapes in the other photos and provides a pattern and structure. I am not drawn to the steel grid, but maybe I can use it later.

The Process Unfolds

I usually work in Photoshop without a firm plan toward the final image, letting much of it develop wherever the process takes me, making decisions as I go along. I like to experiment with various software programs and filters to find new directions to explore. During this project I only used Photoshop with layers and layer masks.

To get started I decided to work with what I am drawn to most in the image of the canyon (Seed Image 3): the distant mountain ranges on top. This will create a good background because of the subtlety of the shapes and colors. To begin, I crop just that part of the canyon image (see Figure 8.1). Figure 8.2 shows the area removed from the image.

Figure 8.1 The area that will be cropped out from the seed image.

Figure 8.2 The resulting image after cropping.

To add more expansiveness I will turn it into a panorama by creating a mirror image of the original. First I double the size of the canvas to accommodate its counterpart (Image > Canvas > Add), changing the width from 3.25 inches to 6.5 inches and selecting the left center square in the anchor box so that the canvas size expands out to the right of the cropped image (see Figure 8.3).

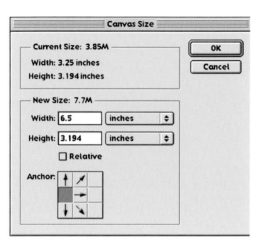

Figure 8.3 The Canvas Size palette shows the settings used to double the size of the canvas out to the right of the image.

Figure 8.4 The resulting new canvas area.

In Figure 8.4 you can see the resulting enlarged canvas with the blank part of the new canvas area on the right.

Next I duplicate the background (Layers > Duplicate) layer and flip the copy (Edit > Transform > Flip > Horizontal). In the Layers palette, I change the Blend mode to Multiply to make both layers visible (see Figure 8.5).

I flatten the image to complete the background shown in Figure 8.6.

Figure 8.5 The History palette and the Layers palette record what is done to the image. The History palette provides an easy way to "un-do" operations, and the Layers palette allows the artist to stack, reposition, and blend images in many different ways.

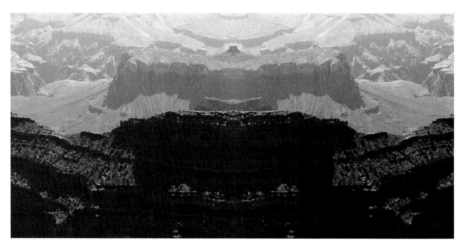

Figure 8.6 The resulting "panorama" is ready for more manipulations.

For more options in developing the image later on, I duplicate this image (Layers > Duplicate) and flip it vertically (Edit > Transform > Flip Vertical). I rename the new flipped layer "Top." I duplicate the background layer again and name it "Bottom." (see Figure 8.7).

Now it is time to bring the photo of the girl into the image. Her clothing is contemporary and not in keeping with the developing mood; therefore, I decide to use the face only. I select just her head using the Lasso tool and eliminate the background (Select > Inverse; Edit>Clear). Before proceeding, I need to do some detailed editing of the face to erase her hand and

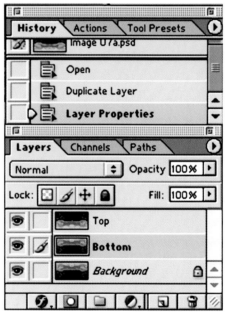

Figure 8.7 It is a good idea to save multiple layers in order to have more options as the piece develops. Unused layers can be turned off until needed.

"repaint" the right side of her face and hair with the Paintbrush and Clone tools (see Figure 8.8). This takes a bit of patience, but with practice and high magnification it is not too difficult.

Then I copy and paste the girl's face above the altered canyon image (see Figure 8.9).

Figure 8.8 The girl's hand is removed from the image by using the Clone tool, the Paintbrush, and lots of patience.

Figure 8.9 The girl's face is brought into the developing composition.

In the Layers palette, I rename the new layer "Girl." Feeling that the color of her face does not blend well with the background, I decide to blend the layers later to resolve this. I add a layer mask to each of the layers (Layers > Add Layer Mask > Reveal All).

Now comes my favorite part, working with layer masks and Blend modes. In the past I used a similar technique when painting in traditional media—layering transparent paint and partially revealing the colors underneath. I like this weaving together of layers, which adds dimensionality and subtlety to the image. To me, layers symbolize the many levels of truth and reality in all their subtlety and complexity. Layers can also weave together different dimensions of time and place somehow related. A work of layers is mysterious and begs closer inspection without yielding its secrets. An example would be to look at an event from the perspectives of science, myth, and consciousness all at the same time.

A layer mask conceals a portion of a layer without actually deleting it, allowing the lower image layers to show through. Erasing the layer mask restores the layer's original appearance so that nothing is lost. There is no fear of ruining the work. Try that with traditional paints; it's just not possible!

I will spend most of my time working in this mode. I do not know which of the layer masks I will use, but having all of them available is convenient. To solve the discordant color problem seen in Figure 8.9, I click on the "Girl" layer and experiment with different Blend modes in the Layers palette. I chose Hard Light and set the opacity at 79%. This number may change later depending on how the layers interact. Figure 8.10 shows the layer order and names as well as the chosen Blend mode.

In Figure 8.11, I like the way the upper part of the girl's face blends with the layer below, eliminating the cool cast of the original photo.

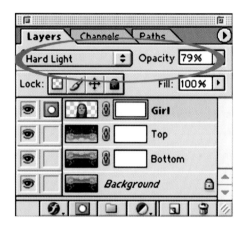

Figure 8.10 With all the layers in place and layer masks applied to all, the image is ready to be "woven" together.

I want to duplicate this effect on the lower part of the face, so I click on the layer mask of the layer labeled "Top" and use a black paintbrush to gradually reveal portions of the "Bottom" canyon layer below (see Figure 8.12).

Figure 8.11 The Hard Light Blend mode has removed the colorcast from the girl's face and has mixed the images together somewhat.

Figure 8.12 Painting with black in the layer mask makes that portion of the layer transparent and allows the image below to enter into the mix in a highly controllable manner.

As you can also see in Figure 8.13, the layer mask of the "top" layer itself has changed in appearance to reflect this process of painting into the layer mask.

To me, the light area appearing in the center suggests rising fog, so I decide to reinforce this effect by using the Smudge tool to blur the light-blue textured area into soft fog. This also provides a welcome change from the highly textured areas of the background (see Figure 8.14).

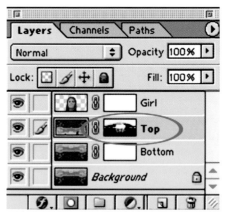

Figure 8.13 The Layers palette shows how the layer mask has been altered by painting with a black brush.

Figure 8.14 A close-up view of the "fog" created by smudging the light blue color around to obliterate part of the natural texture of the canyon.

In Figure 8.15, I have added sweeping textural shapes to the background around her face and chin with the Clone tool. Working directly in the "Bottom" layer (not the layer mask), these shapes show through because of the Blend mode applied earlier. I also paint in a curve of the texture over her forehead in the "Girl" layer to tie in the face with the background. While layers appeal to my cerebral mode of expression, textures have a more physical effect on me. Patterns and textures put me more directly in touch with nature by bringing back the experience of touch in addition to that of seeing. It could be a tangle of roots or the rough pattern of the face of a rock wall, an intricate thicket of new leaves, or waves leaving patterns in the sand. When recreating the textures and patterns of the natural world I feel whole and connected. I often combine layers and textures in one image to further enrich its meaning.

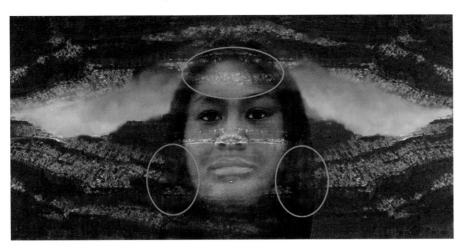

Figure 8.15 Canyon textures are cloned back into the image to add continuity between background and foreground images. Similar texture is applied to the girl's forehead.

I feel the background is finished and it's time to concentrate on the face. I erase most of the light band across the nose by working in the "Top" layer mask but decide to leave part of the narrow band of light dots over the cheeks to add a tribal touch. On her eyelids I reveal some of the color of fog from the "Bottom" layer. Then I eliminate the cool color on the lower part of the face. I also bring down the opacity of the "Girl" layer Blend mode (Hard Light) from 79% to 66% (see Figure 8.16).

After a bit of minor painting and tweaking in the layers and layer masks, I flatten the image and apply a small amount of contrast and brightness adjustment (Image > Adjust > Brightness and Contrast) to the overall image: –3 Brightness and +7 Contrast. The integration of the face and "canyons" is complete (see Figure 8.17).

Figure 8.16 The face is carefully integrated into the image by removing some textures and adding "fog" above the eyes.

Figure 8.17 A close-up view of how the face has been integrated into the final piece.

Last Words

Canyon Fog may be a good title for this image. There is the temptation to increase the contrast and brightness some more, but I think the subdued light is just right for this particular twilight image; it evokes a mystical dimension, a vision of the distant past.

My suggestion to new digital artists: Experiment! You no longer have to be concerned about "ruining" your work by following an uncertain path. One of the most captivating aspects of digital tools is the freedom to experiment with software and plug-ins. By side-stepping instructions you may discover unexpected effects taking your work in a new and refreshing direction.

When I employ predominantly "screen painting" using a Wacom pen and tablet, I call my work "Digital Painting." When combining screen painting with photographic elements and fractals, I choose to call the work "Digital Collage."

Artist Profile: Ursula Freer

Artistic Background or Influences: Classical trained painter turned to Chinese Brush Painting, watercolor, collage, and finally, digital.

System Profile: Power MAC G4 (500MHz, 1GB RAM), OS 9 and OS X, Mitsubishi Diamond Pro 9004 Monitor, Wacom pressure sensitive tablet

Peripherals: Umax S-12 scanner, Sony DSC-717 digital camera, 120GB external drive space, Epson Stylus Color 3000 printer

Software and Plug-Ins: Photoshop, KPT 3 & 5, KPT Effects, Flaming Pear, Lucisart

Papers, Inks, and Other Output Preferences: Legion Somerset Velvet Rag paper, Lyson's Fotonic inks, image size 16" × 20"

Personal Web Site: www.ursulafreer.com

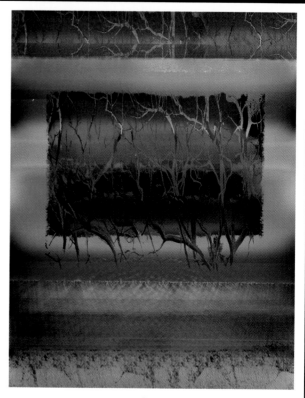

Roots

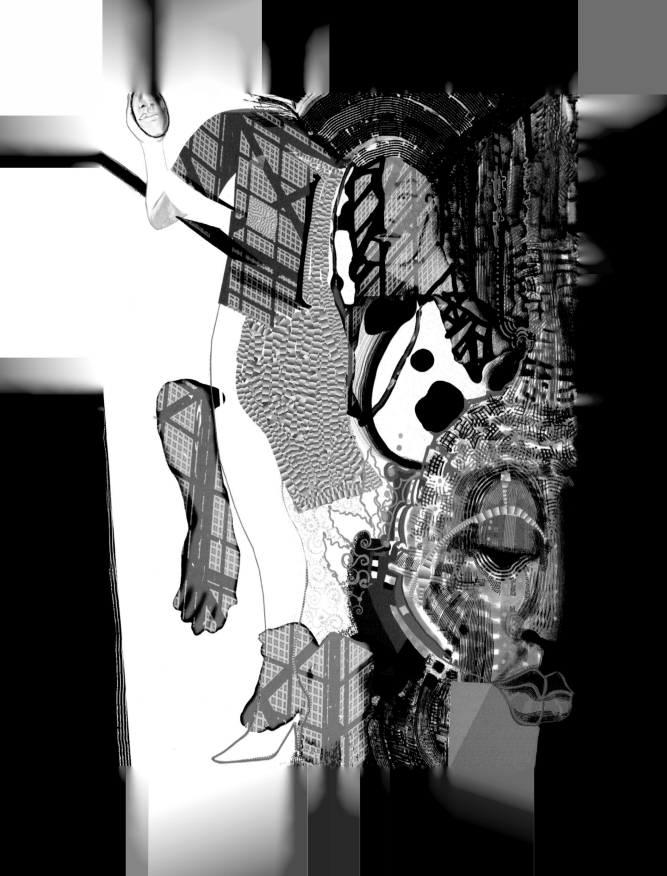

9

Myriam Lozada-Jarvis

Myriam received her art education by attending the School of Visual Arts and Hunter College in New York City, where she received an MFA in sculpture and 2D design. She was first exposed to digital art when using a Macintosh CI and Adobe Illustrator v.1 to create some commercial designs. Realizing the potential of computers to make art but also recognizing the limitations at that time, Myriam did not work digitally again until the early '90s, when she became co-owner of a digital design and printing studio.

Since then her digital work has been exhibited regionally around her southern New Mexico home. Her work is in the permanent collection of the Quinta Gameros gallery in Chihuahua, Mexico and has been shown at the Cork Gallery at Lincoln Center, New York and various group exhibitions in Albuquerque. In 1999, the De Colores Hispanic Culture Festival awarded her "best contemporary art" during their annual exhibition in Albuquerque. In addition to exhibiting her work, Myriam is an art instructor for the Las Cruces, New Mexico Community College District and a freelance commercial art designer.

"My work begins with the human physique, not because I am enamored with figurative art, but simply because it is what I know. It is where I begin—my roadmap. Aesthetic beauty is not necessarily my goal; I prefer to explore the edge between what society allows you to show and what is currently forbidden to be displayed. I am not conscious of creating a particular style rather than fashioning a visual commentary out of the times in which I live."

First Impressions

To me the seed images are familiar and seductive subject matter. The choices seemed logical and I relish the opportunity to work on one or all of the images. Much of my artwork deals with the human figure; therefore, I was immediately drawn to Seed Image 1. The classic pose of the model is reminiscent of the traditional poses set up in figure drawing studios, and the model's cultural mix evoked thoughts of connections between ancient and new.

In New Mexico, Native American-inspired art is plentiful. Often this art overlooks the present day culture and its people for a more mystical and stylized view as seen in movies. I did not want to dwell on the tragic romanticism that often overwhelms that genre of art. Also, I did not want to be obvious in my direction. Yet, this girl holds in her look a strong ancient connection. She has blue eyes, and this suggests an intermingling of cultures, which is also very ancient and human. She could be not just one race but also, in effect, all ancient people. What happens to ancient people as they move across time and cultures to the present? A continuum of the human condition is seen in her face, her eyes, her expression, and her tattoo.

My second favorite image is the steel structure of Seed Image 2. This represents the modern day. I also saw it as a pattern that could be used as a strong design element. As for Seed Image 3, since it keys into the Native American theme I had decided to avoid, I thought I might use it to create a second separate finished image. I am hardly ever affected by such small images of landscapes. I just can't summon up the grandeur in these images that I know is there. I could envision breaking down this image into shapes and maybe using the textures, but I decided to begin with Seed Images 1 and 2 and see what developed.

The Process Unfolds

I started by bringing Seed Image 1 into Adobe Photoshop, and then using the Quick Mask brush I selected areas to be deleted. I was left with only the model's head, arms, and feet, which are recognizable objects, but to me are also shapes that I can build on. I saved this version and brought it into Corel Painter. I made this layer the Clone Source and turned on Tracing Paper. I chose Soft Nib in the Liquid

Ink palette to trace over and color the five shapes taken from the female figure of Seed Image 1. The details and the features of the head, arms, and feet were delineated using the Liquid Ink Nib. Switching to the Soft Edges Brush Look, I stroked over these lines. This affects the lines by randomly spreading areas of black color, as well as softening and blurring my line drawing (see Figure 9.1).

I then placed Seed Image 2 into its own layer and brought down its opacity to 60%, giving the architectural image a faded appearance. I use the Tracing Paper feature mostly when working from a photograph. It serves me in two ways: as traditional tracing paper serves any artist's project and as a new working document once the Tracing Paper feature is turned off.

I clicked Layer 2 containing Seed Image 2 and switched to the Sparse Camel brush under the Liquid Ink palette. I stroked the *architectural* pattern of Seed Image 2 with an ocher, a reddish-brown, and a blue color. Using this brush, I painted the architectural grid

Figure 9.1 Selections from Seed Image 1 are the basis for elements reinterpreted as hand drawn elements using various brushes found in Corel Painter.

pattern into the face, arm, and feet shapes, further obscuring and confusing what they are. I added several large stokes to the upper left side of the line drawing of the face. I look for subordinate elements and shapes that add interest to what I have already established in the work. The strokes I have introduced look like a stylized back and shoulders to me. I like working intuitively, drawing free hand, thinking about movement. After several shapes or lines are laid down, I stop and see if what I have done helps unify or support the composition. This strategy forces me to reconsider the ordinary and frees me from depicting it in a predictable manner (see Figure 9.2).

A new layer is added, and using the Graduated Repeat Pen tool I continue building a shape that indicates the lower back portion of the female figure. This is a turning point in the work, and I proceed to loosely suggest hair and to indicate the back of a woman's head at the very top of the picture. After noticing that the shape I had created could also resemble a skirt, I add a red line, the shape of which suggests the back of a leg with a high heel. What I want to achieve is a visual adventure that is elusive and depicts fragments of the physical world—a chaotic weaving of visual cues that can suggest more than one object or different spaces within the composition (see Figure 9.3).

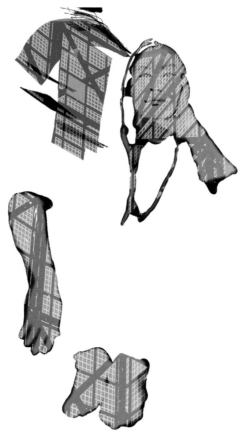

Figure 9.2 Seed Image 2 is introduced into the composition with its layer set to a Blend mode and Opacity that reveals the architectural pattern only where brush strokes of various colors are painted.

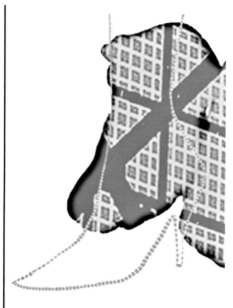

Figure 9.3 Another female figure is suggested by shape and line. At the right is a close-up of the line created by the Graduated Repeat Pen tool.

Switching to the Scratchboard Rake Pen tool, which is adjusted to lay down several lines at one time, I decide to paint in an arch-like structure above the girl's face. I loosely draw "columns," and a suggestion of a temple begins to take shape. Making fine adjustments to Painter's brushes allows me to draw with textures. My training in sculpture directs me toward thinking about drawing or painting in terms of building or constructing an image. The use of layers in Painter and Photoshop complements this working method. Underneath the "temple" I decide to draw a large "mask" using a combination of Pen tools and Liquid Ink at various settings. This mask is much larger in proportion to the temple, so it creates a sense of deep perspective, while balancing this area with the rest of the developing composition. I integrate and unify the temple with the mask by using the Liquid Ink and Graduated Repeat brushes in much the same manner as in the upper portions of the composition. Details are added by reducing the brush size and continuing to overlap textures. I am after a dynamic visual effect that plays off of multiple perspectives, semi-abstraction, and size variation (see Figure 9.4).

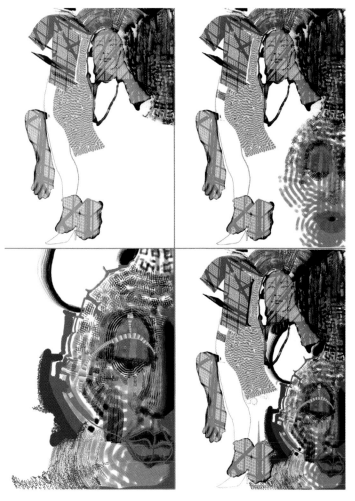

Figure 9.4 The composition takes on more complexity as a number of different drawing tools are employed to add colorful and detailed elements. An underlying concept for the piece also begins to become evident as these elements lend their meaning to the work.

Selecting Black from the Color palette wheel and using a variation of the Dry Bristle brush from the Liquid Ink toolset, two circular and several curvilinear strokes are added to the center of the picture. I partially enclose an area of white space beneath the face and arm of Seed Image 1. These black strokes add contrast to the composition and create a new focal point. I decide to mimic the lines of the steel structure in Seed Image 2. Switching to the Calligraphy Liquid Ink brush, I apply a large black stroke that goes across the white area to the edge of the upper left side of my picture. This helps bring some spatial unity and continuity to the composition (see Figure 9.5).

Figure 9.5 The areas indicated inside the red ellipses are small touches that set the stage for maintaining a good deal of white space as an important compositional element within this piece.

My signature style is somewhat chaotic. I see the visual world in glimpses, the bits and pieces moving around me in no particular order. My working method can be related to in the same way. I arrange bits and pieces to establish an overall design. Periodically I need to take a break from the work, and these breaks help me problem solve. It also allows time for exploring other ideas or frustrations that I may be entertaining. Sometimes these explorations find their way back into the main piece or result in new works altogether. During this project, I had two such breaks in which I explored Seed Image 3 and the face of Seed Image 1.

Side Trips

I must admit that landscape pictures do not inspire me as much as the human figure. However, I opened Seed Image 3 in Corel Painter and cloned the image of the Grand Canyon. I then selected this image as my Clone Source and turned on the Tracing Paper feature. I take a different approach to abstracting this image. By adding a new layer and selecting the Smooth Round Nib from the Liquid Ink toolset, I begin to trace over the image of Grand Canyon, paying particular attention to the line and movement within the photograph (see Figure 9.6).

Figure 9.6 Painter's Tracing Paper feature allows the artist to block out a sketch using another image as a reference.

I apply some base colors of light blue and ocher with the Smooth Round Nib. After turning off Tracing Paper I can proceed to work on the composition without the distraction of the underlying image. The colors in Seed Image 3 influence the direction I take. I continue to apply strokes of orange, purple, and blue using a combination of Liquid Ink brushes. Then, I scratch out bits of color with the Sparse Resist brush and blend other areas of color with the Soft Edge With Color controls. In this way I continue to build up textural contrast emphasizing the color and movement of irregular lines. I like the way this piece looks. It seems to bring out the essence of this grand natural setting, and, to me, suggesting this essence is all you can hope to get from a mere painting or photograph. I think I will follow this lead and complete a separate piece using this image some other time. This side trip has served its purpose in preventing me from "overworking" the original artwork while some subconscious matters are worked out (see Figure 9.7).

Figure 9.7 Here are two variations on the basic sketch begun in Figure 9.6. Both maintain the essential rhythm and space of the photographic reference, but now hold promise for further development as separate, individual works.

My second break from this project occurred because I was having a problem with the small white area in the upper left-hand corner of the picture. As, more or less, another distraction, I decided to explore the face of Seed Image 1 as a mask. The idea of *masks* is a long-term theme within my work that goes beyond painting and sculpture, and I return to this theme when working out problems. Turning back to a preliminary drawing done of the selected body parts, I select a smaller portion of just the face, cropping out most of the forehead, ears, and chin. I brought this selection into a separate document and greatly enlarged it. I cloned the face and selected it as the Clone Source. With Tracing Paper turned on, I look for a brush variant that will respond instantly to my drawing gestures. In this particular case it is the Grainy Variable Pencil. After some initial lines are laid down, I turn off the Tracing Paper and the sketch proceeds freehand. I am pushing (exaggerating or simplifying) the most interesting features of this ethnic face. In this manner, I explore those features as shapes with the potential to become mask-like elements. Sketching in this way is very relaxing, and once one's mind is freed up solutions to problems occur. Finally, I tested some Blend modes on the sketch and decided on a look or two that I liked. I saved this file with the thought of using it in some future project (see Figure 9.8).

Figure 9.8 A drawing is made of the face closely cropped from Seed Image 1, and some variations are explored as seen in one example to the right. Divergent works based on a common image often develop while working digitally.

Wrapping It Up

Upon returning to the main piece, I have decided to title it *Ancient Moderns* in keeping with the concept that first struck me when seeing the seed images. Culture is constructed not only by new developments and technology, but also by the integration of ancient people into modern times. Each carries the other within it.

Toward finishing this piece, I add contrast to the mask in the lower right by delineating the right side of the nose and lips with black using the Smooth Round Nib. I extend the color to the edge of the picture's lower right corner. Where a chin would be, I draw a square and apply a reddish brown color, and then contrast it with a darker shade of the same color in the lower right corner of that square. I add a couple thick orange curved lines to the left of this square, then cover them with texture that ties these elements into the rest of the composition. I feel these orange elements help move the eye back into the composition making the mask appear rounded (see Figure 9.9).

Figure 9.9 Final touches to Ancient Moderns begin with more work in the mask at the lower right-hand corner of the image.

Heading up to the lower edge of the "skirt," I repeated the orange color in a free-hand filigree design. Under that element I use a lighter shade of the blue appearing in the "girders" and hand paint another pattern, which mimics textile. Painting in this area helps to bring the leg forward and gives it emphasis. At this time a black Calligraphy brush from the Liquid Ink palette is used to trace over the girder forms that run across the left side of the girl's face. This helps to integrate this area with the black and white motifs just below it and emphasizes the face while grounding it and visually pushing it back deeper into the composition. I decided to repaint the arches above the girl's head. By doing this, the purple to the right of the face and the shoulder and back areas to the left of the face are separated, and all three elements—face, columns, and shoulder—stand out better. Using the Velocity Airbrush under the Liquid Ink toolset, I sprayed tiny bits of black which add an atmospheric feel and counter some of that pristine look that working with digital tools often creates. This sort of treatment adds a lot of apparent spontaneity to a composition (see Figure 9.10).

Figure 9.10 Some of the white space at the lower center of the composition is filled with light touches of hand painted color and pattern in order to bring the leg at the left a bit more forward in the composition.

Moving to the upper left corner of the composition where my earlier problem area was, I decide to add a line drawing of an arm holding a small round mirror. I add some shading to a small part of the arm to play off of the line's shape and suggest the form of an upper arm. This is one of those bits and pieces that make up what I see. I prefer the enigma created by suggesting shapes rather than rendering them fully. For the same reason, I decide to remove a portion of the upper arm where it meets with the shape of the back and shoulders. I like the way this negative space complements the shapes and sets up a dynamic by which this empty space can be seen either as space or as an object.

It then occurred to me that I could use the rough sketch of the mask/face as a reflection in the mirror. Cutting, pasting, and resizing the sketch into the edges of the mirror achieved this end. After some experimentation, a Blend mode is chosen that makes the face less obvious while lending it the appearance of a reflection in glass. This is exactly how making one of those side trips and getting away from the piece you are working on can pay off. Finally, the lower left side of the composition seems unfinished. But, I hesitate to add anything too elaborate, because I find the white space in this composition to be very important to the look and concept of the piece. I decide to apply a thin black diagonal running nearly from top to bottom along the left side of the composition using the Scratchboard Rake brush that has been used in other parts of the picture. This element is essential in balancing the composition and in that it recalls the girder structure and suggests, perhaps, a page turn—as in turning a new page or looking toward a future that is blank or unknown (see Figure 9.11).

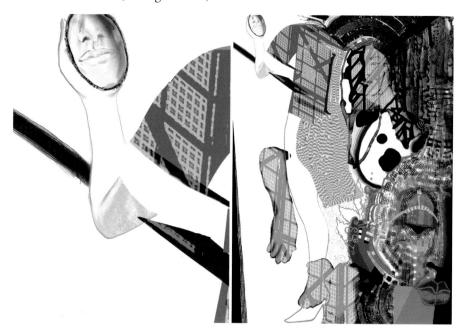

Figure 9.11 To the left is a detail of the arm and mirror that are added to the composition. Here the sketch of the face made during an exploratory side trip has found an important role to play. On the left is the image that was finished by placing a long diagonal along the picture's left edge.

Last Words

This project forced me to closely consider how I work. For me, it is working with texture and breaking up the picture plane. I realized how similar painting with the computer is to how I painted with oils, in that it is about organizing these bits and pieces of my experience, which I combine to create a design. When I look at my work I realize that there are things in it that do correspond to everyday life, but which are more abstract, surreal, or absurd—a sort of chaotic order or ordered chaos. I do not have full pictures in my head when I create art but rather details about which I have been obsessed to some degree.

The two elements about *Ancient Moderns* that I find most interesting are the reflected image of the girl's face and the use of white space. The white space became evident as an important element in the composition about midway through the work process. I also realized that leaving such a large area of white space would be problematic. It could so easily look unfinished, but realizing this makes that space an important aspect of the concept for the piece. Since the future is not finished—or, alternatively, since the future does not yet exist—the white space becomes a metaphor for the future. The jumble of images around this space then becomes the mix of present and past. Within that present and past are suggestions of a human's lineage and, perhaps, genetic memory. The face in the mirror is held out into the void of the future and reflects back to us here in the present. This face beckons to us and reminds us that our identity is made up of more than what we are right in this moment.

Artist Profile: Myriam Lozada-Jarvis

Artistic Background or Influences: The short list includes Hieronymus Bosch for content, Max Ernst for creativity, Alexander Calder for freeing sculpture, Louise Bourgeois for her daring diversity, and Joseph Bueys for social comment.

System Profile: Mac G3 and G4, OS 9.2 and OS X (up to 512MB RAM), Wacom tablets, Sony 21" monitors.

Peripherals: LaCie Silverscan scanner, Nikon digital camera, Epson 4000 and Hewlett-Packard Designjet printers

Software and Plug-Ins: Corel Painter, Adobe Photoshop, Adobe Illustrator, Adobe Streamline

Papers, Inks, and Other Output Preferences: MediaStreet G4 and HP pigmented inks; prints on Tyvek, canvas, and a wide range of coated papers.

Personal Web Site: www.dunkingbirdproductions.com

The Seasons Dance

Dreaming Revisited

10

Renata Spiazzi

Renata Spiazzi was born in Italy, where she received her traditional fine art training in drawing, painting, and sculpture. After moving to the United States in 1952, she taught art in the San Diego Community College District. She also did commission work, mostly sculptures, specializing in reliefs done in wood, bronze, and stone. She began using computer-based software in 1991. About her art, Renata says, "I like abstractions and non-objective works. The reason is that I like the viewer to look at my work and feel, through his eyes, what a piece of music would make him feel by listening to it through his ears. Too often, people looking at a painting get sidetracked by the subject and never get to the real beauty of the work." Renata has received awards in national and international competitions. Her work has been exhibited in the United States, England, Italy, Slovenia, Mexico, Russia, Germany, Canada, and Argentina.

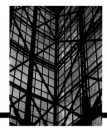

First Impressions

As a lover of abstraction, my first thought was to transform all three seed images with filters, but then I concentrated more on each image and decided to make something more understandable to a viewer.

The girl in Seed Image 1 looks dissatisfied, almost sad. She is sitting on the ground with dirty toes. Through her eyes one can see that she is dreaming, as all teenagers do, of all the things she would like to have and probably never will. This reminds me of a book published in the late '40s titled *How to Be Happy, Though Young!*

So, why not emphasize that look and reinforce that dissatisfaction?

I think I will leave her sitting on the sidewalk (with dirty toes), eliminate some of the tiles behind her, and place a poster of the Grand Canyon on the wall so I will know the reason why she is sad. On the poster will be written "See the World!"

Occasionally I use photographs to create an image. I do not make very elaborate works with them but I like to overlap two or three shots and see what can be achieved. Depending on the selection of Blend modes, the overlapping of two or three images often results in a stunning effect. The procedure overlaps positive and negative, adding mystery to the image.

The Process Unfolds

When working on a subject, it's a good idea to keep it organized, so I sketch out an idea that I can follow. Some of my original thoughts will change in the process of development, but it is good to have a blueprint to work with.

The girl's face has inspired the message of my finished work. Now I have to develop the rest of the objects to reinforce that message. In other words, I have to create a story. Part of the story is conveyed by the shape of the image: If I make the image a vertical rectangle (portrait), the shape tends to denote dignity; a horizontal rectangle (landscape) would denote peace or contentment. My initial thinking is to begin with a square, denoting, in most cases, confinement.

Framing the Grand Canyon

After opening a new file in Photoshop that approximates the size and resolution of the final image, I will work on the background to create a wall of a building. I will use this background to attach a poster of the Grand Canyon.

The finished size of the image I want will be 7" × 7" at 300 ppi. With the finished size of the image in mind, and with the Rulers activated so that I can easily discern sizes, I can make relative sizes for the smaller elements within the overall picture. Initially, I anticipate the wall reaching down two-thirds of the way to the ground (see Figure 10.1). So, I will select approximately two-thirds of the vertical area from the top with the rectangular Selection tool, and color it gray with a gradient that is darker on the bottom and lighter on the top. A close observer might wonder whether the wall will in fact be 7" wide upon completion of the image. The answer is unknown at this point in the process and depends on how the wall will fit into the final image. If you look ahead to the image shown in Figure 10.9, it is clear that the width of the wall does not extend the full width of the image. Another element (the steel panel) ultimately finds its way in front of this wall to provide perspective and a sense of enclosure. But, at this point, that information is not known to me; the blank space is just starting to fill up. My two-thirds guesstimate was simply part of the design in this very early stage of building the image. To make a straight gradient, I hold the Shift key while applying the gradient to the selected area. Once the gradient is applied, I return to the Rectangular selection tool and click within the file to exit the selected area—that is, to deselect the area in which the gradient was applied.

Figure 10.1 Using a gradient to create a wall.

Adjusting the Size of the Grand Canyon

Keeping with the square feeling of the new image I am working on, I need to change the proportion and make a square of the photograph of the Grand Canyon (Seed Image 3). My initial thought is that the measurement of the Grand Canyon image should be approximately 3.25" × 3.25".

Now I plan on widening the Grand Canyon image to fit it on the poster that will hang from the wall I just created. I select the rectangular Selection tool and surround the Grand Canyon image with it (Edit > Transform > Distort). Then I place the cursor on the tiny square on the right side of the Canyon image and pull it all the way to the right to fill the square (hit Enter). I have stretched the Grand Canyon (see Figure 10.2)! Of course, stretching some subjects, such as people or animals, will result in noticeable distortion and should be avoided unless this type of distortion is desired.

Figure 10.2 Stretching the Grand Canyon.

Framing the Poster and Placing It on the Wall

Now I need a frame. It should be unpretentious, just a little something to enclose the image. An earth color should be appropriate; there is a lot of iron oxide in those rocks. The Swatches palette will serve this purpose. I click on an orange-red. It appears on the bottom of the Tools palette. Then I go to Edit > Stroke and change the width to 20 pixels and check the location to Inside. The Blend mode is Normal, the Opacity is 100%. When I click OK, the frame appears (see Figure 10.3).

Now I can add the framed poster of the Grand Canyon to the gray wall I prepared (see Figure 10.4).

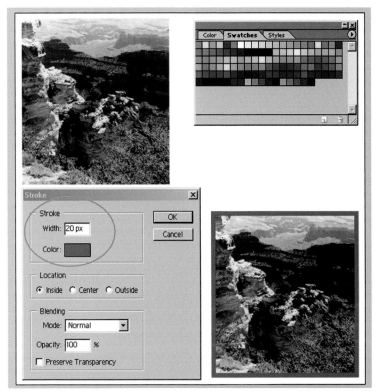

Figure 10.3 Constructing a frame around the poster.

Figure 10.4 Adding the poster to the wall.

Building a Steel Wall

I want to build a wall to form a corner on the sidewalk, to express more of a limitation—like part of a box to represent the girl in a more confined space. I can use part of the steel tower from Seed Image 2 and make a wall with it. So I load the second seed image, "Steel Tower," and select a panel on it with the Polygonal Lasso (see Figure 10.5).

Here I have a ticklish situation. I must be aware of the perspective in the composition. To avoid confusion I will first make a regular rectangle of the steel panel. To achieve this sense of perspective, I will select the panel with the rectangular Selection tool, then Edit > Transform > Distort, and pull the sides into a rectangular shape (see Figure 10.6, A and B).

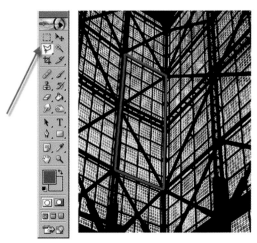

Figure 10.5 Steel tower image selected with a Polygonal Lasso.

I will again select the rectangle with the Selection tool. Now I can click on Edit > Transform > Distort, and pull the two right corners of the rectangle all the way to the corresponding right corners of the support. The left corners will have to be adjusted according to the horizontal line of sight which will fall in the middle of the steel panel and should be completely horizontal (see Figure 10.6 B and C).

In addition to shaping the steel panel, I take several additional steps to darken the bottom area. Light can

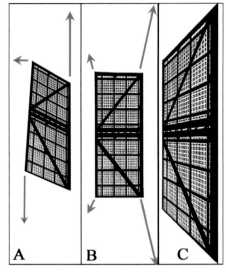

Figure 10.6 Transforming the shape of the steel panel—a two-step process: taking the selected panel from the tower and making it into a rectangle and then reshaping the rectangle to create a side wall with appropriate viewer perspective.

be used to create or reinforce a sense of depth in the image. For this I used a gradient on each small panel to avoid obliterating the entire wall. The dark gives weight to the wall and prepares the darkness of a shadow for the corner where the girl will be sitting.

Now I can move the steel wall into the composition and place the horizontal line of sight at the same height as the two stone mushrooms in the poster of the Grand Canyon, and with the right side of the wall flush with the edge of the image (see Figure 10.7). The third part of the composition is done. I save it as a separate composition for later use.

Figure 10.7 Moving the steel wall into the composition.

Tiles for the Back Wall

As I looked at the image of the girl (Seed Image 1), I noticed two separate elements that I wanted to bring into the composition: the girl and the tile wall. I worked on the wall first, deciding that I needed a wall of tiles about 5.5 inches wide and 6 tiles high.

I prepared a new file that was 5.5" × 2". I selected a strip of tiles from Seed Image 1 and moved it to this file (see Figure 10.8 A). I kept repeating this set of tiles, adjusting them to fit together until a whole strip was formed. I saved this file with the name of "Tile Wall" (see Figure 10.8 B). I can now collapse or flatten the layers that were used to create the tile wall.

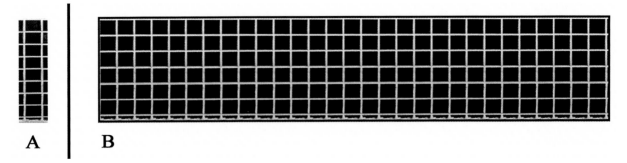

Figure 10.8 Repeating the strip of tiles to create a tile wall.

Placing the Tile Wall into the Composition

I can now move the tile wall into the file of the earlier composition. Just as I placed the steel wall at an angle to give the appearance of depth in creating a 3D space, I need to place the tile wall so that it falls below the poster of the Grand Canyon and jams up against the steel wall to form a perfectly fitted corner. By activating the Transform tool on the layer with the tile wall, I can correct the size of the wall and its direction to give the appearance of a corner of two intersecting walls (see Figure 10.9). I will also save this image as a separate composition for later use. Now the corner is ready to accept the girl.

Figure 10.9 Aligning the tile and steel walls to form an interior corner.

Bringing the Girl into the Picture

With the image that portrays the girl (Seed Image 1), I will have to do a bit of work. I should make a selection of the girl and insert her in the composition shown in Figure 10.9. However, the colors of her clothes and surroundings are too similar to use the Magic Wand or for a Color Range selection. Instead, I will just select the whole image and bring it into the last saved composition.

When the girl is in what looks to be the right spot, I start erasing the surplus edges with the Eraser tool. I use a Soft brush. By magnifying the image, the erasing can be done with more precision. I also erase the spots under her arms to reveal the wall behind her (see Figure 10.10).

Figure 10.10 Bringing the image of the girl into the composition.

The Evidence of Layers

As you can see, every part of the image is on a separate layer—the girl, the tile wall, the steel wall, the gray wall, and the poster of the Grand Canyon. If I want to make corrections, all I have to do is activate the corresponding layer, and my changes will affect only that activated layer. This is why I can erase the tile around the girl and not spoil the rest of the image. To remove any component part of the image and see what the image would look like without the component element, I can click on the eye to the left of the layer in question (see Figure 10.11).

I now save this image as a separate composition.

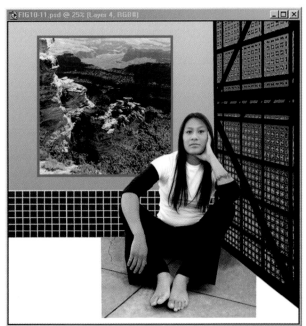 

Figure 10.11 The layers that comprise the emerging image.

The Floor Needs Attention

The floor has to be fixed. I want it to be the same floor—cement with cracks. The best way to expand it is using the Clone tool. To expand the visible floor faster, I can select some patches of the floor and move them to the empty spots. Both the rectangular Selection tool and the Polygonal Lasso are good for this. To make the floor more consistent, a little work with the Clone tool will do miracles. Then I select the existing lines on the cement and extend them (see Figure 10.12).

The Message

I am always thinking about reinforcing the message. I'll add a title to the Grand Canyon Poster: "See the World." This will tell us the girl is dreaming (see Figure 10.13).

I now save this image as Composition #6.

Figure 10.12 Fixing the floor.

Figure 10.13 Adding a title to the poster: "See the World."

The Dream

Now that the representational aspect of the composition is resolved, I can concentrate on the dream. The girl is dreaming of seeing the world. The atmosphere of the image should reveal this dreamy quality.

This is when fractals come to the rescue. Fractals are mathematical formulas that, when inserted in the computer, create images. There is a plug-in based on fractals called KPT 5 (Kai's Power Tools, created by Kai Krause), and one of the facets of this program is Frax Flame. I will use it to create a dreamy atmosphere for the girl.

I was searching in Frax Frame for a circle-styled design for use in expressing my dream concept, but the circle was never in the right spot (see Figures 10.26, 10.27, and 10.28 later in this chapter). I decided to adapt a flame to create the dreamy atmosphere I needed (see Figure 10.14).

Figure 10.14 A fractal with the appearance of a flame.

I used the rectangular and polygonal Selection tools, selected different parts of the image, and clicked on Filter > Distort > Twirl, and the dreamy atmosphere took effect (see Figure 10.15).

Now I can select the dreamy image and drag it into the current composition.

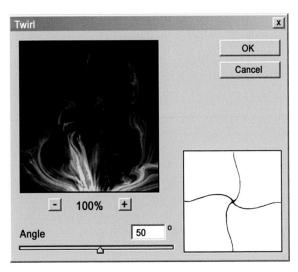

Figure 10.15 Using the Twirl filter to distort the flame.

A Little Secret

At this point I'll have to let you in on one of my little secrets. When I am trying to overlap two images, I like to make the one I will be placing on top slightly larger than the one on the bottom. The reason? I can wiggle it and make it fit better than if I were confined to one position where both layers are already aligned with each other. It gives me room to find the right spot (see Figure 10.16).

Figure 10.16 Placing the flame layer over the existing composition.

Lightening the Image

The overlapping of the two images has produced a darkness I do not want. I lightened the whole image with Image > Adjustments > Levels 190. At the same time, I decide to crop the overlap of the dreamy image since I won't need the overhanging elements any longer (see Figure 10.17).

Figure 10.17 Lightening the image.

I take a close look at the "masterpiece." Does it need any improvement? I think I could have a little more definition of color, so I use Image > Adjustments > Hue/Saturation to push the Saturation level to +15. Now the eye is carried all over the image, but there is not a focus point on the most important part: the face.

A Little Problem

I want to illuminate the face, but here I have a small problem. Earlier I overlapped two images: the girl and the flame. If I now want to illuminate the face of the girl with Layer 5 selected, I will illuminate the flame as well. If I select the girl's layer, I will illuminate the face of the girl but not the flame.

I have several choices: I can click on the black arrow in the upper right side of the Layers palette and flatten the image, or I can fuse Layers 4 and 5 (flame and girl) and work on those two in relation to each other, but leaving the balance of the layers intact. I decide on the latter approach. To accomplish this I select Layer 5, move it down past the "See the World" layer, and place it above Layer 4. Then I click on the black arrow at the upper right and click on Merge Down (see Figure 10.18).

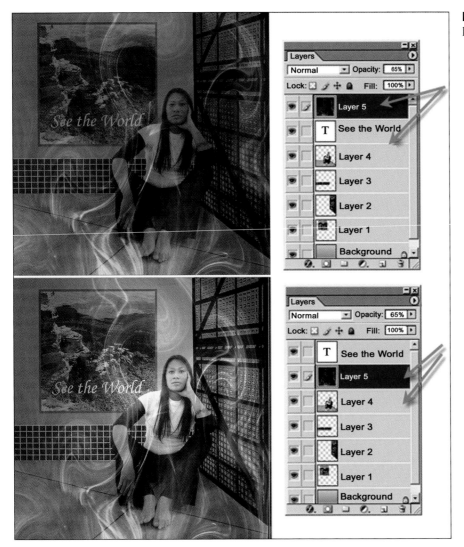

Figure 10.18 Fusing two layers: the girl and the flame.

Lighting Effects

My original thought was to apply Lighting Effects to this fused layer (Filter > Render > Lighting Effects). However, as long as this is the last step to ending the work on the image, I can flatten *all* the layers. This decision will fuse all the layers together and the lighting effects will work for the whole composition. So I go ahead and select Filter > Render > Lighting Effects, and then select Light Type: Omni, Intensity 21, and Ambience 14 (see Figure 10.19).

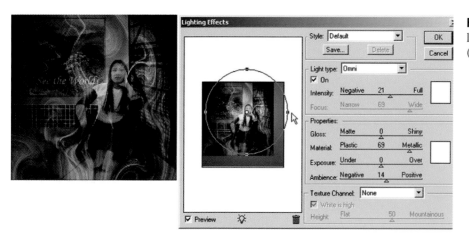

Figure 10.19 Applying a lighting effect to the integrated (flattened) image.

Perhaps a Little Sharpening?

A little sharpening (Filter > Sharpen > Unsharp Mask) may improve the image as well. Now I have it! Her face is in the light, and the corners have been softened with a little shadow—just enough for not letting them be too important.

I decided to print the image. The title could have been *See the World* but perhaps *Dreaming* is better (see Figure 10.20).

Figure 10.20 The initial final image: *Dreaming*.

Looking at the Results

Looking at the results, I find that I am not overwhelmed. Of course, this happens most of the time when I am creating. The final print is a decent work, but for some strange reason it seems a little stiff. That must be my German heritage.

Of course I have to consider that the seed images were chosen by someone else, and this could have influenced the outcome. Then I have to consider also that there are many roles that I play, and in this instance I seem to have chosen the role of being a teacher. My descriptions of my working processes give the reader quite a bit of technology, but artistry…?

Another side to my personality is that I prefer abstractions, or even non-objective subjects. Very seldom in my paintings or photographs will you see human beings. I feel more comfortable with lines and shapes and colors put together to resemble beauty and harmony, and I like to portray my subjects stressing simplicity. So I decided to continue the process with a greater emphasis on my own interests.

I wanted to try to use some abstract shapes with a human being. And this is when I really learned how difficult it is to harmonize two unrelated subjects. I could have done it by changing aspects of the girl, but then I did not feel I would be following the guidelines provided to me for this project—or at least in how I read them.

I still wanted to keep my original idea. Looking into the girl's eyes I could see that dreamy look, and I wanted to continue with the title *Dreaming*. I decided to be brave and dive into my favorite abstractions: fractals.

Venturing into the Fractal Realm

When searching for soul-stirring shapes, the fractal world is the place to visit. There are several fractal programs available. I like to use Ultrafractal (www.Ultrafractal.com), but there are several other fractal programs available on the Internet. I also use plug-ins. Several of them are the sets of KPT (Kai's Power Tools) 5 and 6 and Effects. They are based on fractals and are fascinating to use.

What Is a Fractal?

A fractal is a fragment of an infinite image. But a painting must be more than just a fragment. To me, it must be a complete entity showing, yes, a fragment of life, a fragment of an object, a fragment of thought, but it must have an absolute wholeness to succeed.

I like to use fractals in my work, but I usually transform them with different colors, lines, transparencies, and filters. I also like to weave them with gradients, fragments of photographs, or more fractals until I reach a certain completeness in the composition that will reinforce my message. Fractals usually take a lot of experimenting. When I have a few spare moments I like to sit at my computer and try to develop just one fractal until there is no more possibility (that would be very difficult). During this process I may get several related images. Some are better than others. I save them on a CD for future use.

There are times when some images seem hopeless, but when looked at with a different state of mind, they may prove to be exciting. Some fractals suggest a need for overlapping, while some suggest that a little twirl could be an improvement. Experiments are unpredictable but very rewarding.

Why Experiment?

While searching a CD that I developed during one of my experimental sessions, I rediscovered the images shown in Figures 10.21 A, B, and C.

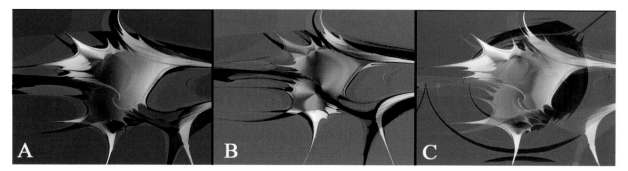

Figure 10.21 Rediscovered fractals.

As you can see, they are all related. With a little tweaking of Figure 10.21 C, I will have yet a different result (see Figure 10.22).

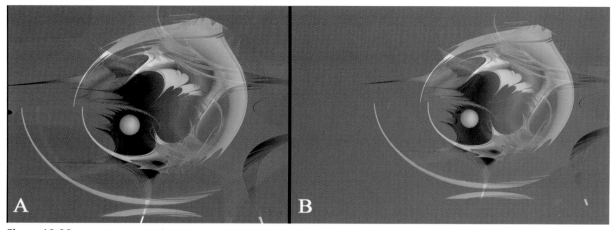

Figure 10.22 A new variation of a rediscovered fractal.

I am sure you can see the relationship between the two images—A and B. The bubble seems to be coming from the right side and pushing toward the left. To make this movement more realistic I should have more space on the left side. The background color of the bubble image is pretty even, so that should not be a problem. All I have to do is enlarge the canvas. (Image > Canvas size) and push the image all the way to the right. I select the image with the Magic Wand and push it all the way to the right and up about half an inch. I pick up the color of the blue background and fill in the white around the image with the Paint Bucket.

I was still thinking about the message in my image. I wanted to continue adding features that will emphasize the dreamy look on the girl's face. I was thinking of sitting her where the little ball is, hoping that this fractal image would give me that dream, but unfortunately it seems to look more like a space ship than a dreamy atmosphere. This means I'll have to go back to the drawing board.

Seeking a Dreamy Atmosphere

In my quest for a dreamy atmosphere I have come in contact with KPT Frax Flame. It is what Kai calls an exploratory filter. The program does not come with much of a tutorial and therefore requires individual exploration (see Figure 10.23). This miracle filter comes with an infinite variety of options. You can choose one of eight different styles, and each style has a myriad of flames. When you find one you like, experiment with it. You can zoom it, reposition it, and when you are satisfied with the result, you can render it. The bigger you want it, the longer it will take to render. Do not expect to see the same flame again.

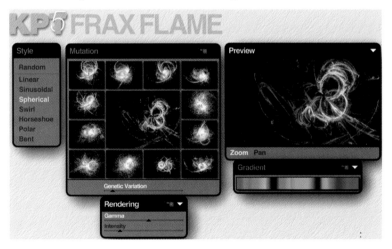

Figure 10.23 A spherical image from Frax Flame.

The beauty of the resulting fractals is that they look like natural phenomena but do not resemble anything I know. So, why not try it?

The first attempts were not too exciting, but when I used different filters and gradients with them, they began to blossom and the one I chose is shown in Figure 10.24.

The colors are not what I would pick for my subject, and neither was the shape, but with a little help from Photoshop, I knew I could change them.

Figure 10.24 The fractal I decided to use.

Decisions, Decisions, Decisions

As the image emerges once again, there are new decisions to make. What color should predominate in the fractal? Should the girl's image be brought in in the same way and placed in the same location? How sharp should the final image look? The continued road to developing the image requires a different set of decisions.

Orange as the Color of Youth

I was still thinking of inserting the image of the Grand Canyon somewhere in the picture. And I know Orange is a prominent color on the Grand Canyon when the sun is shining. But that is not the reason why I would choose an orange. Orange is also a color of youth, so I think a beautiful orange for the dreamy atmosphere should be the thing I want.

The shape I started with was a horizontal rectangle. I think I should change the proportions of the square and make them into a landscape. And for changing the color I will go to Images > Adjustments > Hue/Saturation. When in Hue/Saturation mode, I click on the top choice that says Edit:Master, and a list of six colors appears. In this image I want to get rid of the magenta and turn it into an orange color, so I click on the Hue Level and drag it to the right until it hits +79. Then I go to Saturation and bring it to +44 and click OK. The result is shown in Figure 10.25.

Figure 10.25 Changing the color of the fractal to orange.

I think things are getting exciting! The dreamy atmosphere looks interesting. Now I'll have to insert the girl.

The Girl Enters the Scenery

The girl is still sitting on the sidewalk, with dirty toes, and dreaming. That is the look I want to emphasize. But the dreamy atmosphere will integrate the various elements as a unit. I want to eliminate all the unnecessary lines that will interfere with the dream. I will draw a circle around the top part of the girl with the circular Selection tool. Then I select Inverse and feather it to 80, hit Backspace, and I have the girl almost in a cloud (see Figure 10.26).

Overlapping the Two Images and Making Adjustments

I am now ready to combine the image of the girl and the fractal. I select the girl's image, Edit > Copy, and then select the fractal image and paste the girl over it. In the Layers palette, I click on Opacity and slide it to 40 and start moving the girl until I find the position that will reinforce the message I am after (see Figure 10.27).

The image is a little hazy, so after flattening it I added a little Saturation (+15) and then selected Image > Adjustments > AutoLevels. This seems to work OK here. I then selected Filter > Sharpen > Unsharp Mask, Amount 84, Radius 2.6, and Threshold 16.

This Could Be a Complete Work

Yes, this could be a complete work. It shows her dreaming, but there needs to be something more to this story. When the dream is over, reality is there to meet us. And this is why I put those gates into the image. The gates are telling us that reality

Figure 10.26 Selecting the girl and giving the appearance of being in a cloud.

Figure 10.27 Overlapping the girl and the fractal image.

is not that pretty, or pleasant. It is unpredictable. This is the reason for the gates not being symmetric or pretty. However, they are solidly structured. They are the truth (see Figure 10.28).

Figure 10.28 *Dreaming Revisited* (and framed by the gates of reality).

Last Words

My experience in teaching encourages me to continue to experiment with different tools, different mediums, and different styles. The experimental fever is still with me even in my computer career. I enjoy learning new programs, especially those with new filters and fractals that will give new possibilities to my non-objective work.

I could not have created this image, *Dreaming Revisited*, by depending only on the computer. Without the years spent studying and improving my knowledge of art, my computer work could not be valid. This fabulous box is a great invention, and most of all, it is stimulating. It wakes up dormant ideas in my head in a much faster way than I could without its aid. It gives me a sense of security that I may be accomplishing something useful for those who will come after me. Once a teacher, always a teacher.

The focus of my current work is to deepen the learning of fractals to be able to incorporate them in my creations. In my opinion, most of the time I do not think that a fractal can make a complete composition. I like to use my fractals as beginnings, and then transform them with the use of filters and add more fractals or textures to them to arrive at a pleasing end.

Ever since I can remember I leaned toward abstract and non-objective images. To me, the lines, shapes, and textures placed on a surface are means of excitement, perhaps because I can read their meaning. I do not need a smiling face to know the painting is a happy one. Unfortunately, during my art career I discovered that most viewers are interested in the subject, and when they see a non-objective work, their first reaction is that of being insulted. They think I am kidding and ask, "What is it?"

When teaching, I explain to my students that the subject is not the important part of a painting. It is the treatment of the subject that brings forward the message. If the subject were the important part then I would need only one Crucifixion. Instead I have millions of them, and each one has a different message in it.

The artist has a personal background filled with experiences and, according to his beliefs, he transports a lot of his heritage into his work. A Tuscan artist may put forgiveness in his Christ's eyes, but a Spanish artist, with knowledge of the centuries of invasions in Spain may have in his Christ's face a spirit of revenge, or a message that says "You'll have to pay for what you did to me!"

Artist Profile: Renata Spiazzi

Artistic Background or Influences: I grew up in the eastern part of the Veneto region of Italy, and even though it had Roman roots, it had been occupied by the Austro-Hungarian Empire for many years until the end of the First World War. Walking in the streets of the civic center, one gets the feeling of being in Vienna because of the Baroque buildings, but I was never attracted to the style. It was too rich for me. Instead, I was excited when I walked toward the outskirts of the city and discovered the little churches in the villages surrounding the city. They are buildings of a primitive simplicity, and yet still standing even though they were built in the Romanesque era. That might be my predisposition for simplicity. I find myself trying to express something with great economy of lines, which includes my exploration of the fractal kingdom.

System Profile: Compaq Evo W 6000, ViewSonic Graphic Series G810 monitor, Wacom Cintiq 18SX

Peripherals: Epson 4870 scanner, Epson 3000 and 4000 printers, Encad Novajet 700 printer, Fuji FinePix S 2 Pro, SLR Nikon 6006 with lenses

Software and Plug-Ins: Photoshop CS, Corel Painter 9, Right Hemisphere Deep Paint, Ultrafractal, Auto FX Software: Mystical Lighting and Photographic Edges, MS Office tools, Snag-it, Xaos, KPT 3.0, 5 and 6, KPT Effects, Nik Color FX Pro

Paris Aujourd'hui

Papers, Inks, and Other Output Preferences: I print on different substrates and make editions of 10 to 25 prints each, numbered and signed. Sometimes, when a work lends itself to a bigger size, I print it on canvas which can be stretched on bars, and the work assumes the aspect of a painting. I may also use acrylic brush work after printing on canvas.

Personal Web Site: www.spiazzi.com

11

Melvin Strawn

Mel Strawn has had a long career as an artist, dating back over four decades. "Always a precocious draughtsman and a superb colorist, he has built an impressive record of exhibitions and awards. He has a keen analytical mind, which has stood him in good stead throughout his career. As a student of art, he made probing sketches of master works in accordance with his belief that this method allowed him to truly 'see' and understand. So it came as no surprise to his contemporaries that he became one of the first to grasp the creative potential of the computer" (Sidney Chafetz, in *Transitions*, self-published 1997.)

"In 1981, when many people were wondering just exactly what one might find useful about a 'home computer,' Mel was using his as an art-making tool. His work has evolved in tandem with the development of increasingly complex technology. Some of his pre-computer painterly investigations of finite programmable units began as early as 1977. His first computer art relied on elaborate software programs that he wrote in computer code and viewed on the family television that served as his first monitor. These programs informed and even directed some of his canvases of this time. Later, he began an innovative series of paintings using a limited set of shapes organized on a grid in configurations developed by random combinations generated by a home computer. Although not visually apparent to most viewers, these paintings developed from Mel's fascination with the limitless permutations and configurations possible with simple visual units. His work is evidence of his continued commitment to free gesture and patterned structure." As paint programs with "brushes," ink-jet printers, and more powerful computers were developed, Mel was hooked. Finally, the move to scanned and manipulated imagery brought him even more freedom, including the versatility to incorporate personal sketches into the mix. (Gwen Chanzit, in *Transitions*, self-published 1997.)

First Impressions

Being presented with someone else's material outside of my current direction was a bit new. Not having the choice of source images and all the elements to be employed, the three seed images presented a quandary as to how to use them. Fine art and design (commercial art) were intimately linked in the most influential art education experiments early in the century. The Bauhaus and its American successors put all students through a fundamentals course in design that included experiments in new materials and tools, including photography and any way possible to use light. Art and design became essentially one discipline while creative research into ways to make art embraced anything and everything. The digitizing of images and the manipulation of the digital "stuff" of colored light to generate new images was just a matter of time. The time is now, and this experimental educational heritage is common to both commercial designers and fine artists. So, this challenge is similar to the sort of requests that commercial digital designers receive on a daily basis. The challenge will be to allow the images to reveal a personal meaning, while fulfilling the design of the assigned exercise.

The Process Unfolds

The influences of an artist's teachers are always present. Among my teachers is Sabro Hasegawa, one of the first abstract painters in Japan. For an entire day, he had me draw a single, even width, horizontal line from the left edge to the right edge of an 18" × 24" sheet of paper. He then "knew who I was." Tamen Ayamura, a Kyoto Master Calligrapher, had me write the character for "Kaze" (wind) with brush, sumi ink, and paper for more than a few days. Finally, one of my written characters was good, and we drank a small cup of Suntory whiskey to celebrate. One must solve one's problems by doing. Similarly, I simply had to go through the process described in this journal to get beyond the slight impasse that these imposed images represented.

Day 1

The previous night was full of speculating on approaches I would take toward these images. I had even considered printing them and then tearing up the prints into fragments for scanning. This is a good way to discover relationships between objects and items that might not occur by just thinking about the images. The printed image is, after all, just a physical object that can be physically altered. Instead, however, I decided to play with the seed images as digital images on screen. What potential inter-relationships might there be between these three images?

In Figure 11.1, Seed Image 2, the "architecture image," has been inverted from a positive to a negative, and over that the "girl" image (Seed Image 1) has been placed on a layer. The girl's layer has been set to the Difference Blend mode. I had to move the girl image a bit so that her eyes would show up in a dark zone of the architectural image.

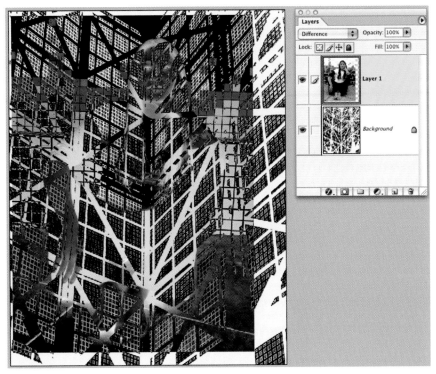

Figure 11.1 The process of exploring the potentials of the seed images begins with inverting the architecture image and applying Blend modes to the upper layer, which has been repositioned within the composite image.

Figure 11.2 shows further image exploration—this time with the "canyon image" (Seed Image 3) in the background layer. The girl image has been placed in a layer above the canyon and the Exclusion Blend mode has been applied to her layer. I decided to have her image revealed only in part, so I applied a Layer Mask and positioned a radial gradient in the Layer Mask. The lightest area of this gradient causes the Layer Mask to reveal the image, while the darkest part of the gradient hides the image.

Figure 11.2 Another experiment—this one with the canyon in the background layer and the girl's image above. A Layer Mask is added and a Radial Gradient is applied to feather the image of the girl into a portion of the layer below. The Exclusion Blend mode accounts for the coloration of the image.

With the canyon still in the background layer, I then brought the architecture image into the layer above and used the Layer Mask with a linear gradient fill to blend the two images from top to bottom (see Figure 11.3). The image now perhaps suggests a "technology-power source," our domination over nature. An interesting formal discovery is made, in that the perspective of the rocks on the upper left aligns nicely with the geometry and depth cues of the architecture. Such formal integration and/or conflict drive meaning and suggest to our mind's eye content or the feeling of significance. This perception often happens unconsciously and gets to the core of my way of exploring what I call my "transactions with the world"—of discovering meaning through the implementation of process.

For the most part, over some 60 years, I've come to accept that I don't have much of anything to "say." When I do, I write or say it. I enter into a discovery process by looking, making drawings, photographing, collecting, arranging, or combining what the world presents. "What the world presents" includes ideas, such as cellular structure (the idea of "structure" itself), or phenomena, such as memory. The world also presents free association of things in time and space and the idea of transparency; all of which became factors in the way I decided to use these three images. And so ends day one.

Figure 11.3 Still another exploration of the seed images—blending the architecture image into the canyon. This time a Linear Gradient feathers the architecture image so that it fades toward the top of the image.

Day 2

Using the girl and architecture images, I noted a slight axial slant toward the left in the girl image, which is similar to the major axial slant near the center of the architecture image. I selected the right half of the girl image along this axis, and copied and pasted this selection to a new layer. I aligned the two axial edges by rotating the layer containing the girl image so that the left edge corresponded to the axis of the architecture. The girl was further locked into the major architectural structure to the right by using the Distort filter to pull the upper right-hand corner of the image upward.

Various possible Blend modes and positive or negative relations of the two layers were explored. A version of these explorations, which leaves the architecture image dominant, was decided on as the next interim step (see Figure 11.4).

Wanting to alter and better integrate the architecture image surrounding the image layer above it, I applied a blue-to-white gradient to a new layer between the other two. Once this layer Blend mode was set to Difference, this effectively inverted the architecture image—the dark beam and girder structure became middle blue to light gray.

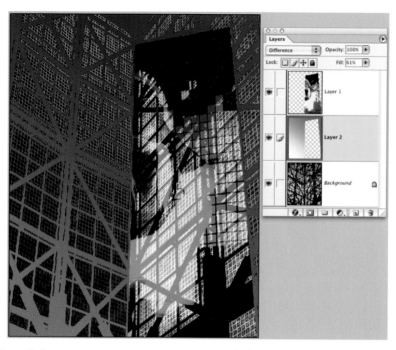

Figure 11.4 A compositional element in an underlying image is used to visually anchor another image layer above it.

Then I selected the empty, transparent space around the girl image (see Figure 11.5). I shifted this selection to the architecture image by clicking on that layer in the Photoshop Layers palette. I applied the Zig-Zag filter and further experimented with settings for that filter until the results that worked were evident.

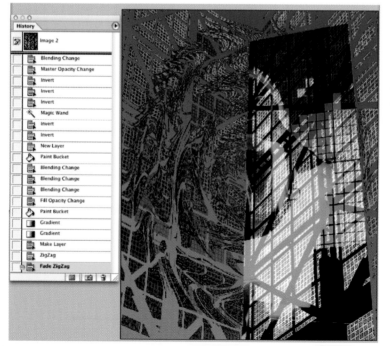

Figure 11.5 The History palette shows a list of all the operations performed on the image. The rhythm established in one layer is reflected in the layer below after a Zig-Zag filter is applied.

The gray color in the lower part of the girl image links visually to the light gray in the architecture image and begins to tie things together. Also, the curves in the girl image are extended and echoed in the now curvy architecture image. In a sense, the girl has transformed the rigid lines of the architecture. Several more Color and Blend adjustments resulted in the image seen in Figure 11.6.

Figure 11.6 After applying the Zig-Zag filter and several Blend modes, a colorful and interesting image begins to emerge, but something is lacking.

At this stage there is lots of structure and strong basic shape, pattern, and color movement giving the image a broad impact. However, it seems lacking in content and meaning, in tension and mystery. Still, it is promising. I am wondering about the "personal style" issue. What is it that moves all this into the realm of *my* imagery and expression? A stained glass effect is hinted at, complete with a "Madonna" image. This is not my usual domain. The demand for a "personal style" as some sort of guarantee of one's artistic authenticity and unique value is a narrowly defined marketing demand—a requirement on the part of critics and art marketers who are not usually artists but rather verbal people who frame the issue in verbal logic. This does not often fit what artists do. I'll let it rest for today.

Day 3

After a few days I returned to the image, falling back on some personal elements— things used in my recent work. I imported scans of three bottle caps, a fragment of screen, and aluminum foil to use as compositional elements. I am mainly interested in placing these elements into dark areas at the top and bottom of the right half of the composition.

Figure 11.7 shows the layer structure at this stage. The left half of the girl's face and hair were cut and pasted into a layer using a Soft Edge selection. A bottle cap serves as a sort of nimbus or halo around her head. As noted, a complex set of Blend modes has been applied to this set of layers. Next, a geometric zone at the lower left is selected and Curves are adjusted to darken and answer a strong planar area at the top right (see Figure 11.8). I use the word "answer" instead of "balance." "Balance" is a static concept while "answer" implies a more dynamic interplay between compositional elements. Now, the larger linear and planar geometry of the architecture image controls the whole composition. At the same time, the organic and curvilinear imagery is allowed to dance through it. For me, the composition is beginning to work.

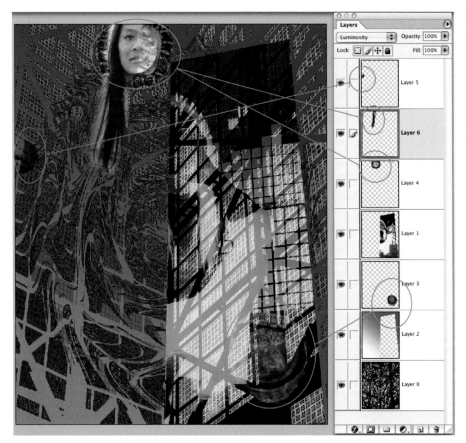

Figure 11.7 The layer structure of the image with some scanned elements added. From the top layer down, the Blend modes are as follows: Linear Burn, Luminosity, Luminosity, Pin Light at 71% Opacity, Lighten, Difference, and Normal.

Next, I decided to take a different tack to see what could be done using all three seed images. Rotating the architecture image 180 degrees changes its perspective so that it opens up toward the top rather than narrowing. The architecture pattern was inverted, causing the small window frames to become black. Using Select Color in the Photoshop Selection menu, these areas were selected and filled using the Colorize mode with a shade of green. The canyon and the girl images were brought in and each placed on their own layer. Only the girl's head and hair were selected from the seed image for placement on its respective layer (see Figure 11.9).

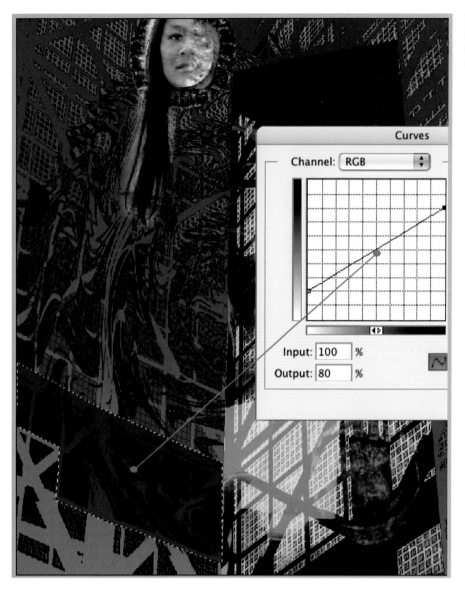

Figure 11.8 An odd shaped selection was made in order to apply Curves to darken this area.

Notice also in Figure 11.9 that a mask has been applied to the canyon layer and shapes suggested from the architecture image have been filled with various shades of gray. These shapes were drawn using the Polygon Lasso tool in the architecture layer. Then, by clicking on the canyon Layer Mask these shapes become active and can be filled with various shades of gray. The different shades of gray affect the degree of transparency by which the architecture is allowed to blend into the canyon layer above it. The canyon layer has been set to the Hard Light Blend mode. The face image on the layer above the canyon is set to the Darken mode

Figure 11.9 Another avenue is explored using all three images. Shapes from one layer are drawn into the mask of the layer above it. Various shades of gray allow the underlying image to bleed through at different intensities.

and repositioned to provide an emotional point of interest relative to the geometric and organic environments of the other two layers. All three images are in some degree of interaction. The architecture details striking the face suggest some sort of tattoo or other such adornment, and I decided to accept that little serendipitous contribution to mystery and to effect meaning. An expressive theme is beginning to announce itself. Figure 11.10 shows various Blend modes applied to the face image, but all these experiments were eventually rejected.

Figure 11.11 shows the final results for this session. The top layer containing the face was adjusted to 32% Opacity. These adjustments are all based on "seeing" and not on any "magic" numbers. I select what I feel are the best results based on the best effect possible. The images are beginning to work together, with none of the three images particularly dominating the composition. More work will be required to see that none of the images is seen as either foreground or background. That is my sensibility, which I will work toward in later sessions.

Figure 11.10 Four Blend modes were tried, but the upper left image was the only one chosen for further development.

Figure 11.11 This version begins to approach a mix of all three seed images in which no single image dominates.

Day 4

A third and, as it turned out, final image was started using the image from Figure 11.11. A duplicate of the whole flattened image was made and became Layer 2. This layer was blurred using the Gaussian Blur filter, and then the Blend mode was set to Difference. This has the effect of making the previously light image appear as a darker negative. The blur has also softened the color and some of the detail.

A second copy of the background layer was made and placed between the two layers described earlier. Adjustments were made in the Curves filter to darken the midtones and shadows, pulling then together. The Emboss filter was applied to the image in this middle layer and the direction of the embossing was inverted. Experimenting with the Blend modes for this same layer led to a decision to use the Luminosity setting to allow the blurred color of the top layer to emerge, while retaining the sharper-edged detail of the embossed layer and creating a strong relief effect. A bit of a surprise! A Layer Mask was added to the middle layer, and the area about the girl's face was painted in black. This allows the layer below to come through without being altered by the Embossed or Luminosity effects of the middle layer, thus setting off the face in a subtle contrasting visual mode.

A few more experiments made by inverting various combinations of layers did not work out to my satisfaction, so the day ended with the image as seen in Figure 11.12. Note the Blend modes from the top down are Difference, Luminosity, and Normal. This was the end of today's session.

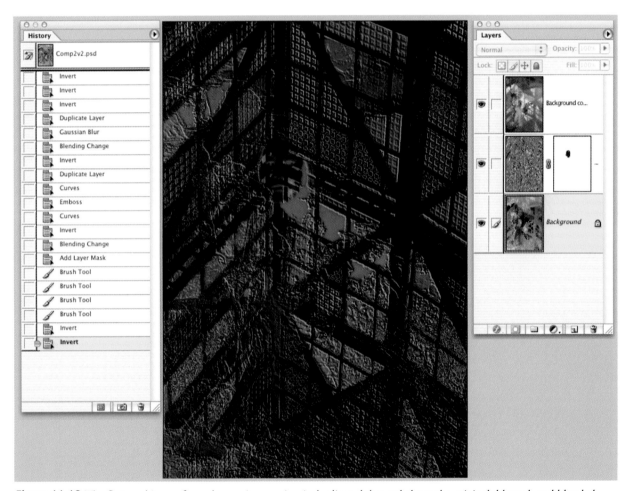

Figure 11.12 The flattened image from the previous session is duplicated, layered above the original, blurred, and blended with the original layer beneath it using the Difference mode. The colors are enriched and the girl's face is brought into the composition in a subtle manner.

Day 5

Figure 11.13 shows the recent version opened with Curves adjusted to "open up" the color range. The curve is steeper approaching the dark zone, which effectively lightens the entire image and allows dark "closed" tones to be illuminated or "opened." I then experimented with Curves set as noted on each of the previous image layers (as shown in Figure 11.12). Working in the background layer yielded little change because the Layer Mask on the middle layer blocks it from view.

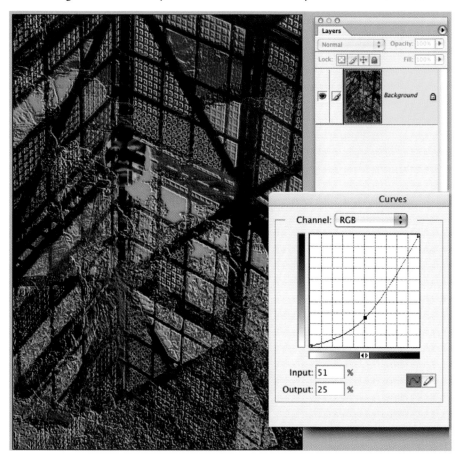

Figure 11.13 Further adjustments to Curves brighten some previously muddy colors and seem to give the image more openness and space.

On Layer 3, by clicking on the layer itself and not the Layer Mask, a Curve adjustment similar to that shown causes a rather surprising alteration. The bottom lightens and there are some other changes. This seems to be the richest and most mysterious total image. Since my objectives are to discover, evoke, or provoke something I've not experienced before, mystery certainly fits that intent. This image (see Figure 11.14) now works for me and is probably the keeper!

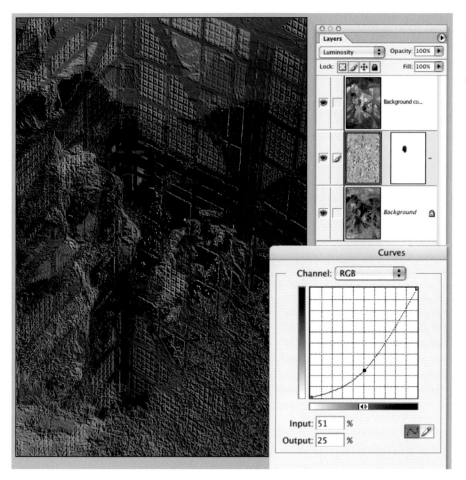

Figure 11.14 Applying a Curves adjustment to the top layer brings the composition into a state that meets the artist's intentions.

Day 6

Figure 11.15 shows, on the left, the flattened image before adjusting Curves compared to the "keeper" image on the right. Some of the soft "erasing-through" earlier Layer Masks now work well in moving the dark zone down along the off-center axis of the composition. The merging of qualities into *one* image in which none of the three source images act as a foreground or background, but rather all interact in a new, overall statement is what makes this work, according to my sensibility…or "style." To the degree that new technology encourages new processes for composing, I think digital image making launches us fully into a very eclectic era in which old notions of technical style relate poorly, if at all, to the work being done.

I will call the finished piece *Seeing Time Through*. The work suggested the title to me. I want my titles to suggest some interpretive lens through which one can consider the work. The word order is disjunctive, which demands a bit of extra attention on the viewer's part. And, like the image, the title can yield more than one "reading."

Figure 11.15 The finishing touches bring unity to the image. None of the three seed images act as a foreground or background; rather, all three interact in an overall statement.

Last Words

This image-making venture started with an alien confrontation—that is, being given three images totally new to me and seeming to have nothing to do with each other or with my own normal ways of selecting subjects or ideas. However, the digital process invites experimentation in depth. It provides means to explore efficiently and widely in search of *possibilities*. One's sensibility and creative habits, the evoking of trial and error, and probes in modifying and inter-relating elements and images are the essential ingredients of any creative adventure. Art has been many things and has served many purposes. Digital processing makes it possible to investigate new, subtle, and unexpected qualities and relations. Optimistically, it even makes it possible to engender new qualities of experience—or new meanings, if one grants that meaning or significance can lie in one's internal experience and not just "out there."

Artist Profile: Melvin N. Strawn

Artistic Background or Influences: BFA, MFA California College of Arts and Crafts, Jepson Art Institute, Otis Art Institute, Chouinard Art Institute. After 32 years of college and university teaching, I am now Professor Emeritus, University of Denver. Among my influences I count Asian calligraphy and art, Goya, Piero della Francesca, Cezanne, Mondrian, Picasso, Matisse, William de Kooning, and a host of others. I have also integrated chance, randomness, and Zen into much of my work. My imagery and "creative process" is a personal amalgamation of modern-abstraction, objective drawing, and object appropriation via scan and camera. Perhaps you could call my work "mixed media," except all elements are now digitally processed.

System Profile: Three Macs: Power Mac G3, Mac "Cube" with OS 9.2 and 10, Mac G4 iBook, Wacom 6" × 9" pressure sensitive tablet

Peripherals: Umax Powerlook III scanner, Sigma Foveon chip digital camera, Olympus 3030 digital camera, Epson 9000 printer, Tektronix Phaser 560 laser printer

Software and Plug-Ins: Photoshop CS, Genuine Fractals, Sigma PhotoPro 2, Umax MagicScan

Pale Horse Riders

Papers, Inks, and Other Output Preferences: Osprey Velvet and Merlin Smooth by Hawk Mountain, MediaStreet G4 pigmented inks, sizes vary (too much, maybe)

Personal Web Site: www.911gallery.org/mels/mels.htm

Spacial Flux

12

Stephen Burns

Stephen Burns has been a corporate instructor and lecturer in the application of digital art and design for the past ten years. He has exhibited digital fine art nationally and internationally, including exhibitions at the SIGGRAPH 2003 Art Gallery, Durban Art Museum in South Africa, Citizens Gallery in Yokahama, Japan, and CECUT Museum in Tijuana, Mexico. He received a first place award in the 2001 Seybold International Digital Art contest.

Stephen is the author of *Photoshop FX & Trickery* and is a contributing author to the *Secrets of Award Winning Digital Artists, Photoshop CS Savvy,* and *Advanced Digital Photographer's Workshop*. He completed a series of Photoshop videos for the creative artist for KURV Studios and writes monthly articles for *HDRI Magazine*, specializing in the latest version of Photoshop and 3D texturing.

First Impressions

The three seed images are simply snapshots—a reclining portrait, an architectural backdrop, and a landscape. None of them exhibit dynamic composition, nor do they portray an artistic vision or statement. They are just quick convenient references of the subject at a specific point in time. The challenge is to create a dynamic composition of something that would be more visually interesting. One of the characteristics of artists is that they can see beauty and life in mundane everyday places that most of us would not give a second look. So let me take you on a journey into my thought process and techniques used to create my own image.

The Process Unfolds

The most dominating imagery is the reclining portrait (Seed Image 1). The human subject is tightly framed, and this makes it ideal as a starting point for experimentation. Understand that I have no preconceived ideas as to where this will end up visually. I will experiment at this point and allow my imagination and gut instinct to take me in a variety of directions. It is important in the beginning stages of creating that you do not get emotionally attached to the image. Allow your instinct to offer possibilities and, most important, allow mistakes to take you in directions that you would not have normally taken. This state of mind requires practice and the willingness to free yourself of the fear of making mistakes.

The Experimentation Begins

The number one rule in working in Photoshop is to duplicate (Ctrl+J) the base layer so that if you make a mistake you can always delete the layer and duplicate the original again to save time. I wanted to see the results of disfiguring the portrait a bit, so by duplicating and flipping the base layer horizontally I added masks to each of them for the purpose of extending the head upward and adding additional eyes (see Figure 12.1).

Figure 12.2 is a continuation of the process to deform the head. I created layer sets to keep things orderly. When you work in layers, it becomes very easy to have quite a few of them, so I recommend that you use layer sets. That is exactly what I did here. I just clicked on the yellow folder on the bottom of the Layers palette to create the set. All of the layers I was working with can now be dragged into that layer set. You can rename it by double-clicking on the folder. Here, I renamed it "body."

I created a new layer from one of the portraits that shows an enlarged view of the foot that is angled on the lower left corner. I felt this would be a good opportunity to play with framing techniques using portions of previously created layers (see Figure 12.3).

Within a new layer set called "background," I merged the portrait images into one single layer and applied some Gaussian Blur (Filters > Blur > Gaussian Blur). After applying a Layer Mask, I added a simple shape to the mask to allow the unaltered portrait to show through in a pattern that complements the tile background. The ovals on the image itself and on the layer show the shape I imposed (see Figure 12.4).

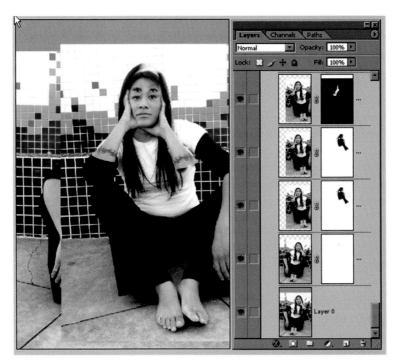

Figure 12.1 The base layer is duplicated, inversed, and masked.

Figure 12.2 The head is extended further.

Figure 12.3 Experimenting with framing.

Figure 12.4 Applying a shape to the mask to allow the unaltered portrait to show through.

Now is the time to add some variety to the mix. I chose to bring in the architectural backdrop (Seed Image 2) and change its Blend mode to Darken. This mode will allow the dark pixels to remain untouched but will make the white pixels transparent. To keep the backdrop from completely obscuring the portrait, I applied a mask to allow the face to come through unaltered (see Figure 12.5).

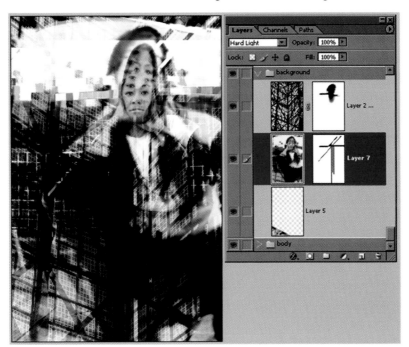

Figure 12.5 Adding the architectural backdrop.

Moving Beyond Predictability

At this stage the composition is still predictable. For me, the predictability arises when much of the original imagery is recognizable. So I experimented further. Duplicating the merged portrait, I applied Polar Coordinates (Filter > Distort > Polar Coordinates) with the Rectangular option checked in the Polar Radial box (see Figure 12.6).

I then applied a mask to give the finished look of an egg-shaped composition. I next applied the Hard Light Blend mode (see Figure 12.7).

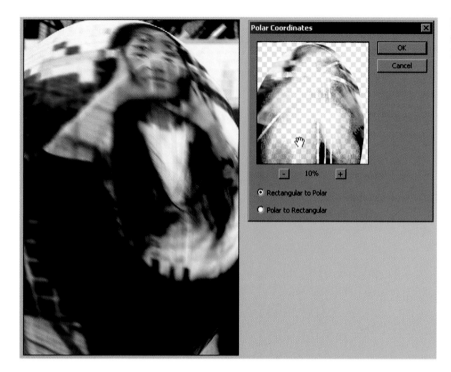

Figure 12.6 Applying Polar Coordinates—from Rectangular to Polar.

Figure 12.7 An egg-shaped mask is applied.

Adding a Sense of Motion

Duplicating the layer again, I applied Polar Coordinates again, but this time with the Polar to Rectangular Radial box checked. I was looking for a way to give the image some energy. I used this layer to apply a sense of motion. Using my Layer Mask, I applied the effect to selected areas. I then set the Blend mode to Lighten (see Figure 12.8).

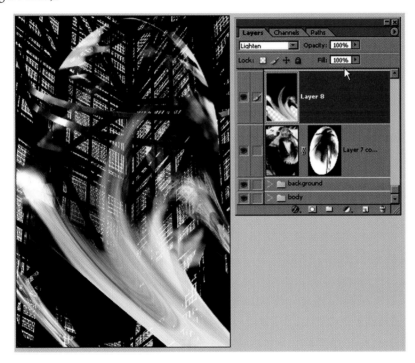

Figure 12.8 Applying Polar Coordinates—from Polar to Rectangular.

Figure 12.9 shows the same steps applied sequentially to add further movement to the piece. Each layer is offset and rotated to assist in giving it more of a spontaneous look.

Figure 12.9 Sequential application of Polar Coordinates, offsetting and rotating each successive layer.

Enriching the Tonality of the Image

I added a Burn and Dodge layer to control the tonality of the piece. This is a new layer filled with medium-gray with its Blend mode set to Overlay. Using the Burn and Dodge tools will enrich or brighten your image (see Figure 12.10).

Bringing in the Grand Canyon

The Grand Canyon landscape image (Seed Image 3) is ideal for adding some color variations. I set the Blend mode to Overlay and further accentuated it with Motion Blur. (Filters > Blur > Motion Blur). Next I placed the layers, creating the Whirl Effect, into their own layer set called "Color Whirl" (see Figures 12.11 and 12.12).

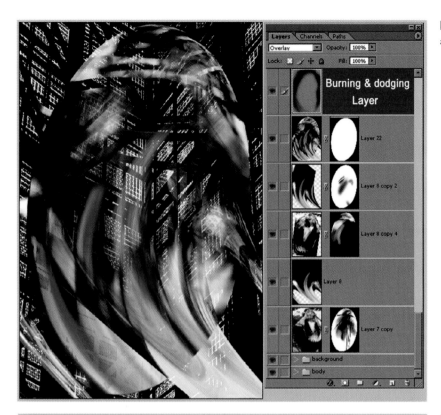

Figure 12.10 Adding a Burn and Dodge layer.

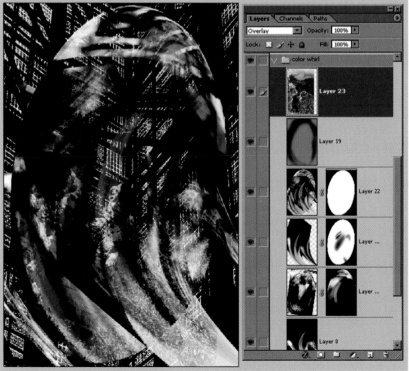

Figure 12.11 The Grand Canyon landscape is used to add color.

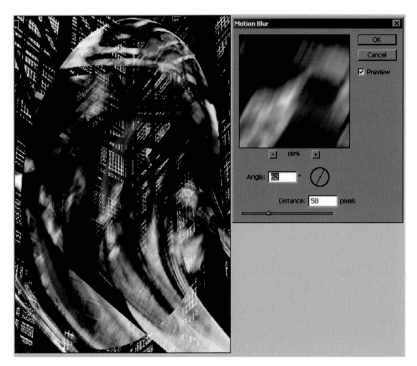

Figure 12.12 Motion Blur is applied to the Grand Canyon landscape.

Framing with the Architectural Backdrop

I wanted the viewer to be drawn into the composition. So, starting from the foreground, I added some framing techniques using the architectural backdrop (Seed Image 2). I first applied Shear to the layer with the architectural backdrop (Filter >Distort > Shear), focusing on the lower right-hand corner of this layer (see Figure 12.13). I then set the Blend mode to Darken. This allowed the rest of the background to show through the light areas and to push the viewer's focal interest away from the lower right-hand corner with this darker, curved architectural shape (see Figure 12.14).

Next, the sheared backdrop shown in Figure 12.13 is duplicated twice, but this time the Blend mode is set to Normal. Each version is offset to allow their respective lines and tonality to catch the viewer's eyes, leading them on a visual journey into the image (see Figure 12.15).

If you recall, I advised against getting emotionally attached to the image during the creation stage. This is where that advice applies to me. Although I like the colors at this point, they do not help with the overall composition. I decided to alter the colors by applying a Hue & Saturation adjustment layer to make the shape more monotone with a sepia-like effect, restricting the results with the egg-shaped mask (see Figure 12.16).

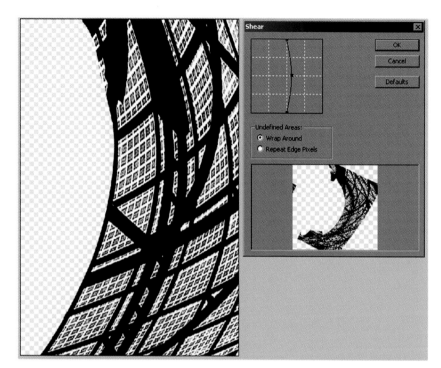

Figure 12.13 Shear is applied to the architectural backdrop.

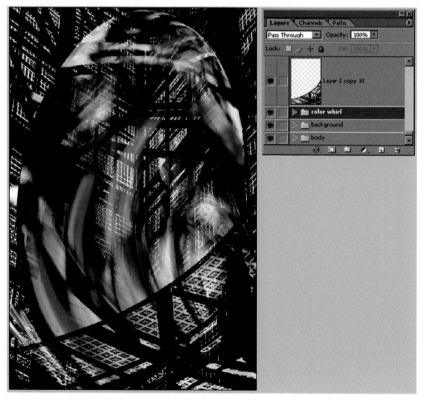

Figure 12.14 Framing is applied using the newly reshaped architectural backdrop.

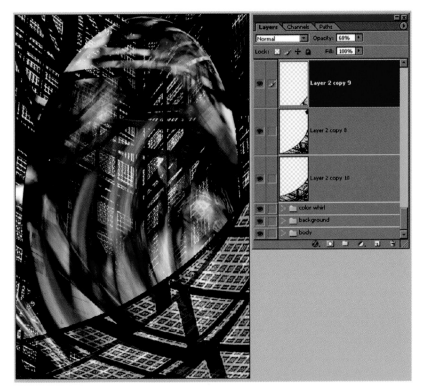

Figure 12.15 Replicating and offsetting two versions of the reshaped architectural backdrop.

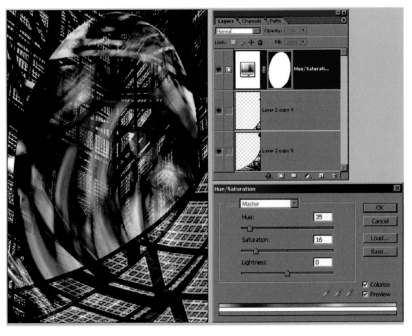

Figure 12.16 Applying a sepia effect.

I liked how this step worked, but the highlights were still too bright. So, with a Curves adjustment layer, I muted the highlights and brightened up the shadows a bit. I placed these layers into a layer set called "Frame" (see Figure 12.17).

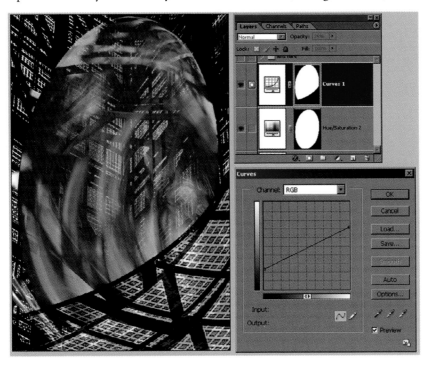

Figure 12.17 Applying a Curves adjustment layer.

Providing an Energy Source

The overall feel of the piece is starting to become energetic, but it still needs a source from which the energy emanates. I used Lens Flare (Filters > Render > Lens Flare) to provide some of that energy source. Placing the Lens Flare on a medium-gray layer with its Blend mode set to Hard Light gave me the flare itself (see Figure 12.18). This is only the beginning of applying the energy, so these were placed into the "Flare" layer set.

Continuing with my experimentation, I wanted to add a 3D-like environment. I used the Pen tool to create a shape that matched the flow of the circular center piece. A selection was created with a Ctrl+click on the Path layer (Windows > Paths; see Figure 12.19 A). I copied a section from the original portrait and placed it on its own layer. Finally, I applied a Bevel effect to give it the 3D look I was looking for (see Figure 12.19 B). To balance the piece, I created two shapes and placed them against one another. I added Color adjustment layers to the shapes to give them more saturation than the background. This is what I was looking for (see Figure 12.20). Once again, I placed the shapes into a layer set called "Sculpture" to keep organized.

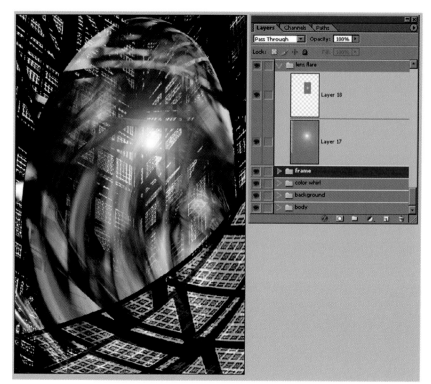

Figure 12.18 Applying Lens Flare.

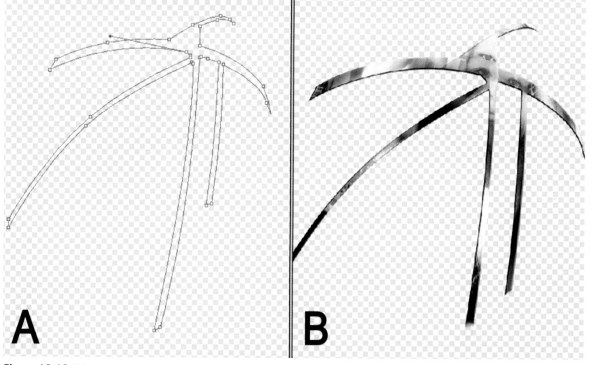

Figure 12.19 (A) Creating a Pen Path. (B) Appling Bevel to the Pen Path.

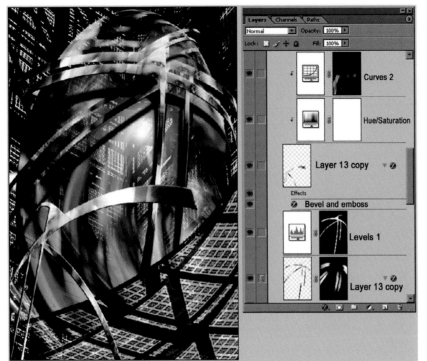

I added some lighting streaks from the Lens Flare source. Since my goal was to use the three images, I duplicated one of the Swirl Effect layers. With the Paint Brush tool activated, I used the Dry Brush to apply the streaks on the mask (see Figure 12.21).

Finally, the background is masked out with a sepia tonality to support the circular shape. After some additional work with the Paint Brush, the energy I was looking for came to fruition (see Figure 12.22).

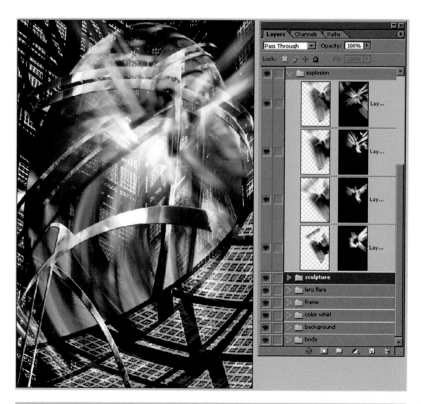

Figure 12.21 Applying light streaks.

Figure 12.22 Applying a sepia tonality and using the Paint Brush to emphasize the sense of energy.

Last Words

I enjoy visual challenges because they provide opportunities to create in an untraditional manner. When I was asked to create a piece based on three predefined photos, I considered what viewers would want to see. My instincts suggested that their expectation might be to see a direct connection to the original images. However, my rebellious nature pushed me to take a different direction. Why should I allow the portrait to remain a *portrait*? Why not destroy it and allow my subconscious awareness to reconstruct it in a more aggressive and unpredictable manner?

My advice is to experiment abundantly and not to get too emotionally attached to the image during this stage. Listen to your gut instinct and allow it to tell you when to change the technique, when to add more content and detail, and when to stop.

Artist Profile: Stephen Burns

Artistic Background or Influences: I discovered the same passion for the digital medium as I did for photography as an art form. I began as a photographer 25 years ago and over time progressed toward the digital medium. My influences include the great abstractionists and surrealists including Jackson Pollock, Wassily Kankinsky, Pablo Picasso, Wilfredo Lam, Franz Kline, Mark Rothko, Mark Tobey, and Lenore Fini.

System Profile: Prostar Computer (800MHz front system bus, 3.6GHz Pentium 4 with Hyperthreading, 2GB RAM, Geforce 6800 video card with 256MB RAM, 200GB hard drive), Wacom Intuos 3 tablet

Peripherals: Epson R1800, Nikon 8000 slide scanner, Howtek drum scanner, Cannon A2E, Sony VX 2000 digital video camera

Software and Plug-Ins: Adobe Photoshop CS, Illustrator CS, InDesign CS, LightWave 8, Toaster 4, Flash, Dreamweaver MX 2004, After Effects 5.5

Papers, Inks, and Other Output Preferences: Hahnemuhle German Etching

Personal Web Site: www.chromeallusion.com

Digital Ecstasy

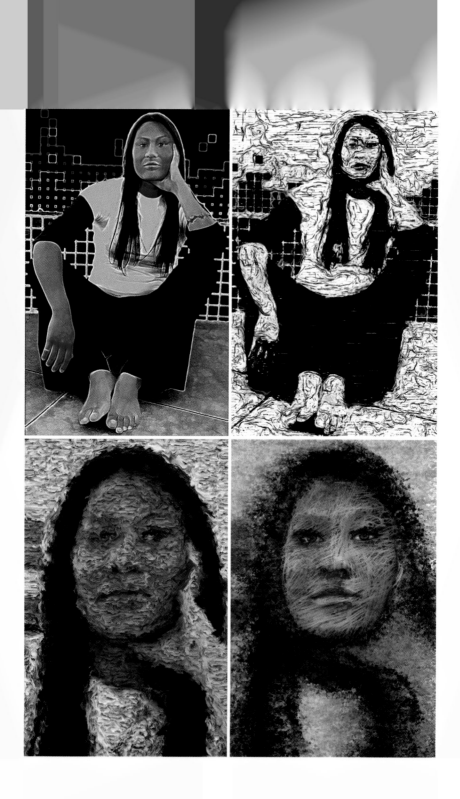

13

Michael Wright

Michael Wright is a painter who began to explore digital media in the mid 1980s on an Amiga computer. He exhibited his first digital prints in 1989 and continues to work in both traditional and electronic media. He has exhibited digital and traditional works on a national and international level over the past 35 years. Michael is profiled in *Computer Graphics Companion* (Palgrave Macmillan, 2002). His digital work is represented in *Computer Graphics World: 25-Year Retrospective of Digital Art* magazine and its portfolio section "Pixel Perfect: Michael Wright," as well as in *The Computer in the Visual Arts* (Addison Wesley, 1999) and *CyberArts: Exploring Art & Technology* (by Linda Jacobs, 1992). He and his work have been featured in *Wired Online, Micro Publishing News, IEEE Computer Graphics & Applications,* and *Agent X,* Television Tokyo. Michael has also been a featured artist at exhibitions and conferences including *ACM1: Beyond Cyberspace, CyberArts X,* and *The Impact of YLEM: 20 Years of Art, Science and Technology.*

Howard Fox, curator of modern art for the Los Angeles County Museum of Art has called Michael Wright's digital work, "Down and dirty, with underlying tension." Elizabeth A.T. Smith, former curator at the Los Angeles Museum of Modern Art, called his work, "Powerful, evocative, an equally charged carrier of meaning about memory, time and transformation." Michael's digital prints are in the collection of the Victoria and Albert Museum in London and the State Museum in Novosibirsk, Russia. He is an associate professor in the Digital Media and Liberal Studies Programs at Otis College of Art and Design in Los Angeles. He also instructs on a regular basis for the Los Angeles County Museum of Art and is the recipient of the Otis Award of Excellence in Arts Education. Michael served as Art Gallery Chair for ACM SIGGRAPH 2003 in San Diego, California.

First Impressions

The project seed images arrived at a chaotic time in my life. It was just two days before my semester started at Otis College of Art & Design, and I was in the middle of a studio move after being in the same location for 17 years. This whole project occurred while I was moving in and trying to get settled in my new studio and while I was teaching six classes. Another issue for me was the method of working. I've never worked from photographs—traditional or digital. I've always worked with frame-grabbed video imagery at low resolution due to the familiar sense of the "TV Eye" that permeates our culture. I've always made the video artifacting integral to the work. I usually have an idea for my work, but it's most likely to be vague, which gives me the freedom to find unexpected depth and layered meaning in the process. In this case it was really my first time working with someone else's digital photo without the artifacting and personal depth of taking your own images.

After spending some time looking at the images, I decided to work with only one, the young woman (Seed Image 1), due to my interest artistically with the figure and the portrait. We artists had been given a timeline of 40 days for this project. I chose to approach the project as a monotype. A traditional monotype implies a series of individual prints based on the same subject and composition. I decided to do one finished image per day for 40 days and then to edit the work to 24 images. The idea of iteration is natural to the way I create on the computer and satisfied my artistic desire to work in a series modality. I don't seek, I find! As a painter, I've spent over 35 years developing my artistic vision. I see composition and the elements of design as though I were taking in a breath of fresh air. It's really a question of perception in the sense that all visual art starts with the eye. Visual artists spend their entire life developing and refining their unique visual eye and view of the world. Keep in mind that all these images are subjective to whoever looks at them. I see them in my own way, and you can see them in yours.

The Process Unfolds

I spent the first 20 days working with the full figure and the second 20 days zoomed in working on the portrait. I began by cropping the image to a composition that put focus totally on the figure. I then adjusted the contrast and color to my liking. Once done with those adjustments, I locked the image into place and began to work my magic. The composition focused on the pose of the young woman and the surrounding tiles, which were like large pixels. The pose suggested a number of things to me. The original image has an androgynous feel. In the pose, the legs and black pants seem heart shaped, with the black suggesting a depth of mystery. The negative space between the girl's feet/ankles forms a V or chalice suggesting her femininity. Her white shirt covers the black and can be seen as surrounding the heart. Her right arm rests on her leg suggesting a passive openness that is neither inviting nor rejecting. The left arm is balanced on the knee, moving up and supporting the head from which all feelings and attitude emanate. The tattoo on her left forearm suggests a harder masculine side. A "Don't mess with me" sign.

Full Figure—Set 1: Looseness of the Stroke

The image shown in Figure 13.1 A represents my early work in which I have simplified the color. This lends a painting feel to the image. Most painting, no matter how detailed, results in a simplification of what the artist is looking at. In this work I achieved an allusion to a looseness of paint that I continued to explore throughout the process. The figure looks harder with the tattoo restricting the forearm—almost tourniquet like—while the negative space between the feet is given a water-like treatment. The whiteness of the forearm gives emphasis to the face, almost lifting it as though it were a mask.

I continued to focus on the looseness of the stroke with an emphasis on the texture (see Figure 13.1 B). Note the change in the face from Figure 13.1 A.

Figure 13.1 (A) Image simplification. (B) Emphasizing texture with continued focus on the looseness of the stroke.

Full Figure—Set 2: From Softness to Emotion

The image (see Figure 13.2 A) exhibits a continued focus on the looseness of the stroke with a painterly look, which adds a softness to the figure of the woman. Note the cross-contour strokes that add a three-dimensional quality opposed to the flatness of the black areas.

Now it gets a little wild (see Figure 13.2 B). Having one of those bad moving days, I wanted to pour out some of the emotion into the work without changing the calmness of the seed image. I chose to use a lot of black lines that swirled throughout the piece like blueberry ripples through vanilla ice cream. I loved the illusion of gooey textures, especially on the ground surrounding the figure. It really captured my feeling that day.

Figure 13.2 (A) A continuation of the loose stroke adds softness to the figure of the woman. (B) Pouring out emotion by adding black lines swirling throughout the image.

Full Figure—Set 3: L.A. Heat

It is the first really hot day in the studio, which resulted in an image that has an emphasis on the texture and flatness to most of the black areas (see Figure 13.3 A). The 220-volt power line for the air conditioning has not yet been installed. I'm running all my high-speed fans. The girl looks sunburned, hot, and happy about it. The heat from her right hand seems funneled right to her face. I feel she is enjoying my discomfort.

The image shown in Figure 13.3 B is a much calmer work that has a mosaic feel to whole image. The eyes are simplified and give a very deep look into the soul. The left hand holds the head as though it were a mask. The black pants seem to bleed into the chalice like negative space suggesting a flow to the foreground. The right hand is very warm and inviting, as opposed to the blues in the surrounding fore- and backgrounds.

Figure 13.3 (A) Heat pouring out of her hand into the face. (B) The black pants bleed into the chalice like negative space flowing to the foreground.

Full Figure—Set 4: The Rains Came

This image (see Figure 13.4 A) is the loosest yet. It's raining really hard today, going for record rainfall. The studio is dark, and I can hear the rain slamming into the glass. The image seems a cross between a watercolor and a deKooning painting. The face still retains a bit of the realism. She doesn't seem to care, and I'm not ready to work the image to further extremes. The work seems to suit the day.

Another rainy day, and I'm feeling contemplative. I'm thinking about what goes beyond mere appearances. I'm thinking about the fractals, the soul, the universe, our place in it, and what it all means. I'm still pushing around and emptying boxes from the move. The image (see Figure 13.4 B) is starting to reveal its structural foundation in the form of an endless web of intertwining lines. In some instances the structure is beginning to disappear. One begins to see into and beyond the image. I'm having a "Men in Black" experience.

Figure 13.4 (A) A cross between a watercolor and a deKooning. (B) An endless web of intertwining lines.

Full Figure—Set 5: Transforming the Chalice

Our girl is happier today (see Figure 13.5 A). The chalice negative space has turned heart shaped, duplicating the black heart of the legs. The paint strokes flow, and she seems willing to let us in. Gray lines float invitingly through the black heart shape. Her feet seem to tap out a rhythm. The paint strokes seem to dance to it throughout the work.

This image (see Figure 13.5 B) is reflecting the turmoil of this day in my life. There is no way she is letting anyone in. The barriers are up. Most of the color has disappeared. The outside influences of the background and foreground have invaded the figure. The tattoo on the left forearm has vanished, allowing an open flow to the head. The chalice shape has been sucked into the black abyss. Lines of gray move through the black areas as though they were horizontal bars keeping feeling from getting in or out. She is not happy and much the opposite of Figure 13.5 A.

Figure 13.5 (A) The chalice negative space has turned heart shaped. (B) The chalice shape has given way to a black abyss.

Full Figure—Set 6: Experimenting with Strokes

The image (see Figure 13.6 A) is opening up again in an oil-paint, watercolor illusion. The whites are calmer with light blue strokes casually looking for a way in. The pixel shapes of the mosaic in the upper background float in space, and the figure although bored seems to be finding her dimensionality again. The tattoo is beginning to reappear slightly integrated with the rest of the paint, still allowing a flow to the head and an emergence of the left eye.

This version (see Figure 13.6 B) is a good illusion of an oil painting. She is bemused and friendlier today even though there is a reminder of her mortality lurking over the right shoulder. The strokes move in a relaxed, playful manner.

Figure 13.6 (A) An oil-paint, watercolor illusion. (B) Movement of the strokes in a relaxed, playful manner.

Full Figure—Set 7: The Electric Queen

In the image shown in Figure 13.7, she is psychedelic, phosphorescent, open to us, and sly—an electric queen of the street. It all starts with the background, which appears neon, pulsating deep into the black while a 3D latticework holds the figure from following. The tattoo radiates heat, which flows into the face through the thumb. A Mona Lisa-like figure for our time if not all time.

A Transition to Portrait

At this point I moved my focus to the face of the young woman. My work has always revolved around archetypal elements—water, light, relationships, and the portrait. I use the portrait as representing humankind's struggle in discovering their spiritual selves in search of spiritual freedom. Moving to the portrait at this point seemed a natural step. The portrait has been a part of my visual vocabulary from the beginning of my art-making career.

In 1991 I was a guest artist at *CyberArts International 2* in Pasadena, California. I did digital portraits of attendees in real time on an Amiga workstation outfitted with a Video Toaster.

In the following year, 1992, I was part of an historic art performance/installation curated by art historian Patric Prince called *Portrait Virus*, which was presented at *CyberArts International 3*—again in Pasadena. The artists involved were Liz Crimzon, Paras Kaul, Tom Pike, Beverly Reiser, and myself. We created portraits

Figure 13.7 A sly, electric queen of the street; a Mona Lisa-like figure of our time.

over networks using different platforms. I captured attendee's portraits in real time using video gear and an Amiga computer, converted the files to a Mac format, saved them to a disk, and passed them to a Mac workstation for painted backgrounds. The images were passed to a second Mac workstation by Ethernet and then were sent from the Pasadena Convention Center to Washington D.C. by modem for further manipulation. The manipulated portraits were then sent back from Washington D.C. to the Amiga workstation, which was connected to a 16-monitor video wall at the Convention Center where they were viewed by *CyberArts* participants. Way cool for '92! Ms. Prince stated, "In an age where data is held to be protected and sacred, we are using the collaborate power of a group of artists to synthesize and expand personal expression through the sharing of data. We hope the *Virus* will transform the portrait elements to project an otherworldly reality that reflects the positive aspects of technological manifestations in society."

Over the years I've continued to present variations of the *Portrait Virus* to include galleries and events such as the ACM1 and SIGGRAPH conferences. In 2004, as guest artist in the SIGGRAPH Guerilla I Studio, I worked with artist Helen Golden who downloaded portraits of Chinese students in real time over the Internet and passed them along to me via Flash memory where I manipulated them. I then passed them back to her and she sent them back over the wire.

So, working with the portrait of this seed image of the seated woman was a very natural process to pursue. In the following sections, note the changes of expression through each iteration of the portrait.

Portrait—Set 1: Zeroing in on the Face

The first thing I did was to zero in on the face, crop it, and lock it into position (see Figure 13.8 A). What I wanted in this first portrait was to give it a painterly feel without losing the sense of the photograph. Mission accomplished. She seems bemused by it all.

In the portrait shown in Figure 13.8 B, she looks a little tougher. I simplified the color areas, taking away some of the detail. The most fun was achieving a palette-knife look in parts of the work, which gives a sense of movement to the static image. There is life buried deeply in the eyes balancing the lack of emotion.

Portrait—Set 2: Fluid Strokes and Spontaneity

I broke down the face to basic black and white shapes, which in themselves are interesting, and then used fluid strokes of the seed colors to suggest coloration (see Figure 13.9 A). The basic facial features retain their strength.

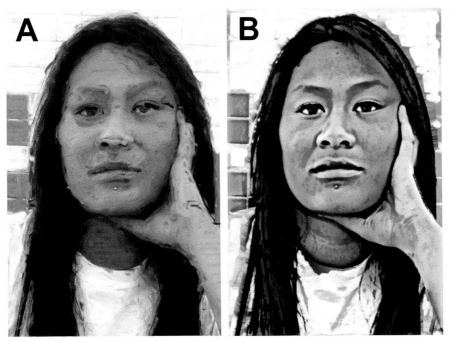

Figure 13.8 (A) Achieving a painterly feel without losing the sense of the photograph. (B) A palette-knife look in parts of the image.

I continue to move away from the photograph and toward the illusion of a painting (see Figure 13.9 B). I found myself attracted to the spontaneity of the work, although she doesn't seem too thrilled.

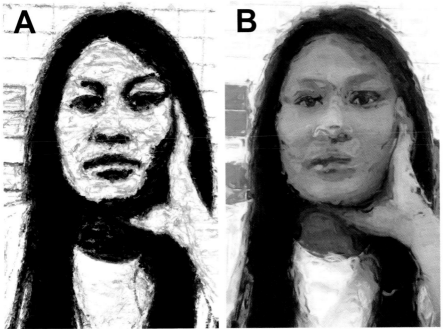

Figure 13.9 (A) Breaking down the face to basic black and white shapes. (B) An attraction to the spontaneity of the work.

Portrait—Set 3: A Smirk and Weariness

The version shown in Figure 13.10 A continues to push the illusion of the heavy-paint palette-knife look beyond that of Figure 13.8 B. The palette is limited, and detail is lost, yet the subtleness of expression is still observed—in this case with a slight smirk.

It's already been a long day when I sit down for this session (see Figure 13.10 B). I'm hoping that the work will energize like it does so often. OK: limited palette, big strokes. Instead of adding, it seems to be peeling off surface appearances and revealing an undercurrent of some sort. She looks as weary as I feel. Session done, and I nod out at the computer.

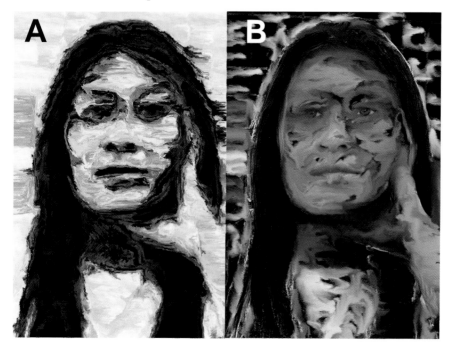

Figure 13.10 (A) The detail is lost but the subtleness of the expression is still observed. (B) Peeling off surface appearances.

Portrait—Set 4: Short Strokes and Colored Lines

I've been thinking about Van Gogh today after having conversations with some of my Los Angeles County Museum adult drawing students about the Van Gogh exhibition of several years ago. The exhibition was a smash hit for the museum. Seeing it, however, was a chore. People were herded through the exhibition like cattle. If it had been a rave, the fire marshals would have closed it down. So this work involved the illusion of very thick paint applied in short strokes with emphasis on the subjective color (see Figure 13.11 A). The work achieves a sort of flatness with all the strokes sitting right on the surface of the picture plane. I had a lot of fun with this one.

The version shown in Figure 13.11 B was achieved with the building of colored lines one on top of another over a reduced black-and-white image. The intensity of the eyes peek out at the viewer, the nose flattens, and the lips thicken.

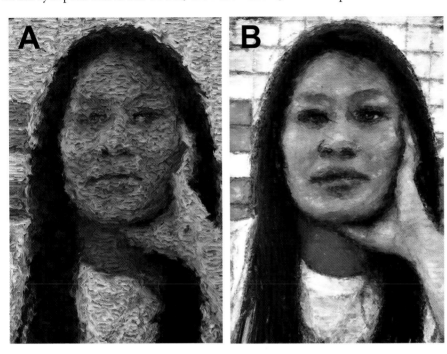

Figure 13.11 (A) Thick paint and short strokes emphasize subjective color. (B) The building of colored lines over a reduced black-and-white image.

Portrait—Set 5: Inner Glow, Mark Making, and Tension

I'm using color to express an inner glow to the figure (see Figure 13.12 A). The light emanates from within rather than from without. It comes up from the neck/shirt area into the face. She doesn't seem to want to reveal this.

Figure 13.12 B is similar to Figure 13.11 B but with bolder strokes and patterns. One feels energy in the mark making, and she seems to be OK with it too. Bits of white jump throughout the face, establishing a tension between the foreground and the background.

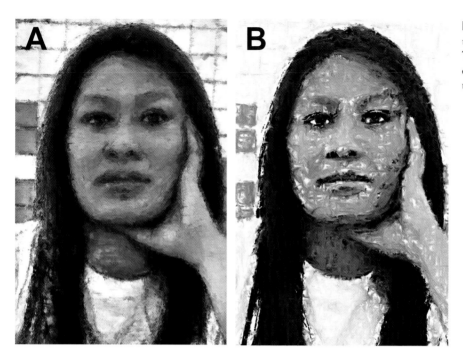

Figure 13.12 (A) Using color to express an inner glow. (B) Tension is established with bits of white jumping throughout the face.

Portrait—A Sense of Energy and Depth

I used several different styles to emphasize the face (see Figure 13.13). It appears that the face is emerging from under water. The lines race throughout, giving a sense of energy and underlying depth.

Last Words

The computer is the perfect postmodern tool/medium, allowing one to explore and create images that are soft deconstructed information, layered, appropriated, and multi-dimensional, almost as fast as one thinks. The changes in the image over time are represented as artifacts. The most challenging aspect of creating digital images is making sure that the art will transcend the hardware and software. I want people to respond to the image, not to how it was created. I've developed a style similar to my traditional work, which is described as a cross between a painting and a photo. My studio is full of traditional media consisting of painting and drawing media, canvas and paper, and old machines with numerous paint boxes. I don't believe one needs the latest fresh-off-the-shelf hardware and software to make good art.

This has been an interesting journey in which I broke out of the pattern of the usual way I do things. Enjoy, and as they say in tinsel town, "That's a wrap."

Figure 13.13 The face appears to be emerging from under water.

Artist Profile: Michael Wright

Artistic Background or Influences: My work looks to represent the spiritual force behind surface appearances using the binary code gleaned from a Chinese dualistic philosophy by Leibniz in the 17th century. I believe that there are keys to the understanding of nature, the universe, and woman/man's place in it. The balance between Yin and Yang and binary math is no coincidence. I choose to see the universal in, as they say in Zen, "the thousand and one things around us." I'm continually in a state of awe at our place in the universal scheme of things. My work attempts to reflect that awe.

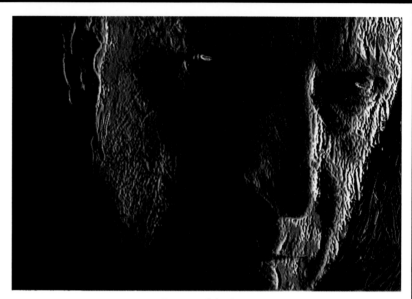

Portrait of the Artist

System Profile: Amigas, Video Toaster, Mac Power PC 8500, G3 Power Book, Two G4s

Peripherals: Several camcorders, a digital camera, and numerous Wacom tablets.

Software and Plug-Ins: Studio Artist, Alpha Paint, Painter, Deluxe Paint 3 and 4, Photoshop

Papers, Inks, and Other Output Preferences: Epson pigmented inks, Epson paper and canvas

Personal Web Site: http://home.earthlink.net/~mrwstudios/

14

John Antoine Labadie

John Labadie has always managed to fuse his formal education with his passions. He feels that his education—a B.A. in painting, an M.A. in perceptual psychology, and an Ed.D. focusing on cognitive analysis of Native American rock art—has had profound influences on the way he thinks about and makes his art. John's career as a scientific illustrator and photographer in the U.S. and Central America strongly brought both the subject matter and the technical methods of archeological research into his work.

John is an Associate Professor of Art, the Coordinator of Digital Arts and Director of the UNC Pembroke Digital Academy. To his credit, he has over 100 international and national juried exhibitions and many articles and essays appearing on the Web and in print. John was able to apply to this project some of the avenues he has currently been pursuing in his own work, with some totally unique results.

First Impressions

After multiple reviews of each seed image, I find nothing particularly inspiring on the *surface* of any of them. None of them offers anything particularly novel, nor is there a "Look at *that!*" image in the group. While scanning these images at high magnification, I am wondering about the reactions these images were intended to elicit. By category, we have: human, human made, and human observation of nature. The canyon image is not sharp, the architecture reminds me of the lobby of an Adam's Mark hotel in Jacksonville, and the young lady has toes like mine.

I've decided to mine the structure and *macro compositions* of these images in search of things that might be valuable to me. Some worthwhile paths to follow are revealed in examining the details of these images. The architectural image seems to have been manipulated previously with a filter. Looks like bits of color in the windows. I have noticed a lot of strong, but also delicate, details associated with certain elements of each composition (see Figure 14.1).

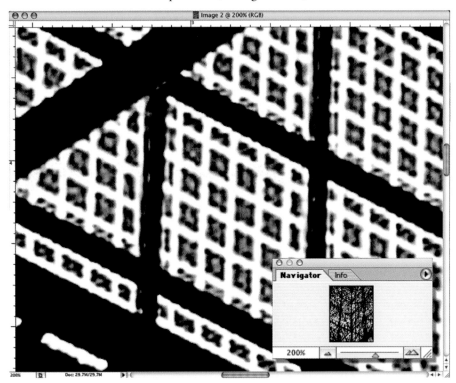

Figure 14.1 Close examination of each file reveals some surprises and offers many possibilities for design elements.

The Process Unfolds

After sampling the range of colors available in each image, and then making some palette comparisons, I've decided to concentrate on structural interests and limit my palette to grayscale, with an emphasis on black-and-white relationships of structural elements. Using black and white clarifies and then more easily merges these details into relatively coherent patterns and interesting visual fields. I've begun to concentrate on only two of the images for my source materials. The Grand Canyon image may provide textural information, but I don't find any valuable structural elements or details there. After a bit of experimentation in mixing and matching *pieces* it seems that there are links emerging between the girl image and that of the interior building structure. The use of black and white is a powerful way to link the two as well (see Figure 14.2).

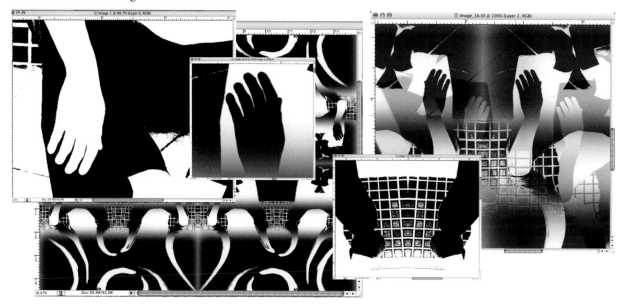

Figure 14.2 By mirroring black-and-white details from Seed Images 1 and 2, a collection of interesting patterns begins to emerge.

New shapes and elements are now emerging from the ever-evolving black-and-white merging of visual information from these photos. For the most part the photos have disappeared and the structural elements and details have become the subject under investigation. I am doing two basic things to cleanly merge and manipulate the disparate objects that are beginning to make up this composition. First, I use Photoshop's Liquify filter repeatedly and at different settings, and, second, I use the Smudge tool to hide the welds between image fragments. Working this way I am able to massage the overall design of the collage and retain sharp resolution of individual items within the composition. I chose the *hourglass* form as a goal for the manipulation in order to introduce dynamic tension into a composition with so many repeated elements (see Figure 14.3).

Surely, the play of opacity and transparency will allow these details to stand out at their best. I've begun a series of experiments to allow the patterns and details to speak for themselves and to each other. I'll decide where to go based on that conversation. A detail from Seed Image 2 is placed in a layer above the image constructed of various patterns. By changing the opacity of that layer, even more shapes and relationships between light and dark masses begin to reveal themselves. Saving each variation develops a rich library of collected shapes, which can be reintegrated into the composition (see Figure 14.4).

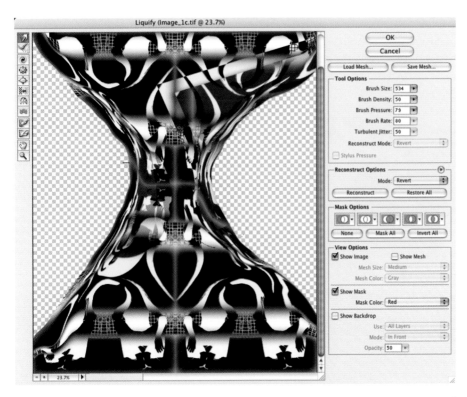

Figure 14.3 The Liquify filter introduces some irregularity and surprise into a design that is essentially made up of many repeated elements. In this manner, *pattern* is employed also as *form* and *line* within the composition.

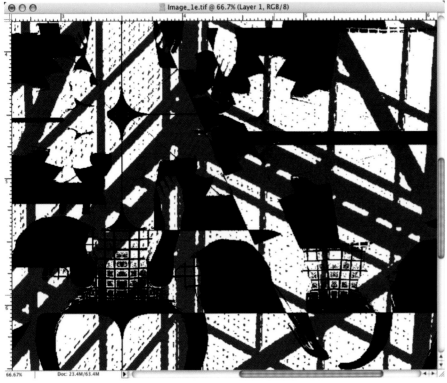

Figure 14.4 Adjusting opacity and transparency between two layers of black-and-white images has a marked effect in creating another set of relationships between picture elements.

There is much to be exploited at the structural level. I see parallels and interest-ing relationships emerging more clearly now. There are so many fascinating pat-terns. These patterns and forms can be used to generate interesting lines as well. While there are specific software (Adobe Streamline) or filters (Find Edges or Highpass) that convert black-and-white forms into outlines, this somewhat *hand-made* approach yields a precise and controllable outline that can be adjusted to create a very mechanical or more *sensitive* quality line.

An image is first run through Photoshop's Threshold filter (Image > Adjust > Threshold) to get the general effect of absolute black or white. This high-contrast image is copied and pasted into a layer on top of itself. With the two identical black-and-white images positioned on top of one another, the lower image is inverted (Image > Adjust > Invert) so that what was black is now white and vice versa. On the layer above, the black portions of the picture are selected using Select > Color Range. This selection of black forms is deleted to reveal the same shapes in white from the layer below. The image looks white on white at this time. Then, by using Free Transform to reduce the size of the image on the upper layer, in which the black areas have just been deleted, the offset between the two identical images will cause lines to appear as the black areas of the layer below show around the offset of the upper image layer. Repeated small adjustments to size and placement will cre-ate near perfect outline drawings of the original black-and-white solid shapes. These outlined shapes are collected for use in the developing project (see Figure 14.5).

I see an architectural composition revealing itself, but not the one I began with. This is a new space and another kind of order. I have been able to use elements of all three seed images in the piece (see Figure 14.6).

Careful placement and control of drop shadows will help define and give the com-position a feeling of openness. Some of the line drawings are inverted to become white line drawings on a black background and placed as rectangular forms, which seem to float over the surface due to these shadow effects. It pays to work dili-gently on creating these kinds of visual depth and texture cues, which in turn cre-ate an almost photographic dimension to the look of a digital art piece such as this. I have gone from photographs of the real world to solid, flat, abstracted shapes and lines, to arrive back in a photorealistic space that resolves both the original forms and the abstracted shapes—a new order (see Figure 14.7).

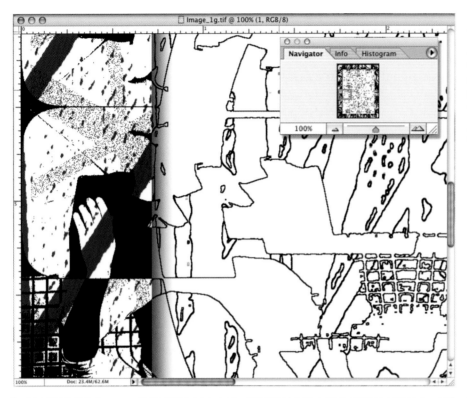

Figure 14.5 Forms and shapes become outlines after a rather handmade process is employed. The resulting line drawings have a lot of detail and energy while still referring to the basic structure of the piece as it becomes increasingly complex and rich.

Figure 14.6 All three seed images have found expression in the developing work.

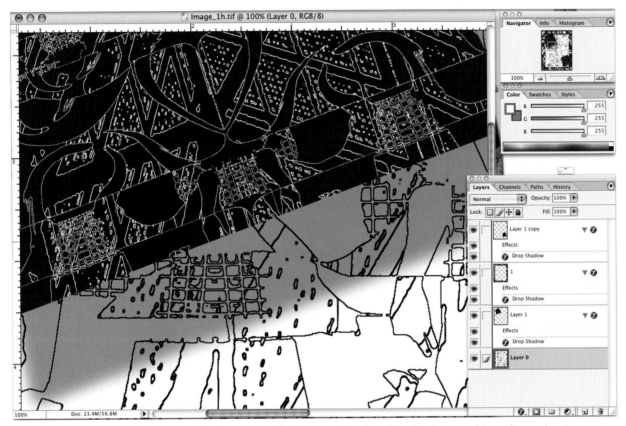

Figure 14.7 Depth cues, such as drop shadows, create the illusion of depth and lend a photographic quality to the piece, which is now taking on a very strong 3D collage aspect in addition to its play of basic shapes and lines.

Deconstruction and Judgment

At a basic level, the elements I've isolated from these images have fallen together with not all that much help from me. I have two complete compositions from which to choose. After much debate, I do what I usually do and throw one out, just to get it out of my head. File deleted. Yes, I've done some graphical surgery but the strength of the imagery, overall, is obvious and it has energy of its own. This project has really gone beyond a mere design exercise. By making the inverted floating shapes a bit transparent, yet another level of detail is added. This detail is likely not to be read immediately from across the room or at normal magnification, but as one approaches closer, more and more detail is discovered. This is key to making art that continues to surprise people as we discover something new in an object with which we imagine we have become intimately aware (see Figure 14.8).

I now have two or three major choices to make concerning compositional variations. I'll have to meditate on the possibilities. I feel as if something else has to happen. While I have enjoyed working in a world of *no color*, the space was too

Figure 14.8 Upon closer examination the rectangular shapes will appear to be somewhat transparent.

flat to be completely satisfying. The shapes that resemble seashells or disks or sunbursts came about in an interesting way that often occurs from *meditating* on a piece in progress. Here is what I do. I either project the digital file large via an LCD projector or make a large print so that I can place it in my environment. This way I have an unobstructed, at-length, *conversation* with the work-in-progress in order to understand where to go next—if anywhere.

This dialogue led to the sense that something more 3D yet still involving shades of gray had to enter the stage. I came to understand that the tension and action needed in the piece could come from the addition of such elements. The shapes themselves are constructed in a freeware program called Cosmic Painter. I had been playing with this program for use in animations but knew that it could produce still images as well. I spent some time with Cosmic Painter and produced 30 or 40 images from which I chose a few that I felt best activated the elements in the composition under consideration.

Beyond being "activators" of the largely flat design, I saw these shapes as an opportunity to introduce into the work a reference to basic life forms, such as diatoms and corals. With the introduction of these elements, together with some relatively subtle drop shadows, the work immediately became alive and nuanced (see Figure 14.9).

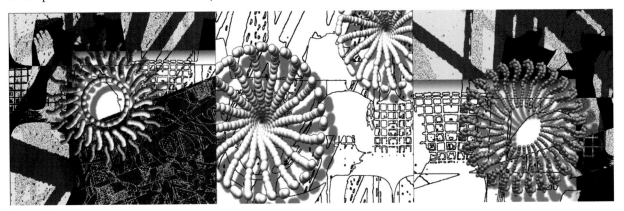

Figure 14.9 Some shapes resembling basic life forms add another sense of space and meaning to the artwork.

Letting Go

So, when is something done? Let's see. **_Finished_**, adjective. 1. Someone highly accomplished or skilled; polished: *a finished artist*. 2. Something exhibiting a high degree of skill or polish: *a painting that is a completed piece of artwork*. 3. a. Certainly doomed to death or destruction. b. Certainly having no more use, value, or potential; washed-up, useless.

OK, I have to go with number 2: something exhibiting a high degree of skill or polish; a painting that is a completed piece of artwork. My sense is that this piece has come a long way from the seed images toward this new visual form. It has been an interesting journey. Now it's time to let this piece go about its business communicating with others outside the art and artist relationship (see Figure 14.10).

Figure 14.10 Keeping picture elements on separate layers allows for a few final tweaks in the arrangement of items, and the piece is complete.

Last Words

I wrestled a bit with the title for this image. Sometimes this is an up-front matter and other times, like this one, it is not so easy. The title I've applied to this piece is *Spawning Run*. I think this title will effectively lead the viewer to consider the possibilities of the various elements separately as well as together as a *story* headed in the direction the title suggests.

Artist Profile: John Antoine Labadie

Artistic Background or Influences: Archeology influences my work as does my collection of Japanese wood-block prints and ethnic art, particularly masks. These all inform my insight into form, color, and presentation. I find working on the Internet to be a daily source of surprises.

System Profile: Mac G5 dual processor (8GB RAM), OS 10.3.8, 23" Apple monitor, Wacom tablet

Peripherals: Epson 1640XL scanner; Nikon D70 and Coolpix 5000 cameras; Epson 3000, 2200, and 1280 printers; HP 800 printer

Software and Plug-Ins: Adobe Photoshop CS; Painter 9; various other software, filters, and plug-ins

Papers, Inks, and Other Output Preferences: Prints from 13" to 54", enhanced matte and watercolor papers, mostly Epson dye-based inks

Personal Web Site: www.steppingstonearts.net

New Bats of the Open Mind

Old Fires Are Burning

15

Margie Beth Labadie

Margie is a photographer, illustrator, and printmaker. Working on her B.A. in Art from Temple University allowed Margie to complete some of her study in Rome and gain a passion for travel. After a career as V.P. of a large printing and publishing company and as an owner of an international travel agency, Margie earned an M.F.A. in Printmaking. She teaches Web design and art classes at UNC, Pembroke, North Carolina and maintains a busy exhibition schedule throughout her southeastern seaboard region. Digital tools and processes have been a growing part of her work since 1997, which she integrates into much of her current printmaking, combining digital and traditional techniques.

"My work in digital is mostly collage, made of gathered images, my sketches, and photographs. I combine my traditional prints and digital images to create works that evoke certain themes and moods. Most of my work includes bird imagery."

First Impressions

I found this project challenging. Using images that have no particular meaning to me left me a little empty. My inspiration for this project came from some rather annoying life circumstances that I tried to illustrate by combining all three of the seed images. I steered away from any recognizable parts of the images and decided instead to deal with texture and mood. I really used only the seed images of the woman and the black-and-white grid. I found the mountainscape to be too soft in focus to use as a source for texture, and I was not inspired by its colors. I decided to focus on Seed Images 1 and 2.

The Process Unfolds

I copied the seed images to my hard drive and made working copies. What to do? What are these images? The black-and-white, geometric, architectural nature of Seed Image 2 is filled with possible directional devices. But it is rather harsh as an image on its own. As for Seed Image 1, with the girl—using the tiles seems way too obvious and again too structured for me. I like the big black shape made by her pants and sleeves. I like the color of the tiles.

I select the black areas in Seed Image 1, including the model's clothing and hair, which will become major elements in the piece. Strengthening the contrast in Seed Image 2 makes it easier to select sharp edges around the grid-like shape (see Figure 15.1).

Figure 15.1 Some key elements are selected using Select > Color Range in Adobe Photoshop to begin the piece.

These two elements are brought together in a single frame. The areas selected from Seed Image 1 are placed in front and resized to fill the frame in a way that helps make those shapes abstract. What was the left pant leg is cut from the shape in one layer and placed into a new layer above. This shape is flipped around its vertical axis and Free Transform is used to stretch the shape and distort it a bit. This, of course, prevents exact repetition of too many shapes and keeps the developing picture interesting. The Smudge tool is used to blend out any ragged or aliased edges and to introduce a little soft color at the tips of these black forms (see Figure 15.2).

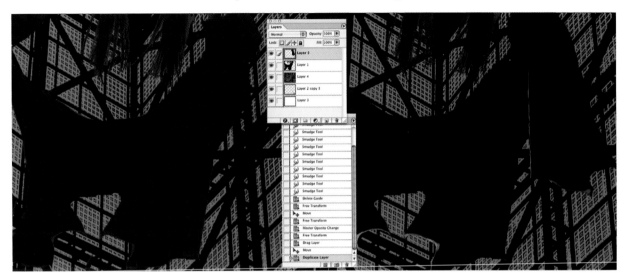

Figure 15.2 In this before-and-after view, the composition takes on complexity as the dark, drapery-like shapes are cut out, duplicated, and repositioned. Some edges are smoothed and color is added by blurring with the Smudge brush tool.

The model's hair, as it appeared in Seed Image 1, is cut from the top of the image and repositioned at the bottom on a separate layer. The hair is flipped so that it faces up. Some color is added—first a rather saturated blue, which is later brought down to almost black, and then some edges around the shape are given a red tint. Two more copies of this shape are made and put together at the point where they reflect one another and seem to become one shape. These operations further abstract the shapes away from any representation of what they actually were at the beginning. They have a life of their own. Creating a set of four *beings*—two floating and two looking up from the bottom right—adds surprise and tension to the developing piece, good elements to have in artwork (see Figure 15.3).

I'm fascinated with the folds in the fabric. I selected what was the model's right sleeve and made the shadow area white by inverting the image in the Curves palette. I colorized the shape a vivid pink and red. What had been shadows now appear as highlighting. The image was duplicated many times to construct what appears to be a billowing curtain from the upper right edge of the frame all the way across to the lower left edge. Each new piece remains on its own layer, with all the previous shapes staying at the top of the layer stack. In this way the piece begins to develop in a three-dimensional way in addition to its two-dimensional layout (see Figure 15.4).

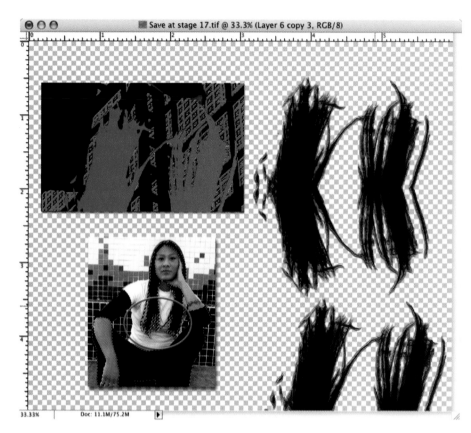

Figure 15.3 Another element is isolated from the original photo and used as material to create some more unusual shapes.

Going back to the fabric-like black shapes, folds and curves in these shapes are emphasized with light touches of color applied by the Airbrush tool. The tips of the shapes are given an accentuated swirl using the Smudge tool. A little color is applied and then dragged and blended to create the apparent swirling tip. Since each shape is on its own layer, smearing pixels in this way does not affect any of the imagery on other layers (see Figure 15.5).

What occurs to me is a separation of two different worlds suggested in this work, so far. The geometric world and the world that the black shapes inhabit are exposed to each other through curtains or veils. I copied one of the legs and repositioned it. After modifying this shape to make stronger folds, I changed the color to pink. Don't ask me why (see Figure 15.6).

I decide that I hate the pink, so I changed the pink fabric to teal blue. That seems to work much better, for now. Fabric folds were added and accentuated using strokes of red and black. Each color is applied to an individual layer so that various degrees of Gaussian Blur can be applied. In this way outlines and shadows are created with a good deal of control. More blur creates a soft shadow effect; less blur creates more edge (see Figure 15.7).

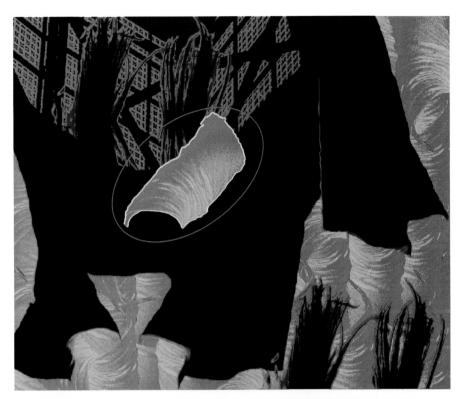

Figure 15.4 The sleeve shape, circled in red, is repeated across the middle ground of the composition.

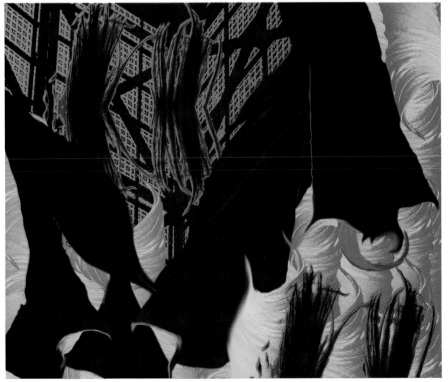

Figure 15.5 The Smudge tool is employed again to create soft swirling edges at the ends of some of the forms.

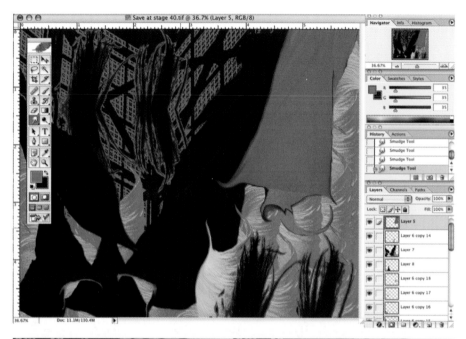

Figure 15.6 The file has gotten more complex with individual layers for nearly each element. This makes for easier shifting of all elements while developing the composition.

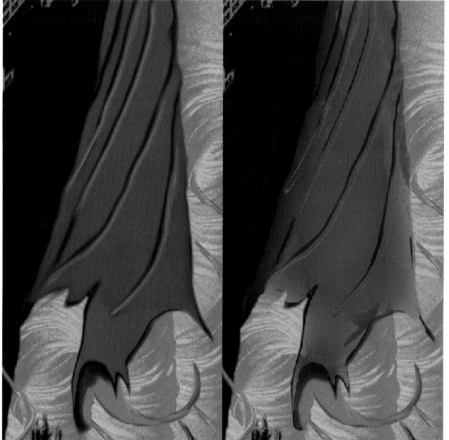

Figure 15.7 Lines of contrasting color become suggestions of folds in fabric by controlling the amount of blur applied to each line.

Going to the geometric image tucked away at the bottom of the layer stack, the color of the grid becomes half deep red and half deep blue-green. I changed the placement of the cloth upon which I had just accentuated the folds by flipping that image on its vertical axis. This keeps that upper right corner open, but with the curtain now helping to better lead the eye into the composition. The "cityscape" background is blurred to create depth, and Gaussian Blur is applied to some of the yellow swirls and to the "flying hair creatures." This process helps to blend elements together, cleaning up some jaggies and giving the piece a softer appearance (see Figure 15.8).

Figure 15.8 Color changes, some repositioning, and blending help to unify and draw the composition together.

I took the large drape just to the left of the teal curtain and changed its direction, using the Free Transform tool. By shrinking the shape back, the whole center of the piece is opened up and some interesting elements that had previously been covered can now be seen. This revealed another section of the geometric grid, which I decided needed to have its color altered a bit. I fixed a "hole" in this "curtain" (see the insert in Figure 15.9) with the Clone Stamp tool. I lowered the opacity on some of the pink swirls to create more depth. Then, I intensified the yellow swirls a bit in order to bring them forward. Am I going too far?

Figure 15.9 More elements are moved around to open up the composition, and repairs are made.

I did not look at this image for more than a week. Getting away from a piece for a while helps, especially if you don't want to over work it. I realized that the main thing for me with this piece was to create a greater sense of depth—not just between foreground and background, but within the foreground. This is achieved by just tweaking a few things. I lowered the opacity of the teal "scarf" and made the black "scarves" more transparent, just to give them an airy feel. I like that a little color shows through them now. I adjusted a few other things, such as the placement of some pink swirls, one behind or in front of the other. A little more of the green color is painted into the "city" grid near the center to bottom area.

The image has become one of wind blowing through fabric, almost like clothes on a line. I like the feeling. But it's rather vast and cold, with perhaps a wild feel to it also (see Figure 15.10).

Figure 15.10 By making some of the forms more transparent and by visually pushing back the "geometric grid" with a darker and less saturated color, a nice active balance is struck in the finished image.

Last Words

"We are what we repeatedly do. Excellence, therefore, is not an act, but a habit."—Aristotle

Artist Profile: Margie Beth Labadie

Artistic Background or Influences: My hometown of Philadelphia, PA was filled with Modern art. Robert Rauschenberg, whose work I saw when I was five years old, continues to astonish me and stop me in my tracks. Art professor Neil Kosh was also very important to my development as an artist.

System Profile: Mac G4 PowerBook, G4 PowerPC, LaCie 150GB hard drive, 512MB RAM

Peripherals: Epson 1200 Perfection scanner, Canon Rebel EOS digital camera, Epson 1280 printer

Software and Plug-Ins: Photoshop CS

Papers, Inks, and Other Output Preferences: Coated inkjet papers, uncoated BFK Reeves and Japanese Unryu paper, pigmented inks

Personal Web Site: www.steppingstonearts.net

What's on Your Hat?

ALL LIVES, ALL DANCES, * ALL IS LOUD

the blue, overhanging
sky
answers me back

—Wabezic
(Ojibwa)

—Red Corn
(Osage)

Hopi Hope

16

Judy Mandolf

Judy Mandolf began her career in traditional fine art photography around 1980, working mostly with hand-colored black-and-white photographs that have been exhibited throughout the U.S. and Europe. Her image of Amish children toured Europe for two years as part of a "Women Photographers in America" exhibition, and in 1984 her figurative studies were part of a cultural exchange with Hungary.

In 1996 Judy passionately embraced the digital medium. "I used to say I photographed because I couldn't draw very well, but the creative spirit released in Photoshop and other imaging software has completely changed my whole approach and opened up unlimited opportunities for me to let my imagination fly. I resent every moment that mundane chores keep me from my Mac." Her images have their genesis in her digital photographs, which are collaged, "painted," and otherwise manipulated by various software programs and printed on watercolor paper. Recently Judy turned to encaustic collage, using this hot wax medium to add dimension to her work. She incorporates her digital work into the collages along with found objects and text.

First Impressions

My first impression was that the three seed images were not photographs I would have chosen. I saw no commonality and little hope for incorporating them into an aesthetically pleasing image. Seed Image 1—Girl: The tile background was ugly and looked like the dreaded public restroom. Seed Image 2—Grid: The grid or fence looked too harsh and overpowering. Seed Image 3—Grand Canyon: There was too much contrast and it was too busy.

I opened the images several times and stared at them for long stretches, idly altering the colors and cropping haphazardly, hoping to come up with some magic transformation. When I cropped out the offending background from the girl and removed the distracting piercing, she reminded me of a Hopi Indian woman I encountered on a reservation in northeastern Arizona. She was selling woven articles from a roadside stand. She was very melancholy and expressed sadness that her people were abandoning their ancient crafts ever since the profusion of gambling casinos on the reservations. (I had heard this same complaint from gallery owners in Santa Fe.) I began to visualize this woman of the present contemplating the destruction of her past.

Now it was clear that the Grand Canyon setting would be a natural for the background image, but it must be softened so as not to conflict with the face and to fulfill my plan of an overall somewhat dreamlike vision. The face would compete for attention with the many textures of brush, rock, mountain, and sky.

The Process Unfolds

I opened Seed Image 3 in Synthetik Software's Studio Artist, which I use occasionally to convert a photographic image to something with a less literal interpretation.

Creating the Painted Desert

In this instance I used the Magnetic Powder option found under Presets > Paint Patch > Default > General, using the source image as the color space and applying the auto action (see Figure 16.1).

Figure 16.1 Applying the Magnetic Powder option in Studio Artist to the Grand Canyon.

At this point I felt the landscape image was still a little too harsh, so I opened the Studio Artist version in Photoshop and applied a LucisArt Winslow filter, using the settings found in Figure 16.2. It was my intention to create a representational background image which hinted at sky and terrain as opposed to a literal desert landscape. At this point I was in the process of making a wrong turn by adding an impasto texture.

I had duplicated the background layer and applied an impasto effect which I had saved in my Styles folder (see Figure 16.3). I often avoid using effects from digital imaging software, preferring to use textures that I've captured photographically. In this case, I wanted to stay within the guidelines of the creative process for this experiment by not using any other photographic material. Texture is very important, and the challenge is to develop a personal style, and it is only in this sense that a canned effect may make the result look less individual.

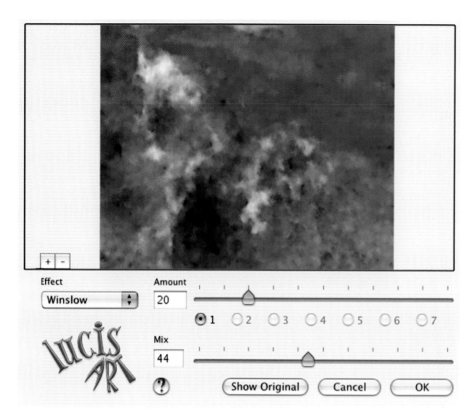

Figure 16.2 Applying a LucisArt Winslow filter.

When I decided that it was a mistake, I had inadvertently merged the two layers. As a way to "fix" this mistake, I opened the digital file in Corel Painter 8 and used the Just Add Water brush to smooth out some of the texture detail (see Figure 16.4). I could have saved myself the extra effort by saving the texture on a separate layer.

Working with the Girl's Face

Now it was time to turn my attention to the girl and how she would blend into the background. Since I was interested in her face only, I had two options. I could select the face portion with the Lasso tool and move it onto the background, but this is the more difficult way to make the transition look natural. Instead I elected to mask out everything but the face. I opened Seed Image 1 of the girl in Photoshop and duplicated the background layer. I next added a layer mask and used a large, soft brush to reveal the face. I then reduced the Opacity of the layer to 70% in order to "see through" it while painting and afterward restored the face to 100% (see Figure 16.5). I cropped the image to improve the placement of the face and to enlarge it in relation to the desert scene. At this point I decided to desaturate the face in order to distort reality a little more. I also used the Clone Stamp to remove the piercing.

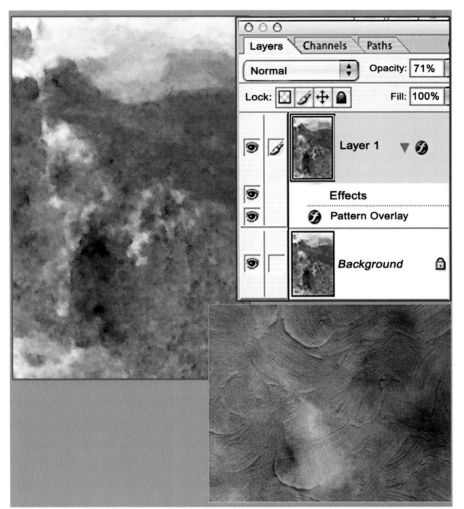

Figure 16.3 Applying an impasto effect from the artist's Styles folder. The detail shows the impasto effect more clearly. The Layers palette shows the pattern overlay at 71% Opacity.

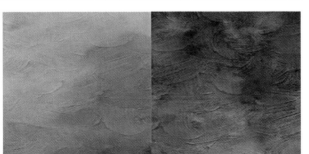

Figure 16.4 Details from the merged layers with the Just Add Water brush in Corel Painter 8.

Figure 16.5 The History palette shows the step-by-step work on the girl's face and the resulting image.

Combining the Face and the Painted Desert

I now want to consider how I might combine the two images. One option would be to move the face image on top of the painted desert and remove the black masking. I chose instead to make the face image the new background and to drag the desert on top to become the second layer. Thus I could add a layer mask (again temporarily lowering the layer opacity) and use black with a large soft brush to reveal her face and hand, leaving a very soft edge. The central portion of the desert scene was also masked out in order to create a separation of sky and earth and enhance the surreal feeling (see Figure 16.6, comment A).

Next something was needed to fill the black void from an aesthetic standpoint and also to convey the connection of the girl and earth. Because I often add clouds to enhance landscape photos, I used the Define Brush technique to create an assortment of clouds and saved them in my Brushes folder in Photoshop (see Figure 16.6, comment B). The assortment of clouds is shown in Figure 16.7.

I used one of the bigger fluffy clouds together with a coral color picked up from the desert image and placed this cloud on its own separate layer so that it could be edited later if necessary. After experimenting with brush opacity, the cloud layer was placed on top of the face to give the illusion of the girl emerging from the

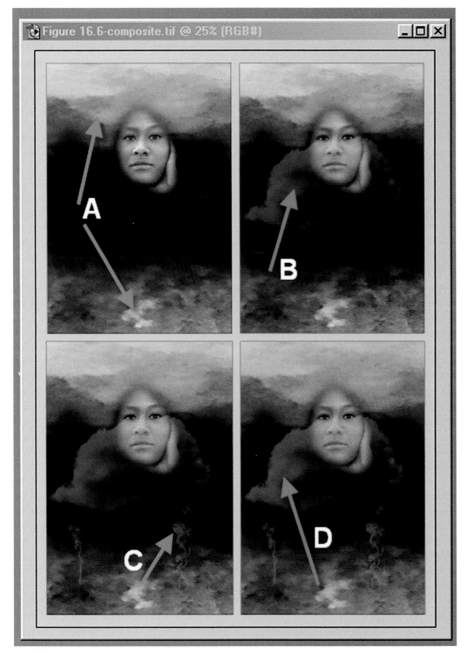

Figure 16.6 This four-fold composite image shows various stages of the face being combined with the desert. Comment A's arrows point to the parts of the painted desert that were masked to create separate sections of sky and earth. Comment B's arrow points to the cloud that was created around the face. Comment C's arrow points to the addition of wisps of smoke added to the image. Comment D shows a Levels adjustment that is most visible in the cloud in the version that became the final prior to the encaustic process.

cloud and allowing the features to show through. Again on a separate layer and with the same coral color, I added two wisps of smoke to lend a "scorched earth" element to the completed image (see Figure 16.6, comment C).

As for the grid image, I felt it added nothing to the story so I decided not to use it.

Knowing that I would be taking this image further into the encaustic process, I made the decision to stop at this point. I planned to collage additional elements to complete the theme and since I would be using hot wax, I needed to take care not to make the image too cluttered.

Figure 16.7 Selections of cloud formations (upper portion) and wisps of smoke (bottom portion) provide the artist with a variety of patterned brushes to apply as needed.

The Encaustic Process

Encaustic (which means "to burn" or "to heat") is an ancient process dating back to the first century Greeks. Perhaps its most famous practitioner is Jasper Johns, who began using it in the 1950s; however, it is still not a widely known medium. I became intrigued by it recently, attracted by its texture and translucency, and determined that it could add another dimension to my digital photography.

Encaustic begins with the application of a mixture of pure beeswax melted with damar resin to almost any rigid substrate. Color is added by using pigment powder, oil paint, oil pastels, or any material compatible with the wax. Each application or layer of the encaustic mixture must be fused with heat to prevent its separating from the next layer. The surface may be scribed to reveal colors or patterns from underlying layers, and objects may be embedded between the layers or on the final surface, so long as they are not too heavy to be held in place by the wax.

This medium is not for the faint of heart. It involves many electrical appliances in order to melt the wax, maintain the temperature of the various colors, smooth the surface, and fuse the layers. My workspace includes two electric griddles, an electric frying pan, a heat gun, an electric knife for cutting chunks of wax, a tacking iron, and a household iron, all of which tend to make the room very warm (see Figure 16.8). Furthermore, the fumes are toxic and good ventilation is essential.

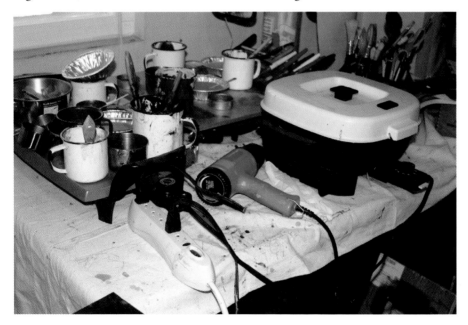

Figure 16.8 The encaustic workspace.

One must work very quickly. The wax begins to harden as soon as the brush is removed and allows for only a few brief strokes before being immersed again in the wax. It is, however, a forgiving surface and may be softened with the heat gun and reworked.

As I worked on the photographic image, I did not give a whole lot of thought to its inclusion in the final encaustic piece since I intended to design the piece to enhance the digital image. However, as I began applying the wax I intuitively began to use my usual palette of earth tones which did not necessarily harmonize with the digital print. At this time I went back to Photoshop and applied the nik Color Efex Color Stylizer filter to the image, which, encaustic inclusion aside, I found more appealing (see Figure 16.9).

Figure 16.9 Applying the nik Color Efex Color Stylizer filter to the image.

My substrate was a smooth, hardwood panel, 16" × 20" × 2". To this I applied a layer of clear encaustic medium and fused it with a heat gun (see Figure 16.10).

Figure 16.10 A heat gun is used to fuse the clear encaustic medium.

The color ground layer was then prepared with a bronze-toned pigment added to the wax (see Figure 16.11).

No attempt was made to smooth the surface since I wanted to maintain a lot of texture and an "earthy" look. The cream-colored "sky" area was created using more pigmented wax, the "clouds" are made from artist's oil paint, and the accent colors are added with oil sticks. A circular sun figure was scribed into the top portion and filled with a metallic gold oil stick. Oil sticks dry much more slowly than wax, which I find makes them easier for applying and blending subtle coloring.

Figure 16.11 A bronze-toned pigment is added.

With the base now fairly complete, I attached the digital image (printed on water-color paper) to the panel using acrylic gel and embedded the following found objects: a dried and pressed flower, four ancient copper coins, and fragments from an old Indian poem, all of which were included in my very large collection of oddments obtained from flea markets, antique stores, eBay, and so on (see Figure 16.12).

The final accents of orange, turquoise, and purple were added with oil sticks and ceramic rub-on paints. I applied black pigmented wax to the sides, allowing small amounts to spill over onto the image surface (see Figure 16.13).

Figure 16.12 Details of oddments embedded on the surface of the panel adjacent to the digital print.

Figure 16.13 Black pigmented wax is applied.

When I first looked at the three source photographs provided, little did I imagine the emergence of this *Hopi Hope!* This has been a long journey filled with baby steps and large leaps and the difficulties of working within someone else's parameters. But a satisfying trip indeed.

Last Words

In 1996 I had been reading here and there that you could do something to photos with a computer. I hadn't the vaguest idea about what this might be and I had never operated a computer, but I thought maybe I could add another dimension to my work. I never for a moment thought a computer could replace my darkroom. Someone asked me if I wanted a PC or Mac, and since I thought the little apple logo was cute, I chose the Mac. Later I was surprised to learn that some people are as passionate about their computer program as they are about politics. Me, I'm just passionate about digital art. I sat down with the computer manual and the Photoshop manual and started at square one. Two days later I produced my first "masterpiece" and I have never looked back. I still feel the same excitement when beginning a new assignment.

The digital camera was very primitive at that time and at first I worked with scanned slides and photos. I loved the immediacy of it and I learned how to work with it. Some images were so pixelated that I had to go around the edges of every object with the Rubber Stamp tool. Some things with fine detail such as branches or fronds had to be scanned in separately and collaged onto the image. A few of these were actually published at 16" × 20".

Art has so many faces. For me, it is all about beauty, about simplicity of form and purity of vision—images that speak for themselves without having to ascribe a complicated explanation. When I begin creating an image, I find myself paring down and maybe paring down some more while Rubber Stamping out extraneous detail.

Artist Profile: Judy Mandolf

Artistic Background or Influences: I was a business major and spent the first part of my life in a corporate environment, mainly as a personnel manager for a manufacturing plant. I considered myself the untalented family member until I was given my first "good" camera around 1980 and immediately became immersed in photography. I quickly added a darkroom in my home. I had never seen a real darkroom so I followed directions from a book. At first I was self-taught but eventually took some college courses and attended many seminars and workshops. The biggest influence in my moving into the fine art field was a summer spent attending a Maine Photographic Workshop in France.

I regret that it took me so long to begin using the left side of my brain, but I guess it is all part of the journey. I have been able to combine art exhibiting with practical contract work—exhibiting in Santa Fe and Taos, New Mexico, the University of Alabama, Arizona State University, and in San Diego, and doing practical contract work for

Pola

Bentley House Art Publishing in Walnut Creek, California where my work is used for greeting cards, journals, t-shirts, placemats, cutting boards, light switch covers, and tapestries, as well as framed prints and posters.

Some of my influences include Andrew Wyeth, René Magritte, Joseph Cornell, Georgia O'Keefe, Henri Cartier Bresson, Jacques-Henri Lartigue, and Jerry Uelsmann.

System Profile: Macintosh G4 Dual Processor, 21" flat-screen monitor

Peripherals: Epson Perfection 4870 scanner, Cannon Digital Rebel and Holgaroid cameras, Epson Stylus Pro 7600 and Epson Stylus Photo 2200 printers

Software and Plug-Ins: Photoshop CS, Corel Painter 8, Studio Artist 2.0., nik Color Efex, Flaming Pear, LucisArt, Power Retouche

Papers, Inks, and Other Output Preferences: Paper: Arches Infinity, Moab Entrada Fine Art, Breathing Color Brilliance 2 (canvas)

Post Processing: May include mounting on wood panel, applying Golden Acrylic Gel for texture, and/or applying encaustic (hot wax) with or without embedded text and/or objects.

Personal Web Site: www.judymandolf.com

(Left) *The Future of the Past*, (Center) *Sky*, (Right) *Indian Country*

17

Björn Dämpfling

Although a life-long art lover, Björn Dämpfling is almost sublimely indifferent toward being an artist. However, this cultivated indifference is actually a deep source for his creativity. For Björn, creativity and freedom are far more important than any resulting artwork. "My production of art is essentially a detached endeavour for my personal enjoyment or empowerment. This is and will be the one and only basis for my making art. Finding out that others like my art too is a nice addition. More important, to find out that others with tastes different from my own also see its quality is the reason for me to market my art now. But this has never been, nor will it ever be, the driving force. Because if I [lost] the feeling of total freedom in making my art, my creative source would just die."

Born in a small town in Northern Germany, Björn has lived in Berlin since 1969. He has lived for short periods in the United States, once in 1983 at Harvard and again from 1987 to 1991 at the University of North Carolina. With a degree in Political Science and a Ph.D. in Economics, up until 1997 Bjoern spent about two-thirds of his professional life on research, writing books, and teaching, and the other third producing art, "drawing on everything, with anything that would make a dot or a line. So, embracing the computer, which I used as an Economist more than a decade before I drew my first digital image, was a natural move for me. I have never had much concern about the material aspects of making art. What texture does the subconscious have? Now, it all ends up on the computer, which plays a 5 to 100 percent role as a tool in creating the final work. All in all, the fact that I can merge every kind of visual input when working digitally and since, from my point-of-view, there is no drawback in leaving behind physical qualities in the making of art, the computer is a perfect medium for my kind of artistic input. I am convinced that only this 'artistic input' is responsible for creating images that have a future and are here to stay."

Currently, Björn finds himself exhibiting his work more often and is seeing an increase in sales of his large format digital prints both in Germany and in the U.S. Björn, like most artists, sometimes struggles with his muse. He goes as far as to refer to the part of himself that creates his work as *IT*. "*IT* makes my art." So when he was presented with the parameters and seed images for this project it was unclear as to what *IT* might do with this sort of challenge. As we see in his three finished works, Björn was as surprised as anyone by the results.

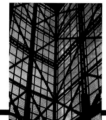

First Impressions

The explanation I found for why this experiment has worked so well for me lies in the fact that I got images I could deal with freely. Better said, *IT* could do what *IT* wanted to do. *IT* does not respond well to making art based on a theme. But this project offered a genuine difference to a "theme" because the limitations are at the onset and do not concern the results. Also, the fact that I have visited a bit of the countryside and culture, including two hikes into the Grand Canyon, was of some importance in my being able to connect with the seed images.

The Process Unfolds

The girl's face and the way she is dressed present obvious associations between past, present, and future. She has many ancestors looking over her shoulder, as she watches over her own future. See Figures 17.1 through 17.5 for notes on the process followed to create *The Future of the Past*.

Figure 17.1 Two copies of Seed Image 1 are pasted in at 50% Opacity. Contrast and saturation were pushed intensely. Then, the image was reversed to display a negative version of colors, lights, and darks.

Figure 17.2 The white portions of the girl's image layer are selected and filled with black. The resulting image is reversed again. Then, Seed Image 2 is pasted in at 11% Opacity.

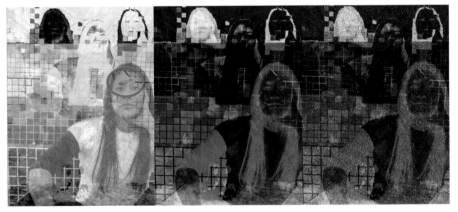

Figure 17.3 Another copy of Seed Image 1 is brought in at 26% Opacity and positioned relative to an element of the girl's sleeve in a lower layer. See the area marked in red. This composite image is reversed; then, Seed Image 3 is pasted in at 16% Opacity and a paper texture is applied to the entire surface.

Figure 17.4 The image is returned to "positive" colors, thus reversing the applied paper texture. Contrast and saturation are pushed to sharpen the image and flatten the colors somewhat. Finally, the texture is smoothed and the Photoshop Cloning Stamp tool is employed to remove some distracting edges (see areas marked in red).

Figure 17.5 After the small distractions are removed and some minor adjustments to the image contrast are made, the piece entitled *The Future of the Past* is complete.

In an attempt to integrate the industrial structure of Seed Image 2 with the organic and natural environment of Seed Image 3, a piece with the ironic title of *Sky* was created. See Figures 17.6 through 17.10 for notes concerning the production of this artwork.

Figure 17.6 Seed Image 2 is pasted in and the colors are inverted to create a negative image. Seed Image 3 is pasted in at 56% Opacity. The contrast and brightness are pushed intensely.

Figure 17.7 Corel Painter's Digital Airbrush is used to paint out details from the white "girder" shapes. These areas are then filled with black. Using first a white Charcoal Brush and then the Digital Airbrush (Straight Lines drawing mode), some gray texture is painted back into these areas.

Figure 17.8 The detail at the far left shows how a white Digital Airbrush is used to create texture in the gray structures. Another detail shows how the triangular area at the top of Seed Image 2 is cleared out. The same area is then filled with sky blue, and the rounded metallic-looking "girders" have been painted in.

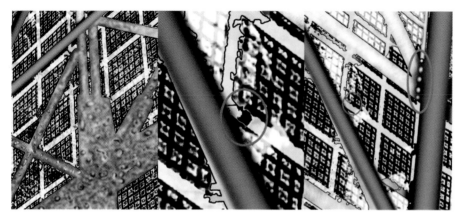

Figure 17.9 More details show the finishing touches. First, bumpy and pitted textures are painted into the gray structures. Then, many small edges that break up the flow of some shapes are located (see the area in the red circle). At the far right, this blockage has been cleared away and additional details in the form of little spheres (rivets?) are painted in.

Figure 17.10 Much of the detail work may not be visible at this size; however, when printed at a large-format size the time spent on the details is rewarded. The image entitled *Sky* is now complete.

A third image came as somewhat of a surprise. Following the guidelines for this project I realized a way to breathe some new life into an old, but not forgotten, drawing I had done over 30 years ago. See Figures 17.11 through 17.15 for notes on how *Indian Country* was created.

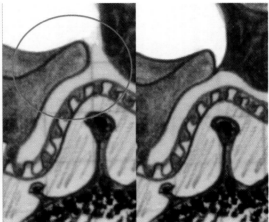

Figure 17.11 A drawing made 30 years ago is scanned and the cleaning process begins. In close-up view the graph paper grid and paper cuts made when the drawing was glued to another sheet of paper can be seen. The same area is shown at the right with some of this cleaned up.

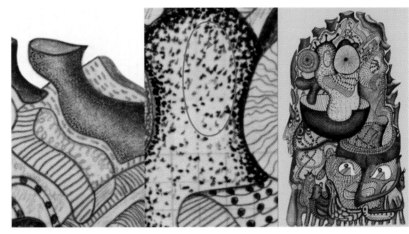

Figure 17.12 Digital Charcoal and Airbrush tools are used to simulate natural materials and to continue to freshen up the drawing. A detail shows how the Digital Airbrush paints in the yellowed paper color to eliminate the grid and intensify and repair the drawing. Minute details such as these are treated throughout the drawing.

Figure 17.13 In a previous step the paper color was filled in around the drawing and now RGB balance is altered to create a different colorcast than the aged paper. The image is adjusted by pushing up brightness and contrast, which gives the drawing a sharper appearance. Finally the restored and enhanced drawing is brought in over Seed Image 3.

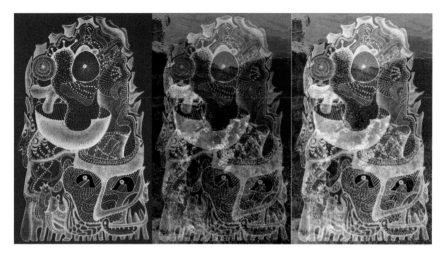

Figure 17.14 Enlarged and now on its own layer, the drawing is reversed into a color negative of its previous state. Setting the Opacity of this layer at 55% allows the seed image to bleed through and interact with the drawing. Brightness, Contrast, and Saturation adjustments help bring the drawing forward.

Figure 17.15 With a final alteration of color balance, *Indian Country* is complete.

"I" had wanted to do something with Seed Image 3 comparable to my signature image, *The Visitor* (see the Artist's Profile). But, instantly I felt that this would become a total disaster. So, "I" gave up, since I had already completed two images for this project. But then, *IT* remembered an old drawing hidden away somewhere. I had made this drawing when I was about 15 years old and was devouring books about archeology and ancient cultures. The drawing made on what was now rotting, 30-year-old, graph paper was influenced by what I had read about the Mayan culture. I am just utterly happy that I found this way to give that old drawing back its tenderness and life. As a bonus to doing this somewhat tedious, detailed work, I now have a pristine digital file of the drawing which may once again find its way into yet another work of art, just as it has here.

Last Words

The best way to describe my work is to say what it is not. My work is not representational, realism, symbolism, or surrealism. I try to stay as far away from any *ism* as one can get. This is a matter of content, which shows formally in substructures below the level of, let's say, the *surrealistic* look of an image. For me, a line is a line and nothing more is behind it. I hardly ever know what a line could mean while drawing it. I am moved by the impression a line makes on me as it does on others who see it for the first time. The difference is that I can react actively to the lines until the image is finished. I do not want to *represent*, by any means, our world or even fictional worlds, so I see myself as creating structures on a flat surface. My goal is to create images worthy of repeated viewing for the rest of my days. The fact that even the greatest *freedom* of art creation is and can only be nothing else but shuffling the bits and pieces of the world one lives in is enough *bondage* for my taste.

On the other hand, any 2D image made today can be fit into one of the *isms* in a formal sense. Because the mathematically possible general modes or "styles" for structuring a 2D image are all *invented* and there is a box for every possible 2D image, it won't be long before computers will sort images by these "styles." But, within these boxes there is endless space to create personally identifiable and essentially new images. I jump into every box there is, all the time.

Artist Profile: Björn Dämpfling

Artistic Background or Influences: Impressionism, Camille Pissaro being a favorite, but I claim no specific influence from art history in my work.

System Profile: PC with AMD 2200 CPU (1GB RAM), Microsoft XP, 4A+ Wacom tablet, 19" Llyama monitor

Peripherals: Epson Perfection scanner, Minolta SLR with macro lens, Canon A4 inkjet printer

Software and Plug-Ins: Corel Painter 6.0

Papers, Inks, and Other Output Preferences: Printing outsourced to Artificial Image, Berlin; IRIS prints on Somerset Velvet 300g/m paper (Natural and Radiant White); Iris Equipoise inks; mostly 30" × 20" and 44" × 30" prints

Personal Web Site: www.creativecreatures.com

Der Besucher (The Visitor)

Canyon Challenge

18

Ken Keller

Ken received his training very early on, "nearly growing up" in his father's dark-room. He has worked professionally as a graphic design artist, photographer, and offset pressman. With an eclectic eye and scientific curiosity, he began his fractal work in 1994. He explores this mathematical world of possibilities with the integrity of his innate sense of composition always leading the way. He also directs his work around a set of restrictions that, in the end, add character to his work.

"My style of fractal art could be called purist in the sense that I rely solely on the fractal image generation program to produce my works. I use as little post processing of the final image as possible and ideally none at all. Yet I do not strive to make prints that can be easily recognized as fractal images. I very rarely use transparency to blend two or more fractals together. As a result, my works can be reproduced exactly at any size or format with no loss of resolution. The innate properties of a fractal image are such that as the size of the fractal print increases the level of detail in the print also increases. This is the exact opposite of what happens when a photograph is blown up or scanned. Using the most advanced commercial ink-jet printers combined with the infinite detail of fractal imagery, I can produce prints that have details beyond the resolving power of the human eye. This is an under-appreciated quality of fractal prints by both the fractal artists and their customers."

Ken's imagery has appeared internationally in advertisements, CD cover art, and book designs. He has exhibited his work throughout Northern California where he occasionally facilitates fractal art colloquiums. Of all the artists featured in this book, Ken is probably the one most encumbered by the rule to use the seed images in the creation of his work. He decided to focus on the feel of a natural environment and let the commonalities of nature and fractal geometry reveal themselves.

First Impressions

To be true to my style I could not use the seed images in any concrete or direct manner. I could not make a collage of the seed images or overlay or paste together different fractals to reconstruct the seed images. That would be the easy way out.

I began this project by spending several days deconstructing the seed images in my mind. I studied the compositional elements of each image and how the complexity values were distributed across the compositions. *Complexity values* are one thing that a fractal artist can control. I burn the seed images into the back of my head until my unconscious must take notice of the intrusion.

I ask, what is fractal-like in the seed images? Canyons are caused by erosion, and erosion produces very distinctive fractal patterns in the earth. Fractal image generation programs can also produce straight-edged geometric complexities, similar to Seed Image 2. Seed Image 1 would be the hardest to interpret with fractal imagery, although I have done fractal faces that express anthropomorphic values. Landscapes contain the most familiar type of fractals that are seen in everyday life. I have produced many satisfying compositions in the landscape category. Considering everything, I decided to work with the Canyon (Seed Image 3).

I then spent several days browsing my image bank, looking for inspiration and looking for "the canyon." I have been creating fractals for over ten years and have built a store of images that numbers in the tens of thousands. The reason that I have saved so many fractal images is because of the experimental nature of fractal art. Each image records certain tweaks to the parameters used to create the fractal. Every fractal is like a visual experiment that would be very difficult to reproduce if one did not have the original parameter file. I use this resource as a painter would in choosing a color palette. I select several of these as *candidate starting images* and begin to manipulate them (see Figure 18.1).

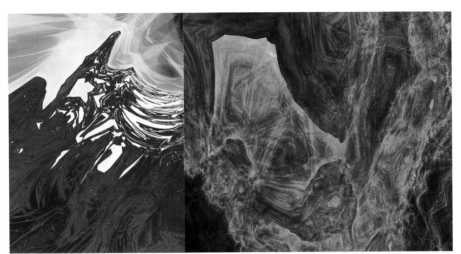

Figure 18.1 These images were selected from thousands of parameter files that are part of the artist's palette of starting images.

The Process Unfolds

I spent an entire week manipulating each of the candidate starting images. This process points out the experimental nature of fractal art. The artist does not know with great certainty what any effect will be on any particular fractal. The artist has to try it and see what happens. Fractals can be very sensitive to small changes in parameters, which can make working with fractal images a very time consuming task. The artist must make minute changes and observe the effects, then apply more fine-tuning, hopefully drawing closer to the desired final effect. I finally decided to use a fractal called *Agate Beach II* as a starting image (see Figure 18.2).

Fractals are generated with a program designed to work with the mathematics involved in fractal geometry. Not all fractal programs are the same, however, and there is very little compatibility between different fractal programs. Usually you must work on a fractal with the program that originally produced the fractal. The fractal program stores the information to regenerate the fractal in a text file called the parameter file. Surprisingly, the size of a parameter file for an infinite fractal shape is only a few kilobytes.

The program I will use for this project is called Fractal Explorer. I use Fractal Explorer because the starting fractal was originally produced with this program. Every program offers its own palette of choices for fractal types, transforms, filters, and other algorithmic controls. Figure 18.3 shows a screen shot of the Parameter window, where much of the manipulation takes place. As you can see, there are several parameters and many selections within those effects. There are many different types of fractals: Mandelbrot, Sierpinski, Newtons, Barnsley, and many more. Each of these fractal types responds in unique ways to particular combinations of adjustments. All fractals start out as an idealized shape. By changing the parameters applied to this basic form, a multitude of effects can be accomplished. Manipulating a fractal means changing its parameters. The actual formula can be changed using the attached complier, if so desired. There is a preview of the fractal in the bottom right-hand side of the Parameter window, and using this preview to visualize the fractal saves much time. Fractals involve millions of calculations and thus can take a very long time to generate at full screen size. It is often advantageous to do the coarse manipulations at smaller screen sizes.

Figure 18.2 After some study and experimentation, this image will be used as a base of operations.

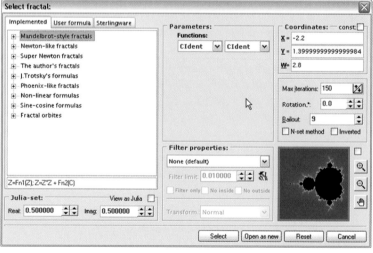

Figure 18.3 The main control panel for the Fractal Explorer software.

You do not need to understand the math to work with these effects; you just have to take the time to see how they all work together. I could use a sentence like: "I punched up the bailout while decreasing the iterations, and upped the color values to smooth out a region of transform." This would mean nothing to the uninitiated, of course, and it is beyond the scope of this project to describe each parameter effect. So I will not attempt to describe the types of changes but only the visual effects of those changes. The above sentence could then be reduced to: "I made the ridges on that edge less rough."

In other digital art techniques, effects are applied to an image, but in fractal art the effect is the image itself. Any manipulation of a fractal changes the fractal *globally*. Traditional digital effects can be manipulated individually without changing any other part of the image. This is usually not possible with a pure fractal image. A traditional digital artist can selectively lighten or darken one small area of the composition, whereas any change the fractal artist applies to the composition affects the entire fractal. A small color adjustment can completely alter the appearance of a fractal. Color is controlled with the Color control box (see Figure 18.4).

In reality, most of my final works are framed views of a portion of a fractal. The total fractal shape (or set) is the fractal as it is viewed with a magnification factor of 1. My final fractal image is actually zoomed into this fractal by approximately 336,000 times, which corresponds to a microscopic level. Figure 18.5 shows the final fractal at a magnification of 1—not your typical pretty fractal.

As you explore a fractal, you must be able to scan the image and look at it from all angles—to envi-

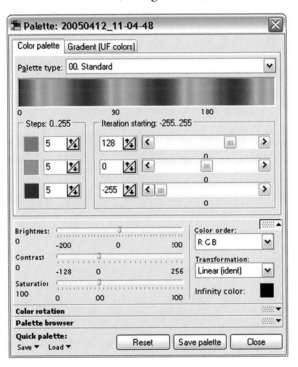

Figure 18.4 The Color control panel for the Fractal Explorer software.

sion it in different orientations, frame formats, and magnifications. The fractal artist is immersed in a weightless, endless, visual universe. This is similar to a photographer exploring a three-dimensional world, but one that is infinitely in focus. Over time, the fractal artist begins to sniff out areas of interesting visual dynamics. Artistic intuition takes over and guides one to success.

I spent several days playing with these fractals, trying random changes, throwing in the kitchen sink, wildly mixing the soup, and seeing what develops. This invites serendipity to pay the artist a visit, and this play produces several images that

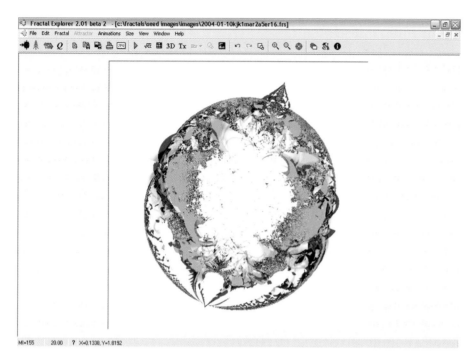

Figure 18.5 At a magnification factor of 1, the entire fractal image, representing the complete set of a fractal equation, can be seen.

occupy me for some time, tempting me to lose focus on the project at hand. I will save these experiments to refine later. Three images that develop from this experimental play are seen in Figure 18.6.

Figure 18.6 Three variations on a particular fractal.

I spent several days exploring *Agate Beach II*, trying not to change the parameters in any extreme manner in order to gain some control over the process. I save almost every manipulation, often returning to an earlier composition to modify the parameters to match an effect that was discovered in a separate combination of effects. I am starting to find and define *compositional scenes* that suggest the general impressions of the Canyon seed image. I am like a bloodhound that just found the scent. Now it gets exciting.

At some point I wonder what I had done to the entire fractal by my manipulations at this small scale, so I zoom out to magnification 1 to satisfy my curiosity. Much to my surprise, the overall character of the entire fractal has become richer. I see new surfaces that look very interesting (see Figure 18.7).

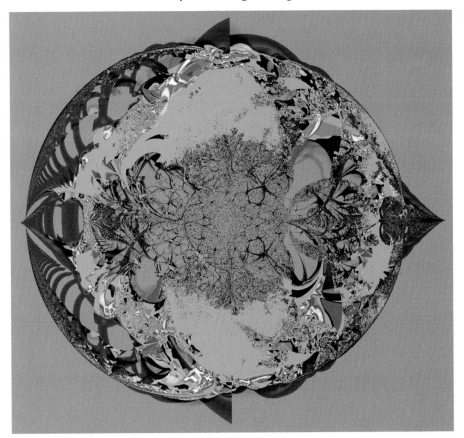

Figure 18.7 The full picture of the fractal as it has been modified up to this point.

Again I zoom deeply into regions of closely spaced transformations. To my delight the qualities I was working on at the small scale are affecting the largest scale. Areas of chaotic complexity are being squeezed closer together—just the thing I was trying to accomplish at the small scale. I spent hours doing shallow zooms near the outside surface of the fractal, working on many compositions and then moving on (see Figure 18.8).

Figure 18.8 The exploration within a specific fractal begins.

The techniques I am using now involve less manipulation of the fractal and more exploration within the fractal. At the end my focus is completely on small adjustments to the composition by moving the frame and zoom in ever finer amounts. I watch the edge of the frames, for this is what I can control. A degree in rotation can make a big difference. Beginning at the edges of the picture, I try to involve the entire picture (see Figure 18.9).

Figure 18.9 The outer frame becomes the only constant point of reference and control as possible compositions are encountered and rejected.

I work a long time on the pinnacle shape silhouettes. Nothing seems to work like I want it to, so I have to compromise. I change the sweep of the transform borders (Translation: I find out how to curve the silhouette edges) in the smallest degrees possible. I can only do so much, however, and I have to compromise again. It is still not right. What is wrong? See Figure 18.10.

Figure 18.10 Zeroing in on an interesting area.

I spent several days intentionally not working on the image. I feel I have hit a rut and need a break. Then it hits me: change the framing ratio; do a wide-angle shot, so to speak. Make the frame ratio more panoramic, like an old western movie or those wide-angle photographs of the canyon lands. Canyons are spacious—wide or narrow, they are always about space. An elongated framing will accentuate the towering forms (see Figure 18.11).

Figure 18.11 Switching to a panoramic view helps the artist sense the wide-open spaces of a natural canyon.

I am happy and work within the panoramic frame for a day or two. Slowly I sense that something is not right. I have refined the pinnacle silhouettes as finely as I can, but I cannot make the layers come closer together to achieve the narrow, vertical feel of the original Seed Image 3.

Then it hits me: Turn the frame on its side. There's the needed verticality. I work a day on the composition with this orientation. I make adjustments to the silhouettes easily now because of my earlier experiments. I refine the composition with slight zooms and frame shifts. It is time to get picky.

Then I sit back for a few days and just look at the final product. I consider everything over again, including the purpose of this project and its deadline. I am very close to finishing this thing. But it still does not seem right. What is it now? See Figure 18.12.

In my work outside this project, at this particular time, I am experimenting with certain levels of color contrast. I now see that I am imposing my personal stylistic evolution to this very specific project. Finally it is only me who is standing in the way of the final expression. The artist must move aside for the work to proceed.

And so I lower the color contrast and adjust the composition again. It takes several hours, but the colors are now right. With a sigh of relief, I feel I can stop here. This project has been a real challenge, so I will call the final piece *Canyon Challenge* (see Figure 18.13).

Last Words

Final preparation of the image includes only anti-aliasing. Anti-aliasing at the maximum 9 points is applied using the native program. Further sharpening with an outside image manipulation program may punch out the image even more for printing applications. I try to always keep in mind that the final objective is to produce a physical print. I visualize myself in an art gallery looking at the final image on a wall. It helps to view the final composition at a small size on the screen to replicate how the final print image would appear in the physical world, actually hanging on a wall.

Figure 18.12 The orientation seems right, but there is still something amiss.

During the late '80s and early '90s, fractal art gained the unfortunate reputation of being purely ornamental, psychedelic, and completely mechanical. The ease of creating such fantastical images from a new form of geometry astounded and intoxicated its cohorts. Fractal art became trivialized by the vast amount of stereotypical images that suddenly appeared on the Internet. Naive practitioners thought that this would enable the artist to produce masterpieces in a week's time. Traditional art critics dismissed the genre as vapid ornamentation.

As a sub-genre of algorithmic art, fractals endure the same malady that all digital art must presently suffer: the general assumption that *real art* cannot come out of a computer. What is not generally appreciated is that all *real art* attempts to transcend the tools that create it. Perhaps fractal art with its particular restrictions can transcend its limitations with its unique attributes. I believe fractal art has a bright future. Computers keep advancing, and more theoretical work continues on fractal geometry. Printer and substrate options increase every year. And while swarming groups of galaxies fall into fractal forms, the tiny human mind weaves these grand patterns into art.

Figure 18.13 With a final color adjustment the composition is complete.

Artist Profile: Ken Keller

Artistic Background or Influences: Impressionism, Abstract Expressionism. (Pollack was doing fractal art before Mandelbrot named fractal geometry.) Pure Abstraction (Mondrian for his grasp of geometry relating to the human mind and eye) and Op Art.

System Profile: "Typical PC" running Windows (512MB RAM), "CRT screens have better light."

Peripherals: Epson 10000 printer

Software and Plug-Ins: Fractal Explorer, Flarium 24, SterlingWare, Tiera-Zon, UltraFractal, Vehira, FractTint

Papers, Inks, and Other Output Preferences: Epson inks, watercolor papers, canvas, Tyvek, adhesive transparent materials, usually output from 16" × 20" to 44" × 66", most popular selling prints are 8" × 10"

Personal Web Site: www.fractalartgallery.com

Ecstasy

A Glimpse into the 31st Century.

19

Helen Golden

Artist Helen Golden is known as a pioneer in the digital art realm. She exhibits her mixed-media/digital art nationally and internationally in solo, juried, and invited exhibitions in galleries, museums, and universities, and she has been cited in newspapers, magazines, books, television, and on the Internet.

In July 1997, Helen was a co-organizer of the *Digital Atelier: A Printmaking Studio for the 21st Century* at the National Museum of American Art in Washington, D.C. There she was an artist-in-residence for 21 days along with the artists of Unique Editions, the digital collective of which she was a co-founder. The event was supported by 31 technology corporations.

Helen's artwork has been accessed by the National Museum of American Art at the Smithsonian Institution in Washington, DC; she is a Laureate of the 1998 Computerworld Smithsonian Information Technology Innovation Distinction; and, in 1998, she was the recipient of the Andre Schellenberg Award in Fine Art.

Helen was the first curator/director at Art At The Pond, a San Francisco gallery that pioneered exhibiting digital art. She has also been an artist-in-residence at the A.I.R. Gallery in New York and at the San Jose Institute of Contemporary Art in California. Additionally, Helen works as a consultant for companies that are creating hardware, software, and media.

First Impressions

"OK," I thought, "This is what I have to start with. What can I do with these three images?" The images were unlike those that I would typically use for inspiration, but I often say that no matter what I am given to start with I will turn it into art. That may be bragging, but I prefer to think of it as a way of saying that my imagination asserts that it can take anything and use it to make art. Sure, I have preferences and am motivated more by some things than others, but I said to myself, "Here we go," and indeed my imagination was off and running and I began making little pencil sketches.

The Process Unfolds

The three seed images felt pedestrian to me, so I figured I would just start fiddling around with them and see where altering them would take me. One of the tools I often use to play around with is the application Lucis, so I proceeded to process all three images in Lucis to see what I could discover or what would start to happen.

The Woman Transfigured

I started with Seed Image 1. I began musing about the shape of the young woman's bracelet and tattoo. I knew that I wanted to spend some time to see where I could go with that. I paid particular attention to that area even while I was making overall manipulations to the entire image (see Figure 19.1).

I came up with three variations of Seed Image 1. These are the ones I actually worked with, but I experimented a lot with the Lucis settings before I settled on them (see Figure 19.2). I felt that by exploring Seed Image 1 I got to know the potential within it. I knew that I could return to the source any time I wanted to create another variation. I noticed the softening and watercolor feel that evolved from the processing, and I looked at the effects that the processing had on the tiles and her face and thought about that.

Figure 19.1 What processing looks like in a Lucis application—the seated woman.

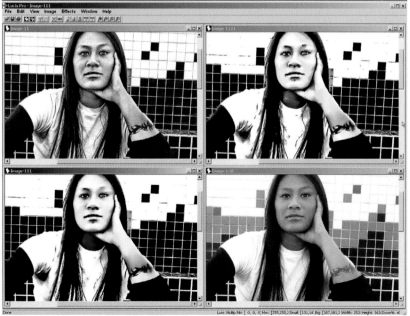

Figure 19.2 Three Lucis variations for the seated woman.

Urban and Country

Seed Image 2 was the one of the three that had initially grabbed my attention. I was raised in a city and love to explore urban themes. I struggled to make something interesting happen to the image, and I did manage to get some interesting contrast going between the stark straight lines and the softened "window" areas. I love drama, and this began to feel like there was working potential (see Figure 19.3).

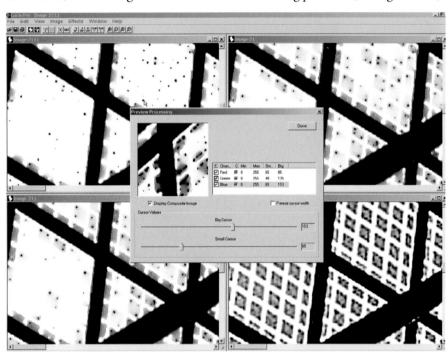

Figure 19.3 Three variations of Seed Image 2 (the grid) with the original at lower right.

At first, Seed Image 3 seemed pretty uninteresting, but I wrestled with it mentally. What could I do with this? I tried a bunch of things in Lucis, and the more radical manipulations began to wring some fun things out of a few parts of the image. I was pleased with the texture that appeared in the bottom area in the second variation from the left, and I really liked the watercolor feeling that I got in the top area in the second sample from the right (see Figure 19.4).

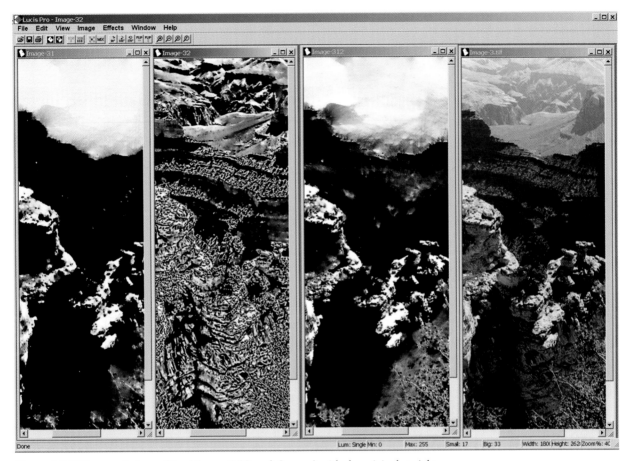

Figure 19.4 Three variations of Seed Image 3 (Grand Canyon) with the original at right.

Transforms of Seed Image 2

I wanted to really work with this already manipulated image, so I set myself up to push it even further. I have tried this little routine before. I enlarged the canvas (not the image). Now I've created enough empty (white) space around the image that I have room to make alterations to it. This is one of my tricks to set myself up to *think out of the box*.

In Photoshop I tried several different things to exaggerate the visual elements of Seed Image 2. I liked and made use of a sequence I often try: Image >Transform > Perspective. The corners of the image acquired handles that I grabbed, and then I had a really good time moving them all over the place to push those straight lines around (see Figure 19.5). Sometimes the distorted rectangle moved into amazingly interesting shapes, which inspired me to explore something I most likely would not have thought of if I didn't have access to this tool.

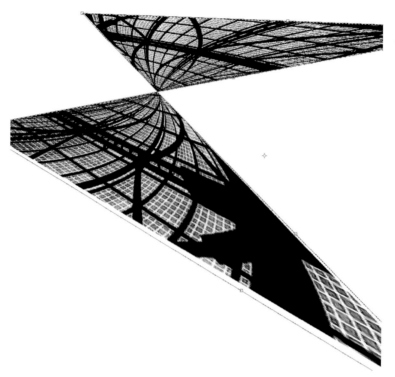

Figure 19.5 Pushing the rectangle around with the Transform tool to explore the linear image.

I took this last flight of fancy pretty far, but this image shows only the tip of the iceberg. By that I mean a considerable size file developed (with many layers) because I played a lot with all the fascinating shapes and lines I got when I distorted Seed Image 2. I had a little story going in my mind that this was about my life as an urban-dwelling child, and the windows, streets, and alleys became those of remembered people and places. After a while I noticed that I was struggling with my *story*. It wasn't consuming enough, but I continued to hang in there for a while until, boom, I just stopped, and said "enough." There was nowhere interesting to go with it, and it didn't satisfy me. I thought about what was going on and what to do, and then turned off the computer (see Figure 19.6).

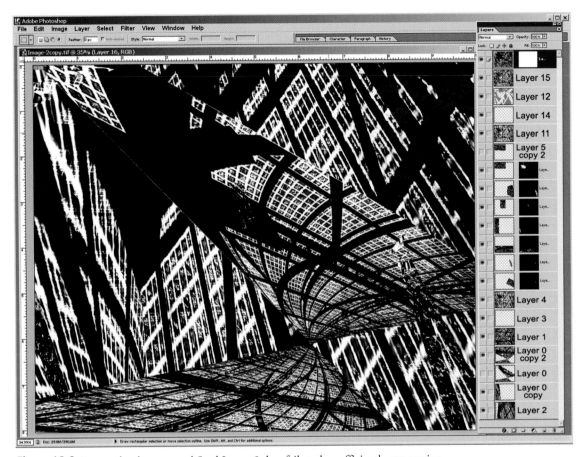

Figure 19.6 A story develops around Seed Image 2, but fails to be sufficiently consuming.

A New Beginning with Zig-Zag and Wave

I returned to browsing some earlier ideas and also looked over those Lucis variations of Seed Image 1. I still was interested in the bracelet and tattoo area. I spent time trying many different Photoshop operations on that section of variations. I particularly enjoyed the design elements that emerged when I repeatedly used the Zig-Zag and Wave filters (see Figure 19.7). I realized I was spending far too much time on this, but I was having great fun. Some of these experiments began to look like a line of dancers, and I stayed with them for a while, even sketching on top of one of them with a Photoshop brush that gave the illusion of charcoal. I didn't exactly know where to go with these, but I persisted.

Figure 19.7 Applying the Zig-Zag and Wave filters in Photoshop gave the impression of dancers.

This next image shows the direction I went in and the image that I worked on for a while. There are many layers and operations preceding this stage, and many of the bracelet–tattoo experiments are integrated in it. I used a piece of Seed Image 3 to create the upper background because it felt other-worldly and sunset-like to me. I had some idea going about the emergence of life forms—maybe a cocoon, I am not sure. Ultimately I got stuck; it got uninteresting, and I left it as I had left an earlier developed file.

I know that I have a rebellious (and not particularly helpful) streak that just doesn't do well when it is given parameters for creating. I prefer to follow my impulses and see where they take me. However, I wanted to succeed at this assignment and wondered what I was going to do after two false starts. I had fun playing with the bracelet–tattoos and I thought I had wrung as much as I could out of them (see Figure 19.8).

Figure 19.8 Another flight of imagination using some parts of Seed Image 3 and several from the bracelet experiments. There was something in mind about early humans, but this was another version that did not satisfy.

Returning to an Earlier Place

I returned to variations of Seed Image 2, and this time as I played with it things began to happen with some ease. I didn't feel as if I was trying too hard to get any-where. Perhaps I had explored the material enough to have a better grip on the pos-sibilities, and as I went a lot further with my *out-of-the-box* routine some interesting things began to emerge, especially when I tried Rotate 90° CW (see Figure 19.9).

I had created layers out of selected pieces of the variations, trying various layer blending modes as I combined them to see what they would do to the linear ele-ments, and I liked what was happening. I especially was interested in the aqua/red color juxtapositions as those heightened the drama of the linear structure (see Figure 19.10). I began to think of this as background for an urban image (there it is again), but it also began to feel futuristic to me and I think my mind shifted into telling that kind of a story.

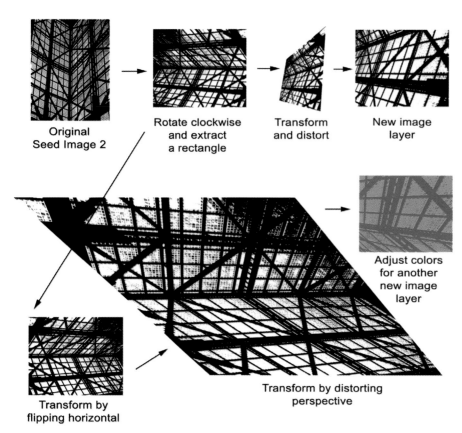

Original
Seed Image 2

Rotate clockwise
and extract
a rectangle

Transform
and distort

New image
layer

Figure 19.9 Making changes to Seed Image 2. These perspective and color changes were done primarily in Photoshop.

Adjust colors
for another
new image
layer

Transform by distorting
perspective

Transform by
flipping horizontal

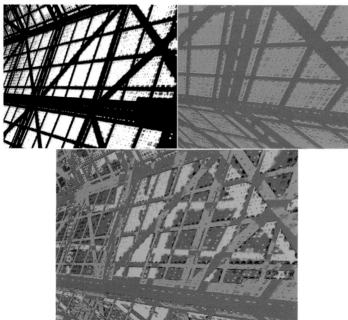

Figure 19.10 Normal Blend mode (upper left). The layer over it is in the Difference Blend mode (upper right). Combining the upper left and upper right images produced the image at the bottom.

Returning to the Face

I knew that I wanted to place a human element into the story, and of course the face of Seed Image 1 came to mind. I didn't want to use the side of the face that was distorted by the hand, and I didn't like that some of the face was hidden by the hand. So I selected the side of the face that was intact, copied it, used Transform > Flip Horizontal, and abutted that half up to its mirror image, and there it was, a new face! I used Transform > Perspective to create a face that felt futuristic—similar to life as we know it yet a bit different (see Figure 19.11).

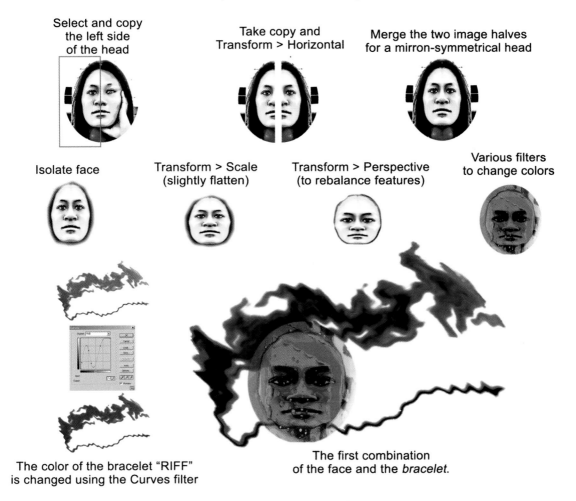

Select and copy the left side of the head

Take copy and Transform > Horizontal

Merge the two image halves for a mirron-symmetrical head

Isolate face

Transform > Scale (slightly flatten)

Transform > Perspective (to rebalance features)

Various filters to change colors

The color of the bracelet "RIFF" is changed using the Curves filter

The first combination of the face and the *bracelet*.

Figure 19.11 Reconfiguring the face and adding a bracelet–tattoo motif.

When I placed the face onto the futuristic urban linear background it felt too isolated. I tried placing duplicates of the face around the image and that didn't work. Then a thought about the 31st century popped into my mind, and I found myself wondering what the human communications apparatus would be like. Would our minds connect to a network or would we be reading each other's minds? I was free to imagine anything I wanted. I saw energy and intelligence coming directly from the head.

I returned to look at the bracelet–tattoo experiments, and one of them looked like it would fit around the head just beautifully. I tried it and it did (although I needed to make color changes in it. See Figure 19.12). Now I was getting excited about my story; the parts were fitting into place, and my imagination was having a good time.

Figure 19.12 An early stage of the combined components.

Energy and Color

I wanted a heightened feeling of energy crackling throughout the image, but the excessive red of the background structure was too dominant. I changed the colors in most of the structure but left some of it red and thus retained the sense of energy I liked, but now the image felt more integrated.

When I began making art using the computer, I began to pay a lot more attention to color in my work. I believe I ventured into this area where I had not been particularly adept before because when I used computer tools I could reverse most of the actions that I took.

In this image I worked on changing the colors by selecting the red areas. Then I used Select > All > Modify > Contract to be sure that I left lots of the existing dynamic red around the edges of the structural element, and I changed the rest into dark, nearly black areas that I felt added complexity and drama. Lots of other subtle changes were made in those areas to increase variety in texture and color (see Figure 19.13).

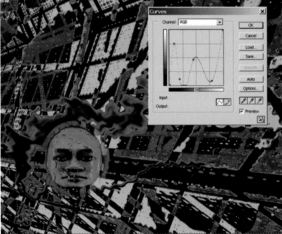

Figure 19.13 The Hue/Saturation layer was added in the Normal mode (top). The Curves layer was added in the Linear Burn mode (bottom).

A 31st-Century Sky

By now the story I was telling myself about this image was asking for a way to connect the statement about the 31st century with the present. I decided that adding a *natural* element such as sky to the top of the picture could give that feeling, so I grabbed a piece of Image 312 (one of the variations of Seed Image 3 that had been processed in Lucis when I started this project). I created a mask that would block everything but the blue areas, and I placed that piece of Image 312, which had actually come from the trees and foliage section, and inserted it in Overlay mode. With some tweaking, I had my *Clouds in the Sky* (see Figure 19.14).

Image 312 (Image 3 processed in Lucis)

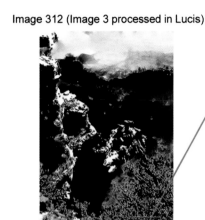

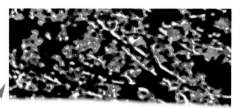

That small piece of Image 312 was scaled up.

I copied a small piece of this and used it to add texture to the top. I had started to think of that as the sky area of the image I was working on .

A mask (the black areas) protect everything except the *sky.*

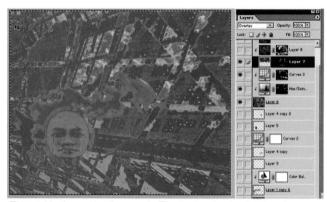

The red is the protective mask. The textural selection has been used in Photoshop in Overlay Mode.

Now I was getting some *clouds* in the sky.

Figure 19.14 Clouds created from trees and foliage.

Adding Dimensionality

In Photoshop, I created a flattened, single layer TIFF file of the image and then opened it in Corel Painter. I really like the dimensional effects that I can get in Painter, and I use variations of those to unify images or to increase the 3D feeling in an image. I was going for the latter in this image by using Effects > Surface Control > Apply Surface Texture > Image Luminance. I got a textural feeling that gave this the dimensionality that I felt it needed (see Figure 19.15). I continued by adding a 3D effect to further add depth and drama in order to unify the image.

I later decided to remove the dimensional texturing effect from the blue "sky" areas as it reduced the illusion of depth in the image. I kept the textures in the areas that feel like they are closer, which retained the impression that one could reach in and touch those surfaces.

Figure 19.15 Adding dimensional effects by flattening the image and reopening and reworking it in Painter.

The futuristic theme provoked questions, and as I viewed the disembodied head I thought why not put three additional eyes into this picture, imagining that they could be surveillance or communication devices (see Figure 19.16).

This image had areas that felt overly pixilated to me as too many jaggy edges were apparent. Typically when I encounter this problem I save a single-layered file with Photoshop in the Genuine Fractals .stn format and resize it to enlarge the file. When this 29.7MB file was opened at 118.625MB there was a filling in or softening effect on the linear elements (see Figure 19.17). I achieved even cleaner transitions by smoothing the edges using the Clone Stamp tool and the Smudge tool.

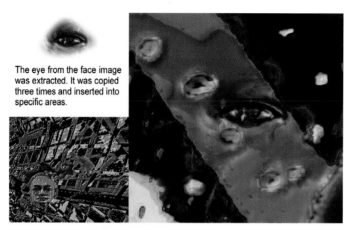

The eye from the face image was extracted. It was copied three times and inserted into specific areas.

Figure 19.16 Adding eyes to the disembodied head.

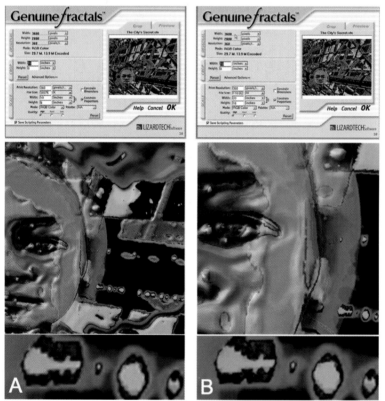

Figure 19.17 Resizing the image in Genuine Fractals resulted in a softening effect on the linear elements. (Left: original image size; right: resized image.)

Last Words

My next steps included using several masks to tweak areas of the image and making additional small but necessary changes. The head had lost its prominence, and I altered and saturated its color to bring it into the foreground again. Next, I saw that the sky area needed more tweaking, and I used a mask to select that area (see Figure 19.18).

Finally, I selectively lightened the "clouds" using Color Range (see Figure 19.19).

Figure 19.18 The mask was used to select an area to tweak the sky.

Figure 19.19 Lightening the clouds using Color Range.

Artist Profile: Helen Golden

Artistic Background or Influences: I was fortunate to have a great liberal arts college education. As an art major I was influenced by studying with prominent abstract expressionists, but fortunately I wasn't pushed into expressing myself in a particular way. I was told that I had to make a living, so I was trained to be an art teacher rather than an artist. Now, I see how lucky I was that I had the great fortune to develop on my own. I have taken courses here and there and benefited from critique groups, but most importantly I have worked and worked to continue making art. I feel extremely lucky that I had the opportunities, the passion, and inner drive to become an artist.

I have been enthralled with and influenced by the paintings of Goya and Rembrandt; the color in Claude Monet's paintings; photographs by Bill Brandt, Ernst Haas, and Andre Kertesz; sculptures by Isamu Noguchi, Henry Moore, Barbara Hepworth, and Alexander Calder; the imagination of Pablo Picasso and Max Ernst; the dances of Martha Graham; and the music of J.S. Bach.

Interiors

System Profile: Two PC computers, 1 Macintosh computer

Peripherals: Wacom Intuos tablet, Epson Scanner, Hewlett-Packard Designjet 5000PS wide-format printer, Epson desktop printer, two digital cameras, one film camera

Software and Plug-Ins: Adobe Photoshop, Metacreations Painter, Lucis Pro, LucisArt, Genuine Fractals, SnagIt, Macromedia Dreamweaver MX

Papers, Inks, and Other Output Preferences: Hewlett-Packard UV pigmented inks, Hahnemuhle digital fine art papers, Innova digital art media

Personal Web Site: www.helengolden.com

Guarding the Grid

20

Bruce Wands

Bruce Wands is an artist, writer, and musician. His artistic energies have been focused both academically as chair of the MFA Computer Art department in New York City's School of Visual Arts and in independent projects such as writing *Digital Creativity* and forming his own video, animation, and music studio, Wands Studio. As a musician, Bruce was the first to give a live performance over ISDN lines on the Internet in 1992. He is the director of the New York Digital Salon, an international digital art organization formed in 1993. *U.S. News and World Report* ranked his department fifth in the nation in multimedia/visual communications. For this project, Bruce engaged the talents of Dave Weisman in building the creative aspect of the image. Dave's work has appeared in *Forbes* magazine and in *The Washington Post*. He teaches interactive media in the graduate computer art division of the School of Visual Arts.

First Impressions

Most of the creative work I do starts with a clear idea. What intrigued me about this project was the new situation. As such, I could take a fresh approach and see what happened. The directive was to take the three source images and combine and interpret them in a creative way. After receiving the seed images, my first task was to print them out and study them. I put them up in my studio and just thought about them for awhile. I looked at each image carefully, and thought about how it could be deconstructed, manipulated, modified, taken apart, and then evolved into a final composite image. Several things came to mind with each image. The grid image (Seed Image 2) immediately offered lots of image possibilities. It had a lot of small graphic elements that could be used as windows for images. It also had strong lines that could be used as an aid for composition of an image. The landscape image (Seed Image 3) was interesting, but fairly straightforward. While there were several levels of depth to the image, it had a fairly uniform blend of landscape elements. It stood on its own as a complete image and statement. The portrait of the woman (Seed Image 1) also appeared to me as straightforward. Of the three images, the grid pattern had the most potential. Based on these observations and thoughts, my plan was to use the grid image as the basis for my new image and somehow incorporate the other two into it. I also decided to use some of my own images as graphic elements. Since the project was about combining the images, I had also settled on creating a collage.

The Process Unfolds

Since I was taking a fresh approach to this project, I also decided to collaborate with a Photoshop expert rather than work alone. The majority of images I create are photographs, and the type of manipulation I do is generally global and related to the exposure and color balance process rather than collage. The abstract *Buddha Light Painting* images I create are done with 3D software and also are not collage. I felt that bringing another creative perspective into this project would give me a more interesting end result. I decided to work with my colleague David Weisman, a New York based illustrator and Photoshop guru whom I have known for many years. When I contacted Dave, he immediately asked me to e-mail him low-resolution versions of the images so that he could get a head start on thinking about the project. The next step was to schedule a session and get to work.

When we met, we talked about what we wanted to do and decided to start with the grid image. We brought all the images into Photoshop and made them layers. Our next step was to work with the composition of the grid and crop it so that it formed a strong foundation for the final image. The approach was to take a portion of it and use the strong angular black lines as composition elements and as a means to direct the gaze of the viewer. Also, we felt that the large grid was a bit too busy and wanted to focus on a portion of it. I also liked the fact that the grid had a bit of an optical illusion property to it, whereby it either looked like it was going away from you or folding into the center. We would later exploit this effect with the other graphic elements of the collage. We resized the grid layer and recomposed it to fit our developing concept and the final print format.

Our next idea was to work with the portrait image (Seed Image 1) and somehow integrate it with the grid. I worked with my Apple Titanium 17" laptop and Dave worked on an Apple G4 dual-processor, dual-1.0GHz machine with 1GB of RAM. We discussed our ideas, and then as Dave was working on the image I would write down what we were doing. This process worked well and gave me a skeleton with which to write the final process description.

Deconstructing the Woman

Next we needed to isolate the woman from her surroundings so that we could position her somewhere in the grid image. As Dave was doing that, I was writing. He completed his task a bit before I did and was playing about with one of her arms (see Figure 20.1 A). When I looked up, I liked it. It gave us both the idea to deconstruct her figure and incorporate it somehow into the grid image. Since one of the hands was open and looked as if it was grasping something, we went with this idea and positioned the arm in such a way that it appeared to be grasping the grid and holding it up (see Figure 20.1 B). This started a whole train of creative ideas regarding the use of different figurative elements.

Figure 20.1 Positioning the arm. (A) The artists begin to build the figurative elements for the final image. Note that the grid pattern has been cropped. (B) It was determined that the goal for the arm was to have it come from "behind" the image and grab the black vertical line.

From a technical point of view, we used the Selection tool to select the flesh color and isolate the woman's arm. The arm was added to the image as a layer. Shift-clicking to grab the proper flesh colors allowed us to get the different composite parts of the woman's figure. We selected her right arm and isolated it. The idea was that the hands would support the grid structure. We were slowly building the image while conceptually merging the human element with the grid element to form the underlying structure and tension for our image (see Figure 20.2).

Figure 20.2 The other arm is added to further emphasize the interaction between the figure and the grid structure. The idea is that the figure is actually holding onto the grid.

Working on the Eyes and Feet

The next step was to look at her eyes. Eyes always communicate and draw attention in an image (see Figure 20.3). In this case we wanted one eye looking one way and the other looking the opposite way so that the image would start to look almost like a portrait. However, we wanted to add a twist by putting one eye upside down. That made the image and perspective a bit more unpredictable and interesting.

Figure 20.3 The next stage was to add an eye looking through one of the window elements of the grid. This relates to the earlier concept of using the rectangular elements in the grid as windows. This image is close to the final arrangement of the figure with the second eye upside down so that it provided a bit of disorientation to the viewer. A small figure of the woman was also added on a girder as if she was just sitting there looking at you.

To make the eye mask, we selected the black of the grid, inscribed it with the Lasso tool, and then Option-clicked with the Magic Wand to deselect the black. This gave us a mask for the grid window. We then put a Perspective Transformation onto the eyes.

The next step was to work with the feet. We decided to put the feet only in the bottom as if one was lying down on a bed and looking down one's body. We also felt that this added a little bit of humor to the image. The feet also supported, and somewhat completed, the composition of all the figurative elements. But after adding the feet, we thought we still needed one more figure element. We decided to take the whole figure and make it very small, almost as if it were sitting on a girder (see Figure 20.3).

Adding Color to Dramatize the Image

After adding the small woman again, but this time resting on the hand, we decided to add some color. I am currently working on a series of fine art images called the *Buddha Light Paintings*. (See the artist's signature image at the end of this chapter.) One of these images had a geometric pattern similar to the grid structure. We brought this image into the composition on its own layer and tried several different color combinations and transparencies and ended up with a more dramatically colored image. It had a much stronger presence and feeling (see Figure 20.4).

The Soldiers, Fish, and a Window

We decided to move the girl out of the hand since the image appeared to be too busy and repetitive. However, the bottom right portion of the image needed some sort of compositional element. We decided to add some other figures. I had recently been to Xian, China and had some photographs of the terra cotta soldiers. We isolated a single figure and then used the Clone tool to duplicate the figures. We created a small row of them standing on one of the girders. Finally, we individually colored the terra cotta soldiers (see Figure 20.5).

At this point the image was beginning to get complex. We decided to take a minute to analyze what we had done and then add a few final elements. We took a short break and then returned. Upon viewing the image, we felt that the top of the image was too dark and simple, and that the composition was drawing the viewer's gaze out of the image, rather than into it. We thought about adding something there.

I had just the image. As mentioned, while Dave was working in Photoshop, I would jot down notes. Another thing that I was doing was browsing through iPhoto and image folders on my disk. I would look at the photographs and images

Figure 20.4 The addition of color. The previous black-and-white grid image with the figurative elements needed color. This stage shows the addition of the Buddha Light painting image as another layer. The geometry of that image reinforced the geometric elements of the grid and added the element of color.

and then pull out those that I thought might contribute to this project. Now that we needed something for the top of the image, I knew I had just what we needed. We took a fish photographic image that I had taken and combined it with the main piece. It had geometrical patterns and shadows that worked well with the composition. We moved it around, re-sized it, and then created a ramped fade so that it would be present only in the top of the image. This worked and we were very happy with it (see Figure 20.6).

Figure 20.5 The soldiers are added on one of the girders, including an upside down gray one in the hand. Once this image was finished, the artists felt that there needed to be something more happening graphically in the top of the image.

Now we felt that the image was basically complete. We wanted to add a window or two to finish it, but without making it too cluttered. Since we had not yet used the landscape image, we decided to put the landscape at the bottom left above the feet. This worked and became one of the finishing touches for the image.

The final step was to make some touch-ups. We replaced the small woman with another version. The Transformation Perspective procedure did not look believable, so we just made her small. The center of the image also needed something stronger, so we colored the soldier figure that was being held in the hand a golden

Figure 20.6 Fish are added to the top of the nearly final image. The composition now felt more balanced.

yellow. As we were doing this, I realized that this also added a narrative element, since one of the original soldiers on the grid was black. The soldier in the hand now connected to the black, or "missing" soldier.

Once this was done, we were happy. While the image is complex, the composition keeps you involved. The elements do form a narrative of sorts and keep your eye and mind involved. After a week or so, I decided to call it *Guarding the Grid*. This was an homage to the soldiers and their role as guardians (see Figure 20.7).

Figure 20.7 The final image. Some clean up work was done, such as fixing the small woman so that she did not look distorted. The landscape source image was included to add some interest to the bottom left of the image and the soldier in the hand was colored to become a focus of interest.

Last Words

This project took me in some creative directions which I do not usually travel. In that sense, it was a success. I enjoyed the challenge presented as well as the collaborative aspects of the project. Creative projects for the future include the *Buddha Light Paintings* series, a photographic exhibition of my travels to Asia, and a series of nature photographs, the first focusing on orchids. In addition, I will continue to write and perform my music and sound art.

It is worth noting that the light source used for creating color is part of my series of images called *Buddha Light Paintings*. They are based on the sacred geometry that underlies Buddhist art and were created using Maya software. The process used is called volumetric light, and the rays resemble theatrical spotlights. The lights are placed at specific locations within the Buddhist geometry.

Artist Profile: Bruce Wands

Artistic Background or Influences: My artistic influences are very broad. From a fine art historical perspective, I am influenced by Monet, Kandinsky, and William Blake. I also draw inspiration from the Victorian, Art Nouveau, and early 20th-century artists. Buddhist and Chinese art also influence my creative work. I have a traditional art studio with a drawing table and a large collection of art supplies in addition to the digital video and music components in Wands Studio. I enjoy working in both traditional and digital media, and my studio gives me the freedom to create whatever comes to mind at the moment.

System Profile: A multipurpose collection of Macintosh (laptop and desktops) and PC computers

Peripherals: OWC Firewire hard drives, HP PSC 2100 multipurpose printer, OfficeJet R80 printer, Epson 2000P printer, Epson flatbed scanner, Nikon slide scanner, Nikon and Canon digital cameras, Sony digital video camera

Software and Plug-Ins: Adobe InDesign, Photoshop, Illustrator, Alias Maya, Microsoft Word, Apple Final Cut Pro, DVD Pro, 32-channel Digidesign ProTools Mix 24 system, Mackie 24-channel mixing board, and a variety of outboard gear

Buddha Light Painting #4

Personal Web Site: www.brucewands.com, www.davidweisman.net

Mosaic of Transformations

21

Seeing Digital Art

Seventeen artists; seventeen different journeys and styles in art-making. Readers will draw their own conclusions, but one likely conclusion is that the digital artists in the preceding chapters appear to be like all other artists: They use their tools and materials to configure and reconfigure the given or imagined reality. In this sense, digital artists would be exhibited together with other traditional media artists. In terms of the broad view of human history, technology permits the artist to use an ever-increasing variety of toolsets while the culture in which the artist lives weaves the backdrop of meaning and symbolism. The artist—digital or traditional—expresses his or her art in particular historical moments with particular tools and materials, not in some ethereal vacuum.

Within the context of the 21st century and an exploding digital technology it would be expected, even mandated, that an artist living in the cultural moment explore the current set of tools. This hand-in-hand relationship between technology and art has prevailed from Giotto through Warhol; there is every reason to believe it will continue.

This chapter will look at several hallmarks in discussing art—the artist's intent and search for meaning, the role of play and experimentation toward uncovering intent and meaning, and an exploration of art styles and techniques focusing on these featured artists and their transformations of the original three seed images.

Text and Context

Throughout this book's artist journals, the artists show a concern for finding a concept or story around which to build their image. The personal history of each artist underscores a long involvement in art making and an involvement with both traditional and digital media. Their art is not naive; rather, it is a result of a mature engagement with making images. This was no random process.

The use of three seed images, unseen by the artists themselves until they began this project, presented an artificial starting point, much like an advertising illustrator might be provided with reference images or, in times past, when a benefactor like the Church of Rome would commission artists to capture a particular storyline or embellish certain personages. The advantage of a known starting point enables the reader to better compare styles and processes than if every artist started in different places and ended where they may. Earlier in Chapter 2, the hypothetical *Black on White* art show underscored the importance of artists' statements and the titles given to works in affecting and shaping the viewer's perception of the artwork. Words provide a context that shapes the visual understanding of what appears to be the identical physical marking—namely, a black line on a white canvas. This point underscores the interaction between words and the artist's marks in shaping the understanding of what is ultimately seen.

In an extension of that argument, the artists in this book were given the same three seed images. Clearly, the seed images are far richer in information than a black line on a white canvas. But the point is the same: The artist's description and expressed intent will shape our understanding of the image created. This shaping informs our understanding and appreciation, going hand-in-hand with the shaping of materials toward the making of art. All of the artists were asked to discuss their initial reactions to the seed images as well as their compositional decisions, both in terms of what meaning they read into the image and the role they saw that image playing in their evolving composition.

The Intriguing Face

Psychologists and social scientists have noted the compelling nature of the human face—from the way we are nurtured from birth, to the attraction in relationships, to the fight-or-flight pattern in dominance situations. Rather than avoid the face as a potentially preemptive fact, the authors decided to find a face that could represent the contemporary association of a polyglot and pluralistic society. The "It" woman with blond hair and Northern European features that dominated the imagery of 20th-century glamour might be recast, today, as a raven haired descendent of an ambiguously defined culture—possibly African, possibly Native

American, possibly Asian. The artists were not given any information about the model in Seed Image 1, but instead worked from their impressions and how they viewed her within their experience of history and culture.

Michael Wright discounted the metal grid and landscape seed images given his background in working with figure and portraiture. The androgynous feel of the model's pose drew his interest. He noted a certain mystery that her legs and black pants created, appearing heart shaped, while other elements such as the tattoo suggested a harder, "Don't mess with me" attitude (see Figure 21.1)

Dolores Kaufman was also struck by the woman's apparent defiance, but she transposed this attitude into Native American symbolism that contrasted with an encroaching urban environment. Her work suggested a truce between the historical loss of the natural landscape of the Southwest Native American cultures and the contemporary urban culture in which this woman now exists.

Figure 21.1 Michael Wright focuses on figure and portraiture with his attention drawn to the model's "Don't mess with me" attitude.

As already noted, the face is a natural draw. Bruce Shortz engaged this immediacy and worked solely on the woman's face, seeing it as a mask reflecting ego, feeling, mystery, and a path to discovery for both the artist and subject. His impression of her ancestral and tribal roots follows the trajectory of human population and his own personal work in deconstructing the established form of portraiture (see Figure 21.2).

These examples illustrate that if drawn to the face, the artist, like any other human being, will project and imagine a personal and cultural space for the subject. In the case of an artist's perception, there might be more to the elaboration of this story, but the face remains an important starting point. Whether the artist's read of the subject is accurate—was she really defiant; was she really Native American or African?—is ultimately unimportant in this artistic venture. What is important are the signals and ideas that the artist identifies and frames within the image-to-be-created. And, to no one's surprise, the subject can be read differently. Each artist is telling a different story or casting a different spell.

The artist's intent and the story being told provide a backdrop and context for the image, but the strength of the image must ultimately stand on its own. The power of the artist's work is then determined by the strength with which the image stimulates the viewer's own imagination, thus passing on the spark of creativity.

Figure 21.2 Bruce Shortz sees ancestral and tribal roots in the woman's face and also sees the face as a mask for reflecting a variety of feelings.

The Urban Grid

Regardless of one's sentiment toward living in a city, the city is associated with civilization—not necessarily in the sense of being civil, but in having specialized occupations, mass distribution of food, and bountiful buildings, along with sewer, water, and transportation systems. But, along with civilization comes laws and codes of conduct, which necessarily inhibit an individual's complete freedom of action and, in some cases, can be seen as oppressive. In terms of human history, urban society can be measured as a mere flicker of time; still, it is an amazing accomplishment. It is with that sense of history that an image of the built environment is an important visual fact. Seed Image 2 provides a sense of the human structured grid of architecture, as well as society. This image proved important to a number of the artists as they considered what kind of image they were going to make.

Bruce Wands found the grid image the strongest in building his composition with lines that would direct the viewer's attention; it also had an optical illusion quality. It wasn't until the end of the image building process that he was able to fix the narrative to a collage of elements. The woman's deconstructed hand, grabbing one of the missing soldiers against the backdrop of the grid structure, provided an allusion to the guardian role of soldiers—hence, *Guarding the Grid* (see Figure 21.3). In this sense, defending the fortress becomes an echo to humanity's building of walls for protection. An interesting outcome, but also illustrative of the way in which the creative process may be characterized as backing into the final result, while not necessarily having the plan fully known at the starting point.

Reminding her of growing up in a city, the grid, and the sense of drama it provided, immediately attracted Helen Golden. She was drawn to a futuristic storyline where the grid can be likened to a communications network in the 31st century (see Figure 21.4).

And, of course, as an image evolves and takes on a new direction, so too may the existing elements. For Renata Spiazzi, the grid first served as a steel wall representing a confined space in which the subject was sitting and dreaming of

Figure 21.3 Bruce Wands uses the grid to organize the disparate elements and to tell a story about *Guarding the Grid*.

Figure 21.4 Helen Golden transforms the grid into a futuristic communications network.

a far off place However, when she decided to continue the development of the image, the grid changed its significance within the story. The dreaming girl now contended with the gates of reality, with the asymmetrical and solidly structured gates pointing to an unpredictable and possibly unpleasant reality.

Let Us Not Forget Mother Nature

The Grand Canyon is overwhelming and impossible to comprehend in a single image. Nevertheless, Seed Image 3 represents the natural environment. Several of our featured artists were drawn to the natural environment—some just for color and texture, but others saw it as part of a storyline or as a backdrop in which the story is set.

Greg Klamt developed a story about a serenade and a goozerfish. The rock environment helped frame this fantastical image. Using a building block approach, he spent scores of hours painting rocks inspired by the Grand Canyon (see Figure 21.5). He first painted in the rocks, and then he eroded them to create open space in the image. In the rocks he embedded eyes and faces.

Figure 21.5 Greg Klamt is inspired to paint a rock formation based on the Grand Canyon image, including the embedding of eyes and faces in the rock.

Imagining the model as a Hopi Indian, Judy Mandolf decided that the Grand Canyon image could be modified to form a natural backdrop for her image. She worked to make the Grand Canyon into a painted desert.

Mel Strawn integrated the canyon with the grid in his image, *Seeing Time Through*, suggesting in his mind a technology-power source as part of humanity's dominion over nature. He found the rock aligned well with the grid and exemplified his exploration of what he calls "my transactions with the world." His rendering of the images also suggested an interpretive perspective to him, so he decided to title his work in a way that would require the viewer to pay additional attention in order to properly read his image.

Of the three seed images, the Grand Canyon, or landscape, proved to be a more muted presence. Nevertheless, just as with all the images, the landscape was another resource for the artists to create a context. For these digital artists, futurism and fantasy are part of the mix of themes, but so too are contexts of self, ethnicity, and abstract forms. Akin to traditional media artists, the creative process for digital artists involves the deliberative use of their respective toolsets and openness to experimentation.

The Process

Does the making of art differ when the composition process is digital? Apart from the mechanics of the different toolset—for example, paint brushes with acrylics versus electronic cursor brushes with a pressure sensitive tablet—would the decision process differ? In this project, the artists were given photographs to start with, which might have been an unusual starting point for some; however, putting aside this difference, what does the creative process look like for digital artists?

Percolation

All these artists described a process for making their artistic decisions. Several artists spoke of a wait-and-get-familiar period, some more explicitly than others. Bruce Wands (Chapter 20) provided the following description: "After receiving the source images, my first task was to print them out and study them. I put them up in my studio and just thought about them for awhile. I looked at each image carefully, thought about how it could be deconstructed, manipulated, modified, taken apart and then evolved into a final composite image."

And Mel Strawn (Chapter 11): "The previous night was full of speculating on approaches I would take toward these images. I had even considered printing them and then tearing the prints up into fragments for scanning. This is a good way to discover relationships between objects and items that might not occur by just thinking about the images."

Ken Keller (Chapter 18) wrote: "I begin this project by spending several days deconstructing the seed images in my mind. I studied the compositional elements of each image and how the complexity values were distributed across the compositions. Complexity values are one thing that a fractal artist can control. I burn the seed images into the back of my head until my unconscious must take notice of the intrusion."

Ileana Frómeta Grillo (Chapter 4) let her mind wander in thinking about how she would use the images. "I played a bit with the order of the images. The composition with the woman in the middle seemed to elicit more free associations" (see Figure 21.6).

Margie Labadie (Chapter 15) explained that her selection of which image to work on was based on steering clear of normal expectations: "I steered away from any recognizable parts of the images and decided to deal with texture and mood, instead. I really only used the seed images of the woman and the black-and-white grid. I found the mountainscape to be too soft in focus to use as a source for texture. And, I

Figure 21.6 The percolation process can take place inside and outside the computer for Ileana Frómeta Grillo. The reflective process continues throughout the work, from making decisions about subject matter to the type of brush stroke that could work best in the evolving composition.

was not inspired by its colors. I decided to focus on Seed Images 1 and 2."

Myriam Lozada (Chapter 9) explained that her thinking and method related to brushwork within her piece: "I added several large stokes to the upper left side of the line drawing of the face. I am looking for subordinate elements and shapes that add interest to what I already have established in the work. The strokes I have introduced look like stylized back and shoulders to me. I like working intuitively, drawing free hand, thinking about movement. After several shapes or lines are laid down, I stop and see if what I have done helps unify or support the composition. This strategy forces me to reconsider the ordinary and frees me from depicting it in a predicable manner."

Experimentation

Creativity for the artist can be analogous to *play*, but it is mature play directed toward composition. In other words, play with a purpose. This experimentation may be guided by an existing style, but there is always present an open-endedness that could lead to movement beyond their current paradigm.

At the start of this project, Greg Klamt (Chapter 6) described his playing with possibilities: "I actually began this project thinking my final image might be a photo-composite. I started layering the seed images in different combinations to experiment with textures, moods, and colors, without any idea where I was going, but the creative process moves in its own strange way."

Stephen Burns (Chapter 12) provides an even more blunt description: "Understand that I have no preconceived ideas as to where this will end up visually. I will experiment at this point and allow my imagination and gut instinct to take me in a variety of directions" (see Figure 21.7).

And not all experiments succeed. Renata Spiazzi (Chapter 10) makes this point: " I was still thinking about the message in my image. I wanted to continue adding features that will emphasize the dreamy look on the girl's face. I was thinking of sitting her where the little ball is, hoping this fractal image would give me that dream, but unfortunately it seems to look more like a space ship than a dreamy atmosphere. This means I'll have to go back to the drawing board."

Ileana Frómeta Grillo (Chapter 4) explains: "I also selected and layered sections of the background landscape and colored it by experimenting with the

Figure 21.7 Stephen Burns experiments and goes with his instinct. The experimentation continues into the detailed moment-by-moment act. *Should I do this? Should I undo that?*

Channel mixer, Blend, and Hue/Saturation options. . . . I combined the two dress layers by experimenting with the different Blend options until I found the combination that fit best. I then used the Eraser tool and the Opacity change in order to blend the tile pattern more effectively in order to create the dress folds."

Ursula Freer (Chapter 8) describes how she re-created the landscape, first by cropping the part she wanted from the Grand Canyon, and then, "To add more expansiveness I will turn it into a panorama by creating a mirror image of the original" (see Figure 21.8).

The artist's exploration can vary in the intensity of journey, desiring to connect the process and vision in an intimate way. Bruce Shortz (Chapter 5) describes this connection in his work: "I know that I can accomplish what I see in the mind's eye as a possible final result very quickly, without using these kinds of filters. But I know, too, that that old darkroom magic exists within experimentation. As I seek the journey of *Everywoman* as she moves from the past to the present, I embark on my own journey and find not only her past, but also my own and a truth within that."

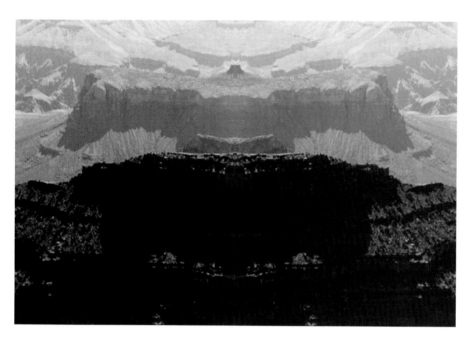

Figure 21.8 Ursula Freer expands the canvas into a panorama by creating a mirror image of the original.

The Blossoming of the Seed Images

There are many, many comparisons that can be made about the step-wise development of the images across and within the artist chapters as well as comparisons of the final images. However, it would be most useful now to consider each seed image—the woman, the architectural detail (or grid), and the Grand Canyon landscape—and the ways in which the artists steered their development. This comparison will be organized from the more literal to the more transformative use of the seed images. The more literal use of the seed image is one in which the original is kept relatively intact and more photographic. By contrast, the more transformative use of a seed image is one in which the original has been processed by other media applications, often taking on an abstract, impressionistic, or nonrealistic semblance. These boundaries are often blurred in practice, but they do provide a starting point for comparison.

As one sifts through these comparisons, other considerations might come to mind, especially the connections between painting, photography, and digital composition. From the digital imaging perspective, photography and painting share a kinship with the advent of digitizing both of these practices. In the digital state, photography and painting are conveyed to the viewer and manipulated by the artist via the same weightless materiality of binary information floating in a sea of code. What this means in terms of the history of art may be more difficult to describe given the enfolding and interaction between these media. After the mid-1800s, photography had freed those painters who had decided to accept that freedom to use their paints to depict more internalized imagery. This trend runs from Cezanne and continues right up to today, forming the backbone of what we call Modernism. Photographers have traveled along multiple paths from an attempt to capture reality with tripods, appropriate lighting, and good lenses, to inventive practices with a candid eye toward capturing movement and objects. But digital artists seem bent on using the photograph as another tool or resource in the wider scheme of finding doorways in and out of perceptual realities. Digital artists appear more inclined to use photographs as part of the democratic pluralism of materials, subject matter, and styles that inform our current art with much less emphasis on reportage about the world. Despite the commonalities that arise when all materials are converted into digital information, there are real differences in sensibilities that have characterized, and in many cases still do characterize, a painter, a photographer, and a digital artist. The following comparisons may help focus this second-tier discussion between the various 2D media, but this is a much larger discussion than can be broached in these chapters.

The Woman

The way the artists transformed the woman's face reveal distinct degrees and styles of transformations. Stephen Burns completely deconstructs the face and composites only parts of it with multiple eyes distributed throughout. The transformation extends to changing her coloration as well (see Figure 21.9, lower right). Greg Klamt goes even further by discarding all elements of the photograph and painting a new face looking off to the side instead of a frontal presentation. The face takes on a surreal aspect (see Figure 21.9, upper left). Those familiar with Ileana Frómeta Grillo's work immediately sense the way she crafts the face and makes the color palette her own, emphasizing a Latin liveliness in her presentation of the woman (see Figure 21.9, lower left). While one can see the woman in Michael Wright's version, the electric and phosphorescent lines that circle and circulate around the image transform the woman in yet another way (see Figure 21.9, upper right).

An obvious point to make is that digital imaging provides the opportunity to recapitulate all art styles—an attitude that says, *yes, I can do it that way too*. However, the discussion takes on more nuances as one turns to the more literal treatments of the woman's face. In the case of Judy Mandolf, the literal portrayal of the woman's face must be understood in the way the artwork is moved beyond digital media into the encaustic process. Digital imaging should not be cordoned

Figure 21.9 Transformative face images: (Upper left) Greg Klamt, see Figure 6.15. (Upper right) Michael Wright, see Figure 13.13. (Lower left) Ileana Frómeta Grillo, see Figure 4.3. (Lower right) Stephen Burns, see Figure 12.20.

off as locked inside the computer, although that feeling is easy to understand in our ever greater digitized existence (see Figure 21.10, upper left). There is also the possibility of integrating the face, by means of collage and/or montage with other figurative elements—perhaps overlaying it with a fractal to give the woman a dreamy look as Renata Spiazzi does, or by superimposing geometric elements and swaths of color in a version that can be called facial graffiti (see Figure 21.10, upper and lower right).

Figure 21.10 More literal-appearing face images: (Upper left) Judy Mandolf, see Figure 16.9. (Upper right) Renata Spiazzi, see Figure 10.27. (Lower left) Bruce Shortz, see Figure 5.14. (Lower right) Björn Dämpfling, see Figure 17.5.

The more puzzling instance is the dual face, which Bruce Shortz creates. Many digital artists have faced the situation where fine art categories reject digital compositions because they are done with a computer—rejected by photographic categories because the structure and surface of the image have been changed with processes not found in the chemical darkroom and, perhaps most surprisingly, often rejected by many digital art shows as looking too realistic. This is an example of an image that could fall through the chasms of misunderstanding except for exhibitions that reject all such categories in favor of simply determining, "Is it a strong image or not?"

Consider some of the manipulations that Bruce Shortz applied to this image. He does more than merely crop the image and superimpose it again at an odd angle. He works along several dimensions: changing the skin tonality, working with image maps in Flexify to reshape the face structure, and using what he calls a high-energy brush stroke in Corel Painter with the objective of recasting this woman as a male/female pair with echoes of an African heritage (see Figure 21.10, lower left). In a very real sense, this approach is highly transformative without appearing to be so.

The Arm

Seed Image 1 focused on the woman, but the artists looked beyond her to work with the tile background, and they also looked at her in pieces—her feet, her tattoo, her piercing, her arm, her clothing, and her hair. A deconstructionist seeks to take apart the object before considering restructuring it. The arm, for example, provides a focus to consider how several artists treated this body part.

John Labadie's desaturation of the images and his collage of bits and pieces take a different path than most of the other artists. However, the use of the arm's shape, but not its surface texture, resembles the treatment by Myriam Lozada. While John focused on light and dark, her treatment of the arm superimposes a piece of the grid image within it (see Figure 21.11, upper left and upper right). Bruce Wands' use of the arm in a disembodied form differs from these more abstract approaches. His selection and placement of the arm supports part of his storyline, in which a golden soldier is rescued (see Figure 21.11, bottom).

A familiar complaint about digital art is that it is too highly rendered—in effect, too perfect looking in the degree of finish—that it is too mechanical, controlled, and polished. A more useful perspective would focus on details, such as this arm, and the larger context. If the standard of image strength is to avoid a too-finished look (perhaps an antagonism to a mass media glamour approach), the imperfect edges around the arm in Myriam Lozada's image (Figure 21.11, upper right) would seem to deflect this criticism. So too the arm in John Labadie's image: The arm is half in partial shade and half in total black, overlapping part of the grid and blocks of black and white in an interesting pattern. Was that planned or accidental? There are myriad thoughts that spin out from this one small detail in the image. Bruce Wands' use of the arm to hold the soldier is clearly an *imperfect*, albeit intended, placement of the soldier that is ostensibly within the hand's grasp.

Whether a *rendered* or *non-rendered* look in the sense described above represents a stronger image is one of the many discussions about how art ought to look. For the purposes of the present discussion, however, our focus is more pragmatic, focusing on the details of the composition and the way they are used in the overall image.

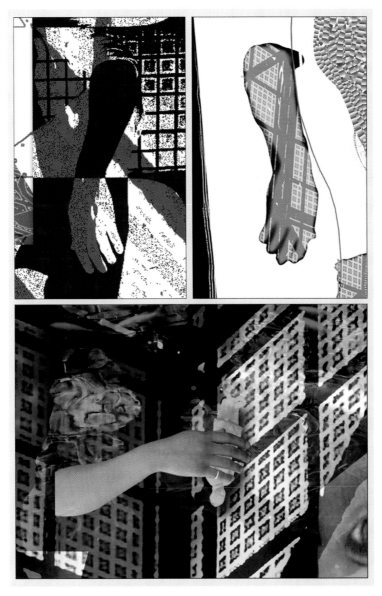

Figure 21.11 Literal and transformative arm images: (Upper left) John Labadie, see Figure 14.2. (Upper right) Myriam Lozada, see Figure 9.10. (Lower image) Bruce Wands, see Figure 20.7.

The Grid

Many of the artists were drawn to the dynamic relationships in Seed Image 2—the grid, or architectural detail. Bruce Wands' initial impression captures this attraction: "The grid image immediately offered lots of image possibilities. It had a lot of small graphic elements that could be used as windows for images. It also had strong lines, which could be used as an aid for composition of an image."

Stephen Burns applied the Shear filter to create a grid curvature and, with added lighting, gave the image a 3D look (see Figure 21.12, lower right). Helen Golden first twisted and reshaped the grid with one color set (upper left) and then altered the size, direction, and aspect of the grid with a different color set (lower left). Both artists used perspective and superimposition to suggest 3D, while Myriam Lozada adopted a flat look, focusing on the relationship of snippets of the grid, and using color and black and white to reinforce those relationships (upper right).

Figure 21.12 Transformative grid images: (Upper left) Helen Golden, see Figure 19.6. (Upper right) Myriam Lozada, see Figure 9.3. (Lower left) Helen Golden, see opening figure, Chapter 19. (Lower Right) Stephen Burns, see Figure12.13.

Several artists used the grid literally as a structural element, such as Renata Spiazzi's first evolution of the image, where it served as a side wall to create a sense of interior space in which the woman was seated (see Figure 21.13, lower left). Bruce Wands hung various elements on this structure to tell his story (see Figure 21.11, lower). Other artists used the grid somewhat literally, but in a broader transformative context. For example, Mel Strawn and Björn Dämpfling both montaged the grid with the Grand Canyon image, but in startlingly different ways, both in perspective, section of the grid selected, color, and blending modes (see Figure 21.13, upper right and lower right, respectively). Margie Labadie's use of the

Figure 21.13 More literal-appearing grid images: (Upper left) Margie Labadie, see Figure 15.5. (Upper right) Björn Dämpfling, see Figure 17.7. (Lower left) Renata Spiazzi, see Figure10.9. (Lower right) Mel Strawn, see Figure 11.15.

woman's clothing swirls in front of the grid as if it were some distant cityscape (see Figure 21.13, upper left).

As one views each image, the wealth of variation is substantial—and not just variation, but rather a highly focused composition connected to the style and intent of each artist.

The Grand Canyon

Picturing the Grand Canyon is always a challenge, especially its immensity. The literal way in which Renata Spiazzi worked with this challenge is one common to our everyday experience—make it into a travel poster. The poster helps the storyline with the woman dreaming of another place (see Figure 21.14, upper left). For Bruce Wands, the Grand Canyon (as landscape) is a small window just above the large foot of the woman, providing balance to the elements within the grid (see Figure 21.14, lower left). Here the immensity of a landscape icon is but a thumbnail—the irony of a modern world where nature appears to give way to the environment of the grid.

Figure 21.14 More literal-appearing landscape images: (Upper left) Renata Spiazzi, see Figure 10.7. (Lower left) Bruce Wands, see Figure 20.7. Transformative landscape Images: (Upper right) Judy Mandolf, see Figure 16.3. (Lower right) Ileana Frómeta Grillo, see Figure 4.14.

The Grand Canyon landscape may also be understood in a variety of transformative styles. Judy Mandolf creates an impressionistic mood that surrounds the woman's face. The impasto stroking of the image as well as the earth tones lends a softness to the image (see Figure 21.14, upper right). By contrast, Ileana Frómeta Grillo is telling a different story and casting a different mood—much livelier in texture and color as she embeds the landscape into the surrounding floor on which the woman sits (see Figure 21.14, lower right).

The last set of images demonstrates an even bolder group of transformations. Greg Klamt paints rock formations inspired by the Grand Canyon, much as painters would use a photograph as a reference. But here there are living creatures and eyes embedded in the rocks, not some distant archeological fact (see Figure 21.15, upper left).

Figure 21.15 Transformative landscape images: (Upper left) Greg Klamt, see Figure 6.19. (Upper right) Dolores Kaufman, see Figure 7.16. (Lower left) Myriam Lozada, see Figure 9.7. (Lower right) Ken Keller, see Figure 18.13.

Dolores Kaufman uses a Hyper Tiling program to create a very different effect from this landscape image. She is reminded of the U.S. Southwest, her personal travel to the Pueblos, and the history of the Native Americans within it—the transformation of the landscape mimics the transformation of cultures occupying the land. Her decision to embed the historical landscape into a modern (digital) context proved to be a resolution to her personal storyline.

"In order to blend an ancient culture with the modern, I must take into consideration the technology of the present and of the future. Once that concept took hold, I began to steer the Hyper Tiling process in that direction. . . . But then, while I was working with Seed Image 3 (the mountains) I got another idea, more subtle than the first, and I began to steer the Hyper Tiling parameters to create forms from the mountain scene that combined the colors of the earth with precise and hard edged forms that vibrate with the energy of technology." (see Figure 21.15, upper right).

Myriam Lozada and Ken Keller both solve the Grand Canyon *problem* in different ways, but both produce easily recognizable and understandable transformations. Myriam Lozada creates an intense and vibrant color impression of rock and mountain, taking advantage of the nuances of nature's own stratification (see Figure 21.15, lower left). Ken Keller also reduces the grandeur of the canyon to elegant and simple lines, but creates a more moody atmosphere with the muted colors in each cutout section.

Taking the Next Step

As you have seen, artists make art for many different reasons—whether simple, direct expression of feelings and emotions, or more complicated communication and story telling. Making art is but one aspect of the larger continuum of Art, with a capital "A." At the receiving end, there is the creative act of looking at art. Without that, why bother? If the spark of creativity is not passed on from work to eye, from the artist's mind to the viewer's imagination, there would be little point to making art.

And, seeing art is not an end either. Once you have seen art and have been charmed or shocked, validated or challenged, or just made more curious by the experience, the natural response is to want to know more. Art is not just one thing, but rather a complex network of nearly all things we experience as human beings. This is where study and talk and classification begin—after experience comes analysis of that experience. That, too, is what art does. Making distinctions becomes an important part of that process. That is the way our gray cells work. By putting things into more manageable, albeit often arbitrary, groups (or gestalts), we gain a foothold in the overwhelming experience of sensory input and thoughts that engulf us in the act of being.

So, how does digital art fit into the arc of art history? How is it to be classified? How does one get a handle on the question of digital art?

22

Categorizing Digital Art

Something big is happening in art and in the world at large. As the artists of post-World War II America looked about them they realized that, as the main focus of people's attention and activity, the natural environment had given way to something completely different. Supermarkets, billboards, highways, and mass media were replacing the environment of fields and forests, villages, and local town newspapers. As our primary daily concern, nature was being replaced by mass culture. Art reflected this change by introducing new subject matter, new media and processes, diverse cultures, and developing new forms of expression through which art is made. Painting took on aspects of sculpture. Sculpture got off the pedestal and filled entire rooms with *installations*. And, as people were drawn into interacting with art, installations became theater in the form of *performance*. New forms of expression were developed and exhibited at such a rate that no single style could hold sway for very long. Modernism, in the form of regular advances by the *avant garde*, gave way to the simultaneous styles of a democratic pluralism.

What's Happening

Toward the end of the last century, another wave of change washed over culture and art. The mass media of the second half of the 20th century was, and is, being fractionalized by the introduction of the amazing new tools of binary information processing. Media, which was once fed one way to the masses, has seen those masses take up these tools and begin to feed themselves. Today we can see a new state of media that can best be described as *hypermedia*. The tools for capturing, organizing, and disseminating information about one's personal environment and experience to a world-wide audience continues to improve in quality while shrinking in size and cost of operation. As we digitize more and more of our experience, the culture of mass media makes way for the culture of hypermedia. In this hypermedia culture, democratic pluralism reaches a feverish pitch. An all-embracing, simultaneous, nonhierarchical value system seems to be coming into place. Art has responded and even fed this process by placing value on media, mixed media, and new media. People, groups, and cultures once outside the traditional European/North American mainstream are awarded space in galleries and museums, as are the handicrafts, outsider arts, and commercial design that were once considered minor endeavors to the world of fine art. As the sheer volume of divergence and change turn under the clearly defined system of aesthetic values that once dictated the way in which art is appreciated, art lovers are more likely to set their own standards. A simple world organized around a certainty of standards and procedures no longer exists.

Simulation, Mimicry, Facsimile, and Illusion

It is probably not possible to draw a cause and effect scenario between the implementation of hypermedia tools and the rise of democratic pluralism. These are more like simultaneous events brought about by a long history of invention within technology and culture. But, the current crowning glory of these converging paths is digital computing and the conversion of so much of our experience and creativity into the common material (or commodity) of binary information. What is possible to see at this early stage is some of the underpinnings of the developing aesthetic of hypermedia art. And, what we see is that as these new tools and processes find implementation in nearly every creative endeavor, the primary challenge for these tools has been to prove that they are as good as the traditional tools. We see this in music where the challenge for digital has been to simulate the richness and warmth of analog musical instruments. We see this in film and animation in which the drive for digital images to mimic photographic realism is continually refined and pushed. In art and photography, we see the need for digital tools to create facsimiles of traditional media and production procedures. We demand seamless mimicry of the traditional, and we also expect these upstart binary devices to go beyond the creativity of the past and dazzle us with newer and better illusions. Thus, one underpinning of a hypermedia aesthetic recognizes the major role played by simulation, mimicry, facsimile, and illusion. We see these aesthetic principles in the wide variety of 2D digital art, examples of which have been presented in this book. And, true to another hypermedia principal of simultaneous mix or synthesis, a sense for the all-in-one, the traditional principles of composition, content, and context remain in effect. Traditional aesthetic principles are not thrown out but are altered to integrate into a mix where old and new are of equal value.

One of these varieties of digital art is *digital painting*, which can be divided into natural media and works utilizing the filters and algorithms inherent to digital processing. Natural media artworks exhibit the appearance of having been made using traditional tools and media such as oil, pastel, ink, or chalk, among others. The resulting images are built up one mark at a time, with each mark input into the binary mastering system through a pressure-sensitive tablet that allows the artist to control how each tablet gesture is registered as a corresponding brush-stroke in the piece. In form and in practice this is painting. What has changed, as with anything done digitally, is that *materiality* is altered and replaced by the fac-simile and feedback of an onscreen image (see Figure 22.1).

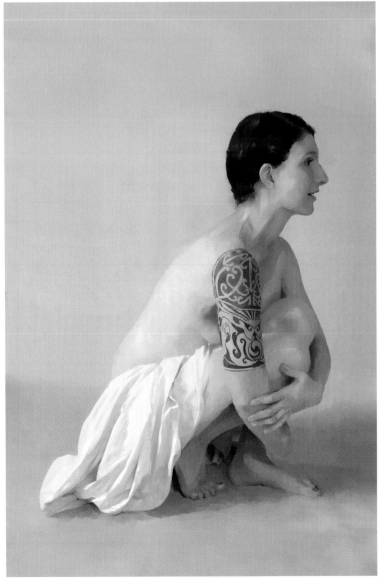

Figure 22.1 *Outside the Box* by Donal Jolley (www.s30d.com). Digital painting software is used exclusively in producing this contemporary take on portraiture and the artistic treatment of the human figure. According to artist Jolley, "The model's tattoo is often considered outside the box of societal norms—as is the electronic method of producing this work. The title is meant to reflect the reproduction of traditional mediums by non-traditional, or *outside-the-box* methods."

In the case of *algorithmic digital painting*, filters and procedural manipulations driven by mathematical operations are performed on the distribution of screen pixels. The digital painter enters into a symbiotic relationship between the tools and the process of his own aesthetic decisions. In this way, the digital artist, like the artist using traditional media, selects a process or working environment that produces random but controllable results. Splattering or dripping paint is a random but somewhat predictable activity that is both under and outside the complete control of the individual. So, too, does the digital artist employ the use of a *filter* with the added advantage of being able, in many cases, to preview the results of this action upon the developing composition. The digital artist can accept, reject, or further alter the results in order to build up to a final image. This is not your father's painting but is a process by which color, line, and form are developed upon a two-dimensional ground; it is a new generation of ways to paint images (see Figure 22.2).

Fractal art is essentially a hybrid of algorithm painting, but it produces such a unique and identifiable imagery as to warrant its own category, or genre, of digital art. The term *genre* is appropriate both in its use to signify *a type or style of art*, and as a term for *the realistic depiction of the natural, everyday environment.* However, the natural environment depicted by fractal geometry is not of nature itself but of the math around which nature is organized. It is the visual representation of a particular and peculiar set of mathematical formulas that make up the ordinary everyday environment of today's digital computer. Fractal geometry, which got its name from Benoit Mandelbrot, serves as the basis for much of the processing of binary files into viewable and printable images. These formulas, which present infinitely enlargeable details distributed in patterns folding back into and repeating themselves, create images of a strange but recognizable nature. This is because fractals describe the organized chaos of many natural objects such as seashells, clouds, and the distribution of leaves and limbs within trees. Although highly abstracted in appearance from these natural objects, fractal images contain the rhythm of nature combined with breathtaking coloration. In this respect, fractal images are eye catching and may suffer from appearing trite unless the artist is willing to make some hard aesthetic decisions—for example, the type of decisions that recognize that beauty in and of itself is not necessarily art, or that art based on process alone does not often generate sufficient human emotion or empathy. But *fractal art*, in that it is imagery residing in and inherent to the digital computer itself, is possibly the most original of all digital imagery. The fact that this imagery offers the artist the sharpest edge to tread between what might or might not be considered art is also what makes fractal images so challenging and important (see Figure 22.3).

Photo manipulation is by far the variety of digital art most often practiced by digital artists and seen by the public. We have witnessed this sort of imagery in advertisements, tabloid journals, movies, and TV for many decades. In certain works

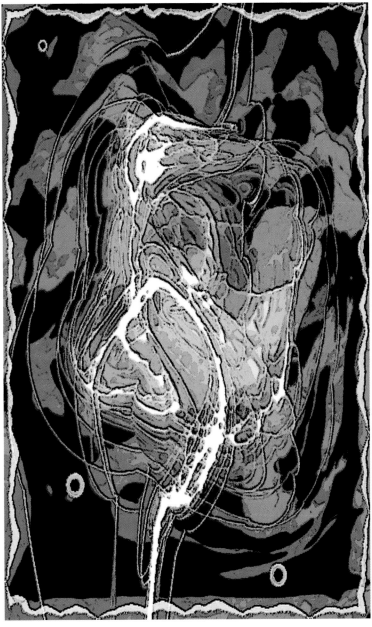

Figure 22.2 *Digital Deflection* by Ansgard Thomson (www.ansgardthomson.com). The artist used a combination of KPT FraxPlorer, Wood Cut, Image Warp, Curves, and Accent Edges filters in painting this abstract image full of energy and mysterious color.

of Pop Art this vision and practice has already made its way into the language of fine art. One reason behind this seminal interest in photo manipulation was suggested by Walter Benjamin in his essay, *The Work of Art in the Age of Mechanical Reproduction*, in which he ascribed a "cult aura" to photography by virtue of a picture's ability to represent a person, place, or period that has been frozen and removed from the flow of time. Coupled with the cultural understanding that reality and often truth is recorded and contained in photographs, a potent field of

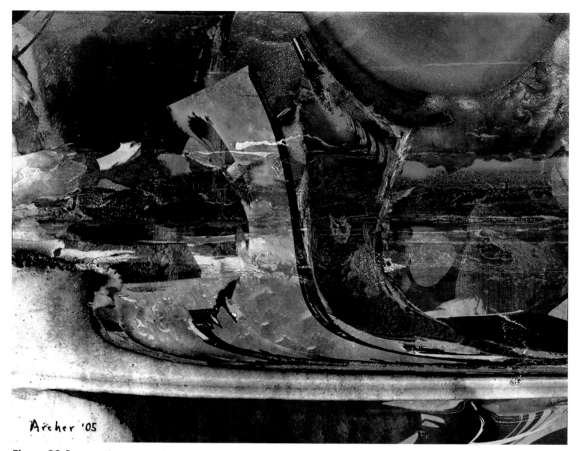

Figure 22.3 *50501* by Don Archer (www.donarcher.com). Exploring the "sparse and ragged edges" of a common Mandelbrot set, the artist utilizes a fractal that bypasses the normal lyrical beauty of fractal imagery for a more powerful and active piece. Here the basic fractal is embellished with texture, some cutting and pasting, and other layering techniques that most fractal "purists" try to avoid.

magical thinking and belief is generated by nearly any photograph. By manipulating photographs, we suggest manipulation of reality. What artist, shaman, or thief can resist that opportunity? Today's digital art is filled with some degree of manipulated images acquired by photographic or other means of appropriation. These images are combined, colored, distorted, and composed into the widest range of images from highbrow to lowbrow art and all the brows in between. The gamut runs from freakish scenes of self-mutilation and distortion to the saccharine tableaux of babies nestled in flower petals, such that the term *to photoshop* is now a recognizable and understood verb.

The digital art of *photo manipulation* can be divided into the familiar forms of collage and montage. Both involve combining images in a particular way, and through the application of digital tools and processes each can take on various degrees of distortion. The difference is that with collage the individual elements of the overall composition are kept separate as seen in the variations of texture, color, size, or even outlines of these image units (see Figure 22.4). Collage involves obvious cut and paste techniques, which is the root meaning of *collage*—that is, "to glue." A more seamless integration of disparate image elements, which shoots for a believable arrangement or association of these elements, would be called a *montage*. The goal of montage is to make the resulting image appear as if its parts were originally together as a unit. Images are blended together and made to appear to share lighting, coloration, placement, and texture in such a way as to appear real and unified (see Figure 22.5). By taking advantage of our recently evolved tendency to see photographs as representations of reality, collage and montage combine the patina of reality with the shock of the improbable much to the delight of our human eye.

Figure 22.4 *Leaf Portal* by Peter S. Gorwin (www.pgphotographics.com). A collection of disparate objects brought together through digital collage to form a tight composition in which each element retains much of its own identity. The simulation of actual objects, a leaf and paper, make this seem much like a mixed media assemblage, until one is struck by the appearance of open sky at the center of the composition.

Figure 22.5 *The Ascension of Miles Archer* by Jim Respess (www.greenflashphotography. com). Three elements—an alleyway, a pub, and a cloud—combine to create a magical scene full of imagination and mood. The seamless nature of this tableau belies the fact of much attention to detail and manipulation of the original photos in its creation.

As a variety of digital art, *3D Modeling* is a subset of algorithmic and fractal art and digital photography. By employing advanced modeling software, the artist can create believable, often astounding, visual simulations of landscapes, architecture, interiors, and human figures. *Sculpting*, in a digital sense, is achieved through the mathematics of algorithms and fractal formulas, but is controlled by the artist through various, complex interactive interfaces. Once the artist has sculpted a mountain range, an abstract combination of shapes, or even a 3D model of a human form, lighting and atmosphere can be added, and a point-of-view, a virtual camera, can be placed inside the scene. After the viewing angle of this camera is maneuvered into an optimal framing, the scene is rendered in photorealistic detail. This sort of art ranges from abstraction to realism to fantasy art. In this same way, some artists install abstract arrangements of elements into a virtual space, apply color and texture to these elements, and light and render these constructions into highly detailed digital prints. Any number of images, photographic or otherwise, can be mapped to the virtual surfaces of these non-material objects, heightening the realism or surrealism of the resulting frame. At the high end of this art is the further animation of these virtual forms and cameras into what we see in many films produced today. Here again, as with digital collage and montage, we experience the intoxicating ability for these digital arrangements to fool the human eye into seeing the most improbable of compositions as a reality worthy of the suspension of disbelief. Of course, it is not *photography* per se, but there is no better traditional way to describe it. It is perhaps *digital constructivism* in that it makes use of virtual materials manufactured and available in the interior world of digital computing (see Figure 22.6).

Figure 22.6 *2003.1a* by Kenneth A. Huff (www.kennethahuff.com). A digital sculpture is created using forms designed in 3D imaging software. Subtle texture, surface treatment, and lighting are applied to this digital installation in virtual space and then framed and "photographed" by means of high-resolution Raytraced rendering. Output as large prints or animated for onscreen presentation, this work is evocative of an unusual and unique imaginary space.

At the end of the dialectic process is *synthesis*, a new form born out of the integration of an original idea (thesis) with its opposite (antithesis). As a variety of digital art, the term *synthesis* implies this notion of something more than the sum of its parts and that this type of art comes from mixing all of the forms mentioned above into the making of a single work of art. The term *integrative* has also been applied to this sort of digital art, in that it describes bringing all these working methods and visual genres into play when creating a digital piece. *Integrative* or *synthesis* digital art fulfills the hypermedia principle of utilizing and placing equal value on all tools, procedures, styles, cultures, aesthetic frameworks, and genres that an artist might require to make work that is unique and particular to the manipulation of binary data as an art-making material (see Figure 22.7). As noted before, a potent power of *digitization* allows previously separated crafts such as music, filmmaking, visual art, or literature to share similar material and creative processes. Practitioners of all these previously separate arts now share certain procedures and sit before essentially the same toolset to create their work. *Integrative digital* art opens the door to a wide potential of visual statements and collaborations. This art is shaped by and is inclusive of all styles, tools, and procedures; which is to say, it is work that stems from the emerging culture of hypermedia.

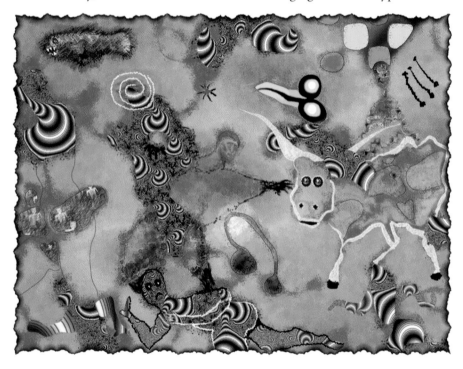

Figure 22.7 *Carnival* by JD Jarvis. Algorithmic paint programs, hand painting in Corel Painter combined with fractals, cut and paste techniques, Texturize, Burn, and Liquid Metal filters were employed to create this piece.

Why Categorize Digital Art?

A fair question to ask is why, in light of the all-inclusive methodology and visual style of digital art, does one even bother with categories? It is true, with what we can see emerging around the implementation of digital technology, that the time is coming when it will be a simple matter of *Art*, with little concern for *this kind* of art versus *that kind* of art. No matter how it is made or what tools are employed in the making, it is all *art*, after all. This is and has always been true, even for all traditional art as well. But, the democratic pluralism of today, the simultaneous appreciation for all sorts of expression, makes this concept a more highly visible reality. Many of the digital artists featured in this book will agree that they would prefer their work to be considered art first with only passing regard for the tools or techniques employed to make it. That day appears on its way and would be a recommended concept to hold close when viewing and appreciating the breadth of today's digital or non-digital art.

Nevertheless, during this transition period from mass media culture to one in which there is greater weight given to, or perhaps taken by, the culture of hyper-media, the arrival of digital art has caused many arts leagues and organizations, curators, gallery owners, art dealers, and jurors of art competitions a good deal of trouble. Whether the source of this consternation lies in the effects of a shift in paradigms, computer phobia, clinging to tradition, or overzealous software sales-men, the problem of where to place and how to judge the worth of digital art remains a challenge for many. How does one include something so new within the context of what has been known? Is it good art? Is it original art?

The case histories presented in this chapter speak toward these dilemmas and carry a common thread. We must begin to judge digital art not on the tools or proce-dures used to create it, but rather on the intent of the artist and one's skill in fus-ing concept to image. In a not too distant future, democratic pluralism may supplant the tyranny of stylistic innovation. The need to follow, in orderly fash-ion, only the *new* or *latest thing* is swept away by individuation—leaving many, seemingly, without an anchor. But perhaps this "anchor" was just a weight hold-ing us back—a limiting force created by the *purveyors of style* to maintain status and market control. As with all art before computers, the knowledgeable art appre-ciator asks, "Does the skillful coordination of process, imagination, and presen-tation create art that speaks to and sparks one's own imagining?" The degree of this spark determines the strength of the work. Multiplicity of choice demands greater all-round depth in our ability to make distinctions.

Case History #1

Is It Digital Enough?

An online digital art gallery requires an opinion on some work submitted by a digital artist for inclusion in the gallery's collection. The work is highly illustrative, depicting very nostalgic vintage American automobiles in appropriate surroundings. The illustrations are quite masterfully created in Adobe Illustrator and finished off in Photoshop with apparently few, if any, scans or photos being employed in the final work. At issue is the question, is this work *digital enough* to warrant exhibition in the digital gallery?

The opinion issued on this matter asks, is it less than art to use digital tools to make it? Certainly not. Conversely, is it *less digital* to use these tools to make work that appears to have been made by traditional means? Again, certainly not. If we are to head in the direction in which there is no *digital art* per se, but rather just another way to make art, then we must be prepared to enter and play on the level field of fine art. What purpose does it serve to describe something as *digital art* other than to describe the media used to make it?

This is, however, a digital art gallery. Shouldn't the art look digital? What is really exciting about digital art is the fresh artwork one can create by exploiting the computer's ability to generate its own recognizable and idiosyncratic imagery. This is new stuff and we know how the art world loves *new stuff*. So, a certain sort of imagery is important in that it helps establish and recognize that *going digital* is something fresh on the scene. At the same time, art cannot be judged simply on the basis of mastery of tools. No matter how well rendered, an image on black velvet is often given lesser status as art. So, even materials used to make art sway some in their judgment. To a certain degree, tools and materials do matter as to the question of art.

Do digital artists intend to promote a look or a style representative of all *digital art*, or is the intent to promote a high degree of accomplishment in using digital tools to make a wide range of art? One of the interesting facts about digital art is that all traditional art can be seen and used simply as a visual device or underlying process in the making of digital art. But then, is it called *digital art* simply by virtue of the tools used to make the imagery? Should we then call everything made without a computer *not-digital* art?

In the final analysis, the gallery was reminded that the first widespread use of digital means toward the making of art was in commercial illustration, design, and page layout. In that respect this artist's work goes back to the roots of current visual digital art.

This artist's work was included for exhibit in the online digital gallery.

Case History #2

When Does Digital Photography Become Digital Art?

An art association located on the east coast is forming new screening policies and guidelines for an art competition and exhibit featuring the range of art being made in their region. The committee wants to include traditional photography, digital photography, and digital art but could not decide, when does digital photography become digital art?

The opinion offered in this case acknowledges that a decision, which might seem arbitrary to some, has to be made. But this decision can be made based on observable criteria. In fact, observation of the art itself, regardless of the tools and processes used, is essential. Since two separate classifications of photography, separating *wet* photography and digital photography, has already been made by this association, the distinction concerning when to categorize *digital photography* as *digital art* lies in the image itself and not the means by which it is made. Therefore, it is the degree of manipulation and the artist's intentions that could place an image in either category.

Whether or not to call a piece digital photography or digital art would have to do with how closely a piece is true to the presentation of an original photograph (the *photograph* being an image captured when light passes through a lens). Or how far, in terms of distortions, montage and collage techniques, does the artist go to create an image further away from the *depiction of reality* (the *depiction of reality* being the traditional niche for photography since *Modernism* got its name). An image offering a realistic depiction that adheres to standard darkroom tactics but has achieved those ends using digital tools ought to define the category *digital photography*.

If the artwork offers an apparently *photorealistic* environment, but that environment is indeed either constructed or surreal in appearance, as with figures being shown in environments or situations that could not actually be real, then that work edges into the area of *Surrealism*, which is traditionally placed in the wider arena of fine art. Again, this is not to say that traditional photography or even digital photography cannot possess a surreal quality or that some such photography might be considered surrealism. It is the degree of manipulation, as well as the intent of the artist, which must be known and gauged here. The intent of the artist to either use digital tools to mimic traditional photography or to push beyond those boundaries is the best indicator for where to draw the line between these categories.

There are cases where simply mapping a paper texture to the entire surface of an image or running a single digital filter on a photographic image in order to make it appear to have been *hand painted* will appear and present itself as art. Work of this sort may be too trite to consider as either photography or art. Look beyond visual effects to determine if the actions mentioned above support a concept or create a unique context for the image or whether it just "artifies" the picture. Commercial success aside, this is probably not strong art and certainly not a photograph; it is the black velvet of digital art.

More to the case in point, however, is not the boundary between digital photography and digital art, but the continued boundary between traditional, or *wet* photography, and digital. If the digital photographer is using his tools to adhere to the traditional presentation of images captured through a lens, then the distinction ought to be between *photography* (digital picture *plus* wet development) and *digital art*. Why distinguish wet photography from dry, traditional from digital, when it is getting harder and harder to tell the difference based on materials. With the advent of digital photo print technology, such as LightJet, Lambda, and others, a digital image is exposed via laser light to standard wet-processed photo materials. What the image looks like and the intent of the artist is the only place we will soon see any difference between how photos are made.

Case History #3

How Many Categories Are There in Digital Art?

A museum with considerable experience in international fine art exhibitions has decided to do a digital-only international competition. Previously, the museum had only all media shows, not wanting to fall into the trap of a crayon–art show, a brush–art show, and so on for every possible medium. However, an *all-digital* show represented an opportunity to develop funding from corporate sponsors—a wedding of new media and new technology interests. The transition from slide submission to an Internet and digital file submission for artist entries would require some familiarity outside the museum's normal community. Who better to lead the way than artists versed in digital media? Who better to ask than the digital artists who had volunteered their efforts in making this show a success?

Even for these insiders, the decisions about where to draw the boundaries proved problematic. The group polled its members, and responses varied from the work must be 100% digital to at least some aspect of the submitted work having been digitally sourced or composed. The majority leaned toward a low threshold for defining *digital*. Sentiment among the members forming these categories was that traditional shows tended to exclude digital works, causing resentment among digital artists. Given that resentment, these digital artists did not want to be guilty of committing the same sin of exclusion.

But, establishing a low threshold for defining appropriate submissions still resulted in a variety of categories:

- Digital painting
- Photo manipulation
- Fractal (or algorithmic)
- Collage and montage
- Mixed media
- Digital photography
- Digital sculpture

The New Surface

Among the most logical solutions for categorizing digital art is to consider the ways and means by which most of this imagery is presented. As an object consisting of ink on a supporting material, or a *ground*, which displays an image transferred from a *matrix* upon which the image was created and stored, to the selected substrate, digital art is at this moment largely the art of printmaking. All 2D static digital art could rightly be classified as prints regardless of whether the techniques of *digital painting, photography, collage, montage, fractal art*, or combinations of all of these are employed to create the image. Some printmakers agree, others do not, but most everyone will have to admit that, today, there is a new surface upon which art is widely created and presented. In the near future, given the promise

By leaning toward the low threshold, it was easy to allow *digital photography* simply because a digital photograph, even without manipulation, is 100% digital. At the same time, *photo-manipulation* could be limited to distorted images. Of course, *collage* and *montage* could be accomplished both as an extension of *digital painting* as well as *photo-manipulation*. One of the group's members creates digital paintings by limiting himself to Photoshop software, presumably a *photo-manipulation* oriented software program. This caused some confusion in the committee, since he was not painting inside a program with the word Paint or Painter associated to it. Some argued all work described as *photo-manipulation, digital painting*, and *collage* or *montage* should merge into the larger rubric of *digital composition*. The committee agreed that a low threshold would result in more entrants to this competition. And, everyone recognized that the importance of selecting the pieces to be included in the exhibit required a second, more traditional threshold—namely, an emphasis on whether the submitted image itself represented strong and thoughtful artwork.

A running insider joke was that this premier all-digital show might also be the last. After all, digital artists simply want to be included among all other media. Might this exhibit yield an eventual merger with all other 2D artists? This all-digital show might serve to make that point.

Still, regardless of a future of inclusiveness for digital artists, it was important to resolve the issue of categories for this particular show. It was decided that the artists would self-select the category for their work by checking off a box with their submissions. This information would be used only for statistical purposes and for tracking how many submissions fell into each category. Subsequent digital art competitions could be more exacting, if desired.

This exercise in definition-making was shown to be a somewhat fruitless search for perfect boundaries. Such boundaries are especially ineffectual in light of the digital artist's tendency to move between several computer programs and across all styles and to dispatch limits or rules standing in the way of making a digital image. The decision to stay with a loose grouping of art styles, along with a low threshold for *how much* digital composition was required, made for a pragmatic and less contentious way of increasing participation among artists working with the conglomeration of toolsets and technologies known to *digital art.*

of high-resolution flat screen technology, we may see a debate emerge as to whether static 2D visual art displayed in such a manner could still be called a print? Does the use of paper and ink fully constitute the meaning of the word *print*, given such a technological environment? The film industry already uses the term *answer print* to describe something that is neither paper or ink. Doesn't digital art exhibited on a screen meet the above mentioned criteria for *printing*, while simply taking advantage of a new surface for art making and display?

This new *surface* goes beyond the materials described and represents the technological patina that separates digital art from the immediate world. The look of digital is that of the *once-removed*. The best art reflects the artist's awareness of this dynamic when viewing digital artwork. Where is the *surface* of an artwork that has no easily discernable, original object-hood? What is the nature of an image's texture if that image resides in a state of non-material potential awaiting some form of display technology to bring it into the light of day?

While there is no common look to the art being made, every digital artist has to share two basic modes of display. That is, the work can be expressed on a monitor or as a digital print. Since the original work occurs and resides in the digital matrix of computer memory and storage systems, this *original* is essentially immaterial and virtually non-existent until expressed in either of these two display modes. Due to its infinitely reproducible binary nature and the fact that some form of *reproduction* or, better said, *production* is required to materialize the original into *any* visible form, digital art is simultaneously an *original* and a *reproduction*. Digital art is truly and unashamedly the art of illusion. The expressive nature of the artist's imagery belies the fact that either of the two basic modes of display offer a flat, mechanized image largely unaffected by changes in ambient light conditions and absent of truly tactile texture. The line between detached mechanical production and expressive, handcrafted artistry that was explored and blurred by Pop Art is blurred to the extreme in digital art, because it is, in fact, both.

Will digital art become interactive? Will large flat screens replace stretched canvas and framed prints? Will cable and/or some other sort of distribution method deliver *art packages* to the high-resolution monitors mounted on our kitchen appliances, thus revolutionizing the concept of *ice box art*? Yes, in fact all of this and more is happening right now. Will art as we know it disappear while simultaneously becoming more important and more pervasive than ever? Will *painting*, once again, be pronounced, "dead-on-arrival," only to rise again to haunt and inform us? Will the cream rise to the top of a churning global pluralism? Yes, all this and more. Whether or not our technologies or dreams are practical, human beings are driven by the potential of the instruments we create and the dreams we materialize. Culture and art in their newfound digital state are already more than we can imagine.

Afterword

by Robert Bersson

An Appreciation of Digital Art: Multiple Perspectives

Digital art is firmly grounded in, and is a product of, the present and recent past. Like photography, the radically new art form introduced to the world in 1839, digital art emerges from a particular artistic and socio-cultural context. Just as photography was born in an urban–industrial society and within a cultural and artistic milieu that valued naturalism and realism, positivism and materialism, freedom and individualism, and within a rapidly industrializing, increasingly urban society, digital art emerges from its own special life-world: one that is intensely consumerist and computer-based, post-industrial and intercultural, dominated by global mass media and instant communications, and driven by corporate capitalism of an international scale. This unique life-world, with its own deep roots in the past, spawned art forms that embodied and expressed its unique character. From the latter half of the 19th century through the early 20th century, photomontage, collage, cinematic montage, mixed-media assemblages and constructions spoke to simultaneity, instantaneity, multiple perspectives, the mixing of media, collagist sensibility, and composite composition, all essential ingredients and prefigurations of the coming digital art. Like photography before it, digital art has a richly complex *prehistory* and very deep bases in our own time. As a writer on art, culture, and society, I look forward with anticipation to the revolutionary and evolutionary manifestations—artistic, cultural, and social—of our youngest and most pervasive art form.

In my role as a writer I came to interview two digital artists (also longtime friends and colleagues) whose insights led me into the world of digital art. Eliot Cohen and Peter Ratner had each worked for years in non-digital art forms—film-based photography and oil painting respectively—before taking up digital art as their primary activity. Their first-person comments that follow transported me toward understanding and appreciation. What impresses photographer Cohen about digital or electronic image creation? "As an artist," Cohen states, "I am excited by the potential of electronic technology to enhance and expand the way I work. The process is one that combines attention to fine details with a playful approach to creating the work." (Bersson, Robert, *Responding to Art: Form, Content, and Context*, New York: McGraw-Hill, 2004, p. 189.)

Cohen discusses the making of his electronic photo collage, *Muybridge Fantasy*, as extremely labor-intensive, involving the integration of captured images (including Eadweard Muybridge animal locomotion photographs), numerous elements, components, subjects, layers, levels, and techniques in the formation of the final "composite picture." Through Cohen's step-by-step description of the process of creating of his *digital composite*, I came to appreciate that his digital artmaking is simultaneously playful and demanding, imaginative and exacting—and strongly collagist from start to finish.

Peter Ratner compares his personal experiences with traditional media and computer-generated 3D animation as follows.

> *One of the first things that many of us working in this new digital medium discovered was that creating art on the computer was mostly a cerebral experience. It was different from the more physical hands-on artmaking approaches such as drawing, painting, and sculpture. The artistic process that …I dealt with was now situated in the realm of visual perception. It was devoid of any of the sensuous considerations and tactile qualities associated with traditional art media.…Thus, computer art has often been labeled as cold and impersonal. This, however, is a misconception since the computer artist can still infuse the work with emotional content while keeping a more detached viewpoint during its development. The artist and viewer can and often do derive emotional satisfaction from the work even though it may dwell in the intellectual rather than the sensory realm. In other words, the actual artmaking process may be more mechanical and less physical, but the final product can be as emotionally satisfying as any traditional art form.* (Ibid., p. 121.)

Cerebral, supportive of wide-ranging creative exploration, intellectual, situated in a digitized realm of visual perception—computer-generated art, for Ratner, is both different from and related to traditional media such as painting and drawing.

Three-dimensional [computer-generated] *animation and illustration allow me the means to approach artmaking from an analytical point of view while painting with oils gives me the option to create imagery from a sensory position. My background as a painter enables me to give physical body and texture to the images I create on the computer. Conversely, my computer background allows me to plot out images for my paintings on the computer instead of sketching them in pencil, ink, or paint. I find it much easier to explore ideas using the computer. The computer is a wonderful tool for the exploration of lighting, textures, and camera angles. Such wide-ranging exploration and discovery could never be duplicated through the use of simple thumbnail pencil or pen sketches.* (Ibid., p. 122.)

Enter multimedia artist Michael Rush with further insights. He is the author of *New Media in Late 20ᵗʰ-Century Art*. Rush emphasizes that digital art, in process and product, is incredibly malleable, ever changeable, open to manipulation, and partial to interactivity. Traditional artworks and artmaking processes in comparison, he asserts, are much more fixed, static, delimited, and finite. In digitized electronic form, the image is "a dynamic system," a truly revolutionary development. In a stirring conclusion, Rush writes that

As more and more artists of quality turn to the digital world (and they will, for who can resist having their work seen by millions of people with the click of a mouse without waiting for the approval of the gallery and museum system?) a reconfiguring of the meaning of art, of aesthetics, of artists' relationships to dealers and institutions, indeed, of artists' relationships with any kind of market, will occur…For some this has meant the death of art; for others, it has heralded vast beginnings. (Rush, Michael, *New Media in Late 20ᵗʰ-Century Art*. London: Thames & Hudson, 1999, pp. 216-217.)

To Rush's passionate vision of digital art as revolutionary and to Cohen's and Ratner's thoughtful insights about the uniqueness of electronic image creation, I would only add that digital art is in its infancy and open to enormous evolutionary possibilities.

Joe Nalven and JD Jarvis' intriguing book furthers our understanding and appreciation of this youngest art form. It starts with the unusual condition of artists working from the same images, thereby requiring us to attend closely to their artistic processes and personal visions. Seeing their digital art unfold and then critically responding to it requires some fresh thinking for those unfamiliar with the divergent ways of making digital art, but it is a journey well worth taking.

—*Robert Bersson*

Glossary of Digital Art and Printmaking

additive colors
The three additive primary colors are red, green and blue. When these three colors of light are mixed in equal proportions, they will produce white light. Also known as additive primaries.

algorithm
A mathematical routine that solves a problem or equation. In imaging, the term is usually used to describe the set of routines that make up a compression or color-management program and other RIP applications.

aliasing
The visual stair-stepping of edges (jagged edges) that occurs in an image when the resolution is too low. Can be caused by improper image sampling or improper image processing (see "jaggies").

alpha channel
An image-editor channel used to contain a mask or partial picture element or color. Created by Alvy Ray Smith and Ed Catmull at N.Y.I.T. in 1997, the alpha channel is used to calculate the transparency of each color in an image. In a three-color image, the alpha channel would be the fourth channel.

analog
Data consisting of or systems employing continuously variable signals or data, as opposed to discrete steps or levels of digital data.

anti-alias
The process of smoothing and removing of aliasing effects by electronic filtering and other techniques, such as blending of hard edges. Also, blending object-oriented art with bit-mapped art.

archival
Of or pertaining to archives. A term that has been used extensively in conservation literature, but that lacks an internationally accepted definition. General understanding: with characteristics of long-term stability (as in: archival quality). Considered meaningless unless qualified with additional information, data, etc.

archiving

Retention of images, often on CD-ROM. Information necessary to reproduce the print is also archived, including ink, tables, sizes, and media used.

artifact

In digital graphic applications, unwanted visual anomalies or defects generated by an input or output device, or by a software operation, that degrade image quality (*see also* "aliasing" and "moiré").

artist's proof

One of a small group of prints set aside from the edition for the artist's use; a number of printer's proofs are sometimes also done for the printer's use.

BIT

Derived from Binary Digit. The smallest unit of information in a computer, a 1 or a 0. 8 bits = 1 byte. Coined by J.W. Tileu at Bell Labs in 1948.

bit depth

The maximum number of bits that are used to define a pixel. A measure of the defined brightness range. The color depth or pixel values for a digital image. The number of possible colors or shades of gray that can be included in an image.

bitmap

A rasterized graphic image formed by a rectangular grid of pixels or dots.

black

The fourth color in process four-color printing. The "K" in CMYK.

black generation

The addition of black ink to the other process colors when separating an RGB color image into CMYK colors. Black generation is typically handled in one of two ways, GCR (Gray Component Replacement—

replacing some of the CMY with K) or UCR (Under Color Removal—using K only in neutral areas).

BMP file

A Windows bitmap file, with the extension ".bmp," that defines an image (such as the image of a scanned page) as a pattern of dots (pixels). From bit mapping, the process of addressing the pixels on the screen.

bon-a-tirer or BAT (*bone-ah-ti-ray*)

The proof accepted by the artist that is used as the standard for comparing all subsequent prints. Some printers require a signed BAT before production printing can begin.

brightness

The overall intensity of the image. The lower the brightness value, the darker the image; the higher the value, the lighter the image will be (*see* "chroma").

BYTE

A standard unit of digital measurement. 8 bits = 1 byte. Each 8-bit byte represents an alphanumeric character.

calibration

The act of setting or adjusting the color settings of one device relative to another, such as a monitor to a printer, or a scanner to a film recorder. Or, it may be the process of adjusting the color of one device to some established standard.

capture

Acquiring information, such as an image, with a scanner or digital-camera device.

CCD (charged coupled device)

Light-detection device used in many popular scanners, digital cameras, and video cameras that generates electrical current in direct proportion to how much light strikes areas of the sensor.

CD-R (CD-Recordable)
A CD format that allows the users to record data to a disc when using the proper hardware. Recorded data is not erasable.

CD-RW
A CD format that allows users to erase data.

certificate of authenticity
1. A written or printed description of the multiple which is to be sold, exchanged, or consigned by an art dealer. [CALIF. CIVIL CODE] 2. A written statement by an art merchant confirming, approving, or attesting to the authority of a work of fine art or multiple, which is capable of being used to the advantage or disadvantage of some person. [IOWA CIVIL CODE] 3. A written statement disclosing certain key facts about a multiple print.

chroma
A measure of saturation associated with color; degree of color purity; relative brightness of a hue when compared to another.

clipping
The grouping (usually unwanted) of all tones or colors above or below a certain value into one composite tone. The loss of visual information caused by too little contrast, in which certain grayscale values are lost or compressed either into the range of pure white or pure black.

CMY (Cyan, Magenta, Yellow)
Three subtractive primary colors used in color printing. In theory, the combination of pure CMY inks produces black; in reality, black must be added to produce a full color gamut.

CMYK
Cyan, Magenta, Yellow, and Black (or Key) are the four colors used in process-color printing. Also known as subtractive color, the color black is achieved by the presence of all inks.

coating
The process of treating media or substrates to accept inkjet inks. Also, a thin covering providing protection from UV-induced fading, smudging, and fingerprints, which may or may not improve the permanence of the print because most fading is due to visible light.

collage
Collage involves the creation of artworks that include elements that have previous existence as separate items. They may be found elements, transformed elements, or elements created entirely by the artist. Digital collages may be defined as digitally created artworks that involve the bringing together of separate images (which may or may not have existed in non-digital form and which may or may not have been created or altered by the artist) and digitally "pasting" them in place in order to create a new work. Digital collages may also contain digital drawing, digital painting, or other digital media. In both montage and collage, multiple sources are used to create a single image. In montage, the disparity of the sources is invisible. In collage, the disparity of the sources is visible, sometimes so much so that the whole is fractured into separate elements contained within a single area.

color balance
The ability to reproduce the colors of a scene to some acceptable standard.

color calibration
A system of software and/or hardware that adjusts and coordinates colors between two or more digital devices. Color calibration systems commonly compare device color profiles and translate one color model into a device-independent language.

color compression
Shrinking the color gamut of the original to the color gamut a device will represent.

color curve

A graphic mechanism for displaying color measurements and for making color changes to an image. User adjustments to the angle and slope of the curve implement color changes to one or all of an image's color channels.

color gamut

A range of colors that can be reproduced by a given system.

color management (color management system)

An advanced technology that uses profiles of the input and output devices to maximize color accuracy and consistency. Targets that include over 3000 colors are printed and measured with a colorimeter to create profiles for the various ink/media combinations. A combination of software and or hardware devices used to produce accurate color results throughout a digital-imaging system.

color model

A color measurement scale or system that numerically specifies the perceived attributes of color.

color profile

Also called "device profile," or simply "profile." This term refers to the relationship between the color models of the system devices.

color saturation

Color Strength. A measure of color purity, or dilution by a neutral.

color separation

The process of separating a color image into four subtractive colors, CMYK, either by photographic or electronic processes, thus producing a set of four films or a computer file.

color space

Three-dimensional mathematical model enclosing all possible colors. The dimensions may be described in various geometries giving rise to various spacings. The parts of the visible spectrum which can be reproduced in a given medium (i.e., RGB for computer monitors, CMYK for print, web safe index colors for the world wide web).

color temperature

The color spectrum of a "black body" radiator heated to a given temperature on the Kelvin scale. The manufacturer's method of indicating the color of a light source in degrees Kelvin (K); i.e., 2700K (yellow/white), 4100K (white), 5500K (blue/white).

colorant

Any substance that imparts color to another material or mixture. Colorants can be dyes or pigments.

colorimeter

An instrument used for color measurement based on optical comparison with standard colors.

colorimetric

Of, or relating to, values giving the amounts of three colored lights or receptors—red, green, and blue. Adjective used to refer to measurements converted to psychophysical terms describing color or color relationships.

colorimetry

Light measurements converted to a psychophysical description or notation which can be correlated with visual evaluations of color and color differences.

complementary colors

Two colors that, when combined, create neutral gray. On a color wheel complements are directly opposite the axis from each other; blue/yellow, red/green, and so on.

compression

The process of removing irrelevant information and reducing unneeded space from a file in order to make the file smaller. Some types of compression can cause losses and distortion. In Run Length Encoding, rows of pixels of the same colors are stored as a number and color, reducing the file size while keeping the data in tact.

computer-generated

A misnomer that implies that no human, artistic control is required to produce artwork. In general it may mean having come *through* a specific kind of device, but essentially it is understood that computers do nothing without the input and control of human beings.

continuous tone

A photographic image containing gradient tones. For printing purposes, continuous-tone images are converted to dot patterns (halftones).

contrast

Tonal gradation between the highlights, mid-tones, and shadows in an image. High contrast implies dark black and bright white. Medium contrast implies a good spread from black to white, and Low contrast implies a narrow spread of values from black to white. Also, understood in terms of "Rate of Falloff." High contrast implies a rapid transition between black and white, whereas a slow "rate of falloff" produces gradual or smooth transition between light and dark.

crop

To remove part of an image.

DPI

Dots per inch. A measure of the detail of a print. "Apparent dpi" refers to the fact that the eye perceives a giclée as having greater detail than in does in physical reality.

densitometer

An instrument that measures the optical density of a transmitting material, or an instrument to measure the negative log of the reflectance of a reflecting material. Such instruments do not measure color. They are widely used in the graphic arts and photographic industries for process control. It will indicate, in density units or percentage dot, the percentage of a given area that is covered by halftone dots. This instrument is used to ensure consistency and process control.

density (optical density)

The degree of opacity of an image; a measure of reflectance or transmittance equal to log10 (1/reflectance) of log10 or (1/transmittance); the ability of a material to absorb light; the darker it is, the higher the density. Density measurements of solid ink patches are used to control ink on paper.

digital

Type of data consisting of (or systems employing) discrete steps or levels, as opposed to continuously variable analog data.

digital art

Art created with one or more digital processes or technologies.

digital C-print

Another term for digital photo print. These are actual photographic prints that are exposed to laser or LED light then processed in traditional RA-4 wet chemistry.

digital collage

The process of electronically simulating traditional collage techniques by pasting together disparate images into a cohesive visual whole, resulting in a new image.

digital fine art print

A fine art print made by any digital output process conforming to traditional fine art qualifications and requirements.

digital imaging

The process of image capture, manipulation, and final image form, accomplished by digital systems.

digital photo print
One of the major digital printing technologies. Produces actual photographic prints that are exposed to laser or LED light then processed in traditional RA-4 chemistry (*see* "digital C-print").

digital printer
A non-impact printing device that is capable of translating digital data into hard copy output. Typically refers to printing with one of the digital output technologies (inkjet, electrostatic, thermal transfer, or laser photo printing).

digitize
The process of converting analog data to digital information.

dithering
A graphics display or printing process that uses a combination of dots or textures to simulate an original image or an output device. The purpose is to create the impression of a continuous-tone grayscale or color image. (Diffuse dithering: method for printing continuous tone images on a laser printer, in which the grayscale information is represented by randomly located printer dots.)

dot
Dots make up an image in color separations or halftones. Halftone dots will have a fixed density but variable size (amplitude modulation).

dot gain
The phenomenon that occurs when ink expands its coverage during printing onto a substrate; often caused by abnormal or excessive absorption by the substrate.

dot pitch
The distance between the dots on a computer monitor, typically 0.24 to 0.38 mm. The closer the dots the sharper the image on the monitor.

down-sampling
The process of receiving data from another computer, server, or system. The reduction in resolution of an image, necessitating a loss in detail.

dye
A colorant that does not scatter light but that absorbs [and therefore reflects] certain wavelengths [of the electromagnetic spectrum] and transmits others. Dyes are generally organic and generally soluble in water or some other solvent system; or they may exist in such a finely dispersed state that they do not scatter light and behave as though they were in solution. The dividing line between a dye and a pigment may, therefore, be indefinite and dependent on the particular total system involved.

dye sublimation
An imaging process that vaporizes colorant with heat and pressure, and deposits it on to a substrate in order to achieve a continuous tone image.

dynamic range
The measurable difference between the brightest highlight and the darkest value.

edition
The aggregate of identical prints produced from a single matrix (see also "open edition," "limited edition," and "variant edition").

(EPS) encapsulated Postscript file
An Adobe graphic file format. EPS translates graphics and text into a code, which can be read by the printing system. EPS files hold both low-resolution "viewfiles" and high-resolution PostScript image descriptions. A vector-based, computer graphics file format developed by Adobe Systems. EPS is the preferred format for many computer illustrations because of its efficient use of memory and fine color control.

expanded-gamut printing

Printing system wherein manufacturers add additional colors of ink to expand the range of the standard cyan, magenta, yellow, black (CMYK) inkset. Lighter densities of cyan and magenta (LC, LM) and orange and green (O, G) and multiple blacks are the most popular.

fading

A subjective term used to describe the lightening of the hue of a colorant following exposure to the effects of light, heat, time, temperature, chemicals, and so on.

feathering

A technique in many image-editing programs that allows for the softening of the edge around a selection.

filters

Software or subprograms within image manipulation software that employ algorithms to control modifications to digital images by altering the values or arrangement of entire or selected areas of an image.

format

Characteristic identifying size of printer, media, or graphic, according to width of media roll, printer's print area, or graphic. "Medium Format" is generally taken to be between 11-24" in width; "Large Format" (Wide Format), larger than 24" in width; and "Grand Format," larger than 72" in width.

four-color process

A system of printing colors by printing dots of magenta, cyan, yellow and black.

fractal

A mathematically generated pattern that is reproducible at any magnification or reduction, and repeats infinitely.

frisket

A paper or liquid masking device (*see also* "mask").

FTP (File Transfer Protocol)

The method for uploading and downloading files to/from Internet server systems.

gamma

A mathematical curve representing both the contrast and brightness of an image. The steepness of the curve indicates greater contrast calculated as a trigonometric tangent function.

gamut

A finite or limited range of colors provided by a specific input or output device, or by a set of colorants.

gamut compression

The editing of an image to reduce the color gamut so that the image can be displayed or output within the limits of a particular device.

gaussian blur

An image-softening effect used in digital imagery. Named after French Mathematician Carl Friedrich Gausse.

giclée

(1) A print made by a digital process, typically inkjet. (2) A copy (typically identical) of an original work of art (as a painting) that was created separately and then reproduced digitally, specifically by inkjet printing. First used in this context by Jack Duganne in 1991 to describe prints made on an IRIS inkjet printer. Pronounced [zhee-clay].

graphic

A non-text item (illustration or photograph) or non-text component of an image.

graphics tablet

An input device that uses a stylus or specialized mouse to write or draw on the tablet surface to communicate with the computer.

halftone

The process of reproducing a continuous tone image as a series of various sized dots within a fixed grid that can be reproduced with ink. The finer the dot grid, the higher the quality of the reproduction.

highlight

The lightest area within an image. Also called "specular reflection."

histogram

A graphical display that represents the distribution of tones within an image. The horizontal coordinate represents each pixel value possible from black to white. The vertical values indicate the number of pixels in the image that occur at each value level.

HLS (Hue, Luminance and Saturation)

A color model based on these three coordinates of color, where hue is the dominant color, saturation is color purity, and luminance is the light/dark characteristic of the color.

HSB (Hue, Saturation, and Brightness)

A color model that utilizes Hue, Saturation, and Brightness as the three coordinates, where Hue is the dominant color, Saturation is the purity of color, and Brightness is a neutral scale of how light or dark a color is.

hue

The attribute of color by means of which a color is perceived to be red, yellow, green, blue, purple, etc.

impact printing

Process of applying ink to a substrate utilizing physical contact between some part of the printing device and the substrate—e.g., offset, lithography, and flexography (see also "non-impact printing").

ink

A fluid or viscous substance used for writing or printing. In digital printing, the substance in inkjet printing (liquid or solid) that gets sprayed onto the medium; made up of a colorant, a solvent, or vehicle, and various additives.

inkjet

A digital printing technology that uses nozzles to spray ink onto a surface.

inkjet printer

A type of printer that sprays tiny spurts of ink onto coated paper.

interpolation

A technique for increasing the size of a graphic file by creating pixels. Also an extrapolation algorithm. There are two types, sequential and bi-cubic. Note: increasing the size of an image by interpolation does not increase or enhance the ability to resolve the detail in that image. It only makes the details that are already present larger.

IRIS or IRIS print

The branded inkjet printer that produced the early "digital fine art prints" and for which the term "giclée" was first used. Currently no longer being manufactured.

jaggies

The effect caused by images or lines being rendered at too low a resolution. It can easily be defined as a stair-stepped effect giving the line or image a rough appearance.

JPEG (Joint Photographic Experts Group)

Standardized image compression format developed by the Joint Photographic Experts Group. Usually used for compressing full-color or grayscale images.

Kelvin

The name of the absolute temperature scale. Used in imaging to define the quality of a light source by referring to the absolute temperature of a black body that would radiate equivalent energy. Generally, a tungsten reading lamp is rated at 2800 degrees Kelvin, while TV or film quartz lights are rated at 3200 degrees Kelvin, and outdoor light averages around 5600 degrees Kelvin. The higher the Kelvin temperature the more bluish the light appears.

laminate

A clear coating of a variety of possible substances, usually plastic, that is applied to one or both sides of a medium after printing for reasons of durability.

lamination

Bonding one product to another by pressure for protection or appearance.

large-format

A printer, media, or print 24" or greater in width.

laser printer

A laser printer uses a laser beam to write on a photoconductive revolving drum that is coated with toner, which is a fine, black powder. After the image is transferred to paper it passes through a pair of heated rollers or a fuser that melts the toner, fusing it with the paper fibers.

lenticular

A technology to create print images that appear to encompass actual depth and/or animation, by "stripping" the image and placing the printed image behind a specially stripped lens material.

lightfast

Resistant to the destructive action of light.

limited edition

A number of multiples or identical artworks that are produced from a single master or matrix, all of which depict the identical image, and which may bear the artist's signature and numbers indicating the unique number of the specific print as well as the stated maximum number of prints in the edition (*see also* "edition" and "open edition").

line art (or line drawing)

1. Single color diagrams or drawings. 2. An image that requires sharp edges and high contrast between areas of the image that have ink and those areas that do not have ink. A drawing that consists only of black and white with no intermediate grayscale information. These images require a higher resolution to create the sharpness that is necessary.

LPI (Lines Per Inch)

Measurement of resolution on a traditional printing press. The number of lines per inch on a halftone screen. As a general rule, the higher the lpi, the higher the printed resolution and quality.

mask

A special effect that can modify images so that only part of the image can be seen, or so that the image blends into the background.

master

See "matrix."

matrix

Traditionally, the plate or surface upon which an image is inscribed in order to hold ink for the purpose of transferring the image to the substrate or paper. In digital terms the matrix becomes the electronic file located on a computer's hard drive or resident memory or stored on a disk or CD. This matrix is made up of binary encoded information that can describe how the image file should appear on the digital raster screen or print.

media
Another term for substrate; the materials to be printed, such as watercolor papers, canvas, copper, wood veneer, cotton, or plastic. The common term used in digital printing.

microporous
Refers to inkjet media with a receptor coating containing voids that the ink fills, rapidly absorbing the ink within the media rather than simply applying it to the surface of the media. This rapid absorption essentially makes it instantaneously "dry" to the touch.

midtones
Tones in an image that are in the middle of the tonal range, halfway between the lightest and the darkest. Also called "middle values."

moiré
An undesirable artifact or pattern that can appear in output film, or a created special effect. It appears as a regular pattern of "clumping" of colors. A moiré pattern is created by juxtapositions of two repetitive graphic structures. An often undesirable element in a digital scan, but a natural visual occurrence created when similar patterns are superimposed and a third pattern is inferred wherever the two similar patterns do not completely match.

monochrome
An image made of a range of only one color.

monoprint
One of a series in which each print has some differences of color, design, texture, etc. applied to an underlying common image.

monotype
A one-of-a-kind print made by painting on a smooth metal, glass, or stone plate and then printing on paper. The pressure of printing creates a texture not possible when painting directly on paper. Sometimes called a "unique edition."

montage
The seamless combination of divergent images into a singular image.

non-impact printing
A printing process that transfers the ink to the media (paper or other) without pressure (*see also* "impact printing").

nozzle
In inkjet printing, the orifice in the printhead from which ink droplets are ejected.

opacity
The measure of the amount of light that can pass through a material. Also, the property of a film that prevents "show through" of dark printing or marks on a substrate (media). The degree to which a material obscures a substrate, as opposed to transparency, which is the degree to which a material does not obscure a substrate. Also "hiding power."

open edition
An edition or set of identical prints from a single master or matrix that is not limited in number (*see also* "edition" and "limited edition").

optical resolution
The maximum physical resolution of a device. Optical resolution provides better quality than interpolated resolution (of the same number), which uses software to create additional image information.

output
In digital printing technology, to translate information from the computer to an external device (e.g., a printer or monitor); to print. Also, the visual display of digital information or that which is printed or displayed.

palette

The number of colors a device is capable of displaying and producing. Also the tools used in paint programs.

PDF (Portable Document File)

A proprietary format developed by Adobe Systems for the transfer of designs across multiple computer platforms.

photograph

An image or picture made by photography, whether traditional or digital (*see* "photography").

photography

The art or process of capturing an image onto a recording medium (whether photographic film or image sensor/detector) by the action of light or other radiant energy with the aid of a camera or other device.

PICT

A picture file format.

piezoelectric (or piezo)

An inkjet printing technology that uses electricity to "fire" the nozzle.

pigment

Colorant consisting of particles made up of many synthetic dye molecules or carbon black. Generally more stable than dyes of the same color. Pigmented inkjet inks are credited with better longevity and may have a narrower color gamut. Finely ground insoluble dispersed particles that, when dispersed in a liquid vehicle, can be made into a paint or ink.

pixel

Term derived from: **picture**(pic or pix) **element** …"pixel." Refers to the simplest or smallest element of a digital image.

pixel depth

The amount of data used to describe each colored dot on the computer screen. Example: monochrome is 1 bit deep, grayscale is 8 bits deep, RGB is 24 bits deep. Images to be printed as CMYK separation should be 32 bits deep (*see also* "bit depth").

plotter

A term applied to a peripheral unit that, through computer control, prints data via the Cartesian (X/Y) coordinate system.

portrait, portrait mode

The orientation of an image that is taller than it is wide; a setting controlling an output device to properly fit a computer document to the print medium.

postcoat

Clear material applied as a final coat to protect prints or artwork.

posterization

An effect created by having a limited number of levels or gradient steps within an image. This may be a planned/desired effect, or it may be a mistake requiring correction.

PostScript

A page description programming language created by Adobe that is device independent. PostScript is an industry standard for outputting documents and graphics.

PPI (pixels per inch)

A measure of resolution or density of pixels in a digital image.

print

1. In the context of fine art, an original work of art (as a woodcut, lithograph, photograph, or digital print) where the art object or artwork does not exist until it is

printed. The print is made directly from the matrix by the artist or pursuant to his/her directions. Also known as "fine print," "work on paper," and "original print." 2. A physical image, usually on paper, produced by, but not limited to, such processes as etching, lithography, serigraphy, relief printing, photography, or digital methods. Prints are usually, but not always, produced on paper and in multiples. Traditional, photographic, and digital processes can be used to produce prints.

print on demand
The ability of digital printing to produce prints individually or sporadically over an extended period of time, with consistency. This allows orders of a small number of prints when needed—"print on demand."

print permanence
The resistance of a print to physical change of any type, from any source, be it light, heat, acids, etc.

print service provider (PSP)
A commercial, digital printing agency or firm that takes an artist's image file and prints it to the artist's specifications.

printer driver
Printer-specific software that allows a computer to communicate with the printer. If available, provided by the printer manufacturer (*see also* "RIP").

printhead
Part of a digital printer that is directly responsible for applying ink to a medium.

printing
The process of applying ink to a substrate.

printmaker
A person producing actual prints from the artist's master file, under the artist's supervision.

proof
A preliminary print used to evaluate aspects of the image (color, density, resolution, etc.) prior to final printing.

quadtone inks
Special multi-monochromatic (B&W) inksets.

raster
A horizontal row of pixels on a screen. The process of rendering an image or page, pixel by pixel, in a sweeping horizontal motion, one line after another.

raster image
An image that is defined as a collection of pixels arranged in a rectangular array of lines of dots or pixels (see "bitmap").

rasterization
Changing vector-type image information to raster image information.

rendering
Applying shading and lighting effects to a two dimensional image.

reproduction
A copy of an original work of art. In the context of digital art, a copy of artwork that already exists in some other original form or material (painting, drawing, et al.) prior to the fixing of the image of that original work on the current printing matrix (*see also* "giclée").

resampling
Changing the resolution of a bitmap file without altering its physical size.

resolution
A definition of resolution in terms of pixels per inch, or pixel density. Refers to the number of smallest discernable dots or pixels. A measurement of the "fineness" of

detail reproduction given in line pairs per mm, or pixels per inch (*see* "DPI" and "PPI").

RGB

A color model using red, green, and blue; the additive primary colors. Video display systems use RGB data to create screen images.

RIFF (Raster Image File Format)

A storage format used with grayscale images. In Corel Painter the RIFF format is used to save color image files that retain all of the Painter capabilities such as "wet canvas" and active layers. Saving in any other format disallows further modifications and interaction with these tools.

RIP (Raster Image Processor)

"Bridge" software allowing the computer to give specific instructions to a printer. Often includes add-on features such as color-calibration routines and various tools.

saturation

A measure of purity of color. Saturated colors contain pure color only; colors desaturate to gray. Saturation is a measure of the degree of pureness or movement away from gray. The amount of gray in a color. More gray means lower saturation; less gray means higher saturation. If a color has no saturation, it is a shade of gray. Saturation is also the degree to which a color is undiluted by white light (*see* "chroma").

scale

To enlarge or reduce an image by increasing or decreasing the number of scanned pixels or the sampling rate, relative to the number of samples per inch needed by the printer or other output device (*see also* "interpolation").

scan

The process of translating a picture from reflective art or transparency into digital information.

scanner

A hardware peripheral that illuminates, reads, and then converts original text, artwork, or film into digital data. Types of scanners include flatbed, film, and drum.

selection

Any of several processes by which the digital artist can isolate a portion of a digital image in order to perform additional work or protect the selected area from manipulations applied to the remaining "unprotected" areas. Similar to frisket paper and masking tape in traditional painting.

service bureau

A company that typically offers custom print-output production services, which can include digital color graphics.

sharpen edges

An image-editing technique to enhance the edges of an object.

sharpening

1. A picture enhancement making the image have more distinct borders, areas, lines, or tones. 2. An option on some scanners that emphasizes detail by increasing the contrast of the boundaries between light and dark areas of an image.

signed

Carrying an original signature of the artist. In law: 1. Autographed by the artist's own hand, and not by mechanical means of reproductions, and if a multiple, after the multiple was produced, whether or not the master was signed. [*Iowa civil code*] [*Georgia code similar*] 2. The artist signed the print multiple by hand to signify the artist's examination and approval of the print. "Signed" does not mean the act of leaving an impression of the artist's name upon the print by any mechanical process. [*Hawaii civil code*]

SLR

Single Lens Reflex, a form of small format (35mm or 6cm) camera that has a reflecting mirror that retracts when the shutter is released. An SLR allows the photographer to view the image exactly as it will be framed in the photo.

soft proof

Viewing a digital image with a monitor instead of generating a hard copy proof. Can be done from a remote location via the Internet.

stylus

A tool that is used on a graphic input tablet as a drawing instrument, or as a mouse.

subsampling

Scanning at a less-than-optimum sampling rate.

substrate

Ultimately, the material that receives the printed image. Sometimes called "media" in digital printing. The single or multi-layered base material of the medium, which can have a very simple or complex structure and is a carrier for the coating, if present.

subtractive color / reflective color

The color mixing system associated with pigments, as opposed to pure light. The term refers to the CMYK color space used by conventional and digital printing devices to produce full-color printing. Theoretically, when all three subtractive primary colors are mixed together the resulting color is black (*see also* "CMYK").

subtractive primaries

The three colors that are used to create all other colors in color photographic printing (Cyan, Magenta, and Yellow).

thumbnail

A small low-resolution version of an image.

TIFF (Tagged Image Format File)

A file format for storage of digital images.

topcoat

The coating applied to the surface of inkjet or other type media during the manufacturing process. The topcoat enhances ink adhesion and other performance characteristics; it also helps to control dot gain, drying time, and moisture resistance.

ultraviolet light (UV)

Radiant energy with wavelengths slightly shorter than the visible spectrum.

unsharp mask

A sharpening process that first blurs the edges then subtracts the image from the blurred areas to yield an image of apparent enhanced sharpness.

UV ink

Term used in relation to ultraviolet properties in inkjet ink, in two different manners: (1) ink that is resistant to UV light degradation, or (2) ink that is "cured" or dried by exposure to UV light.

UV protective glaze

An acrylic sheet used in framing art. It has ultraviolet light inhibitors capable of filtering out 99 percent of UV rays (one of the causes of print fading).

UV resistance

The resistance of something to change under UV light sources including daylight.

variant edition

A set of prints of the same image but varying as to size, coloration, image consistency, materials, or being otherwise differentiated.

vector

A term given to a graphic drawing, specified as a color, start and end point, and applied to line segments, type, and tints.

vector graphics

Drawing software. Vector graphics files are usually stored in formats such as PICT or EPS. Any of a number of graphics formats including EPS(F) and DXF that describe objects on the screen not as colored pixels but as mathematically defined shapes. Vector graphics can be rescaled to any size without any effect to file size. Typically, vector graphics occupy less disk space than their bitmapped (rasterized) counterparts.

vector image

A computer image that uses mathematical descriptions of paths and fills to define the graphic, as opposed to individual pixels.

water-resistant

A surface that can resist dampness but not a soaking of water such as that tolerated by a waterproof surface. Generally implies a lesser degree of protection against water than the term "waterfast," but still improves the material's resistance to water damage.

waterfast

Resistant to the destructive action of water.

waterleaf paper

Papers made with little or no sizing.

watermark

A faint marking on the back of some photographic papers indicating that the picture was taken by a professional photographer. Also, term for a faint image superimposed on a digital image to protect rights of ownership. An identifying mark or symbol imbedded in the substrate on which the art is made, usually referring to the maker of the substrate.

white

The result of combining the additive primary colors (Red, Green, and Blue). In the subtractive color mixing system, "white" is the result of the absence of any color.

white balance

The balancing of color components to create pure white when photographing or scanning a white object. A substitute for a color temperature setting.

white point

The color and intensity of a device's brightest white. With printers, this is usually the white of the paper. With scanners, the color that when scanned produces values of 255, 255, 255 (RGB). Ideally, the white point is 100 percent neutral reflectance or transmittance (*see also* "reflectance").

WYSIWYG

What You See Is What You Get. Refers to the ability to output data from computers exactly as it appears on the screen.

The authors wish to thank the Digital Art Practices & Terminology Task Force (DAPTTF) and Committee Chairman John Shaw for granting us permission to publish an excerpt of the DAPTTF Glossary. For more information or to view the entire glossary, visit www.dpandi.com/DAPTTF.

Contributors

Robert Ambler	http://home.att.net/~betosart/home.html
Don Archer	www.donarcher.com
Stephen Burns	www.chromeallusion.com
Vijay Bhai Kochar	www.vijaybhai-digitalvisions.com
Björn Dämpfling	www.creativecreatures.com
Jack Davis	www.software-cinema.com/htw/
Troy Eittreim	www.eittreim.com
Ursula Freer	www.ursulafreer.com
Helen Golden	www.helengolden.com
Peter Gorwin	www.pgphotographics.com
Ileana Frómeta Grillo	www.ileanaspage.com
Peter Hammond	www.peterhammond.com
Kenneth A. Huff	www.kennethahuff.com
Werner Hornug	(e-mail) hornug@wanadoo.fr
JD Jarvis	www.dunkingbirdproductions.com
Donal Jolley	www.s30d.com
Gerhard Katterbauer	www.katter.at

Dolores Kaufman	www.dgkaufman.com
Ken Keller	www.fractalartgallery.com
Greg Klamt	www.gregklamt.com
John Antoine Labadie	www.steppingstonearts.net
Margie Beth Labadie	www.steppingstonearts.net
Myriam Lozada	www.dunkingbirdproductions.com
Judy Mandolf	www.judymandolf.com
Joe Nalven	www.digitalartist1.com, www.digitalartguild.com
Ansgard Thomson	www.ansgardthomson.com
Cher Threinen-Pendarvis	www.pendarvis-studios.com
Jim Respess	www.greenflashphotography.com
Bruce Shortz	www.10000cranes.com
Renata Spiazzi	www.spiazzi.com
Michael Sussna	www.sussna.com
Mel Strawn	www.911gallery.org/mels/mels.htm
Bruce Wands	www.brucewands.com
David Weisman	www.davidweisman.net
Michael Wright	http://home.earthlink.net/~mrwstudios/

Index

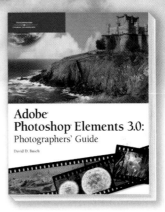
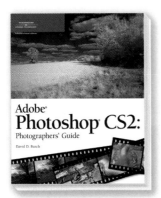
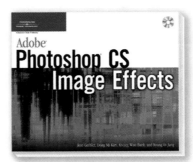

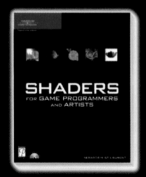

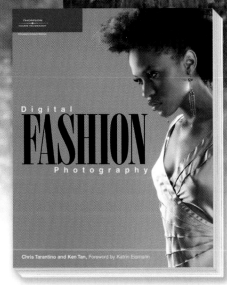
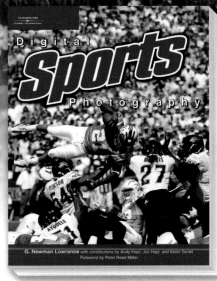

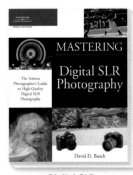

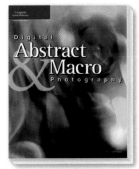

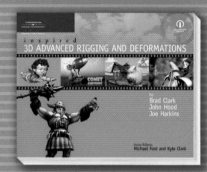

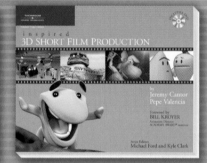